German Unification and t
The Domestic Politics of Integrati

German Unification and the Union o, ...o oome of the most
interesting questions in the study of comparative politics and international relations. The book studies the sources of continuity and
change in German policy toward the European Union, set in the
context of the competing pulls of integration into the EU, and
unification of East and West Germany. Employing a framework of
analysis premised on the interaction of interests, institutions, and
ideas, the book asks: how has the domestic politics of unification
influenced German policy toward Europe? Why has continuity reigned
in some areas, whereas in others significant changes, sometimes
reversals, have been registered? What are the implications of this
checkered pattern of outcomes for Germany and for Europe? Jeffrey
Anderson's book focuses on the political economy issues (such as
trade, internal market, energy, and industrial policy) which represent
key components of both German domestic politics and Germany's
relationship with Europe.

JEFFREY ANDERSON is Associate Professor of Political Science at
Brown University. He is the author of *The Territorial Imperative* (1992),
and numerous book chapters and journal articles on comparative
politics, political economy, and European politics.

TO BE
DISPOSED
BY
AUTHORITY

German Unification and the Union of Europe

The Domestic Politics of Integration Policy

Jeffrey Anderson

CAMBRIDGE
UNIVERSITY PRESS

PUBLISHED BY THE PRESS SYNDICATE OF THE UNIVERSITY OF CAMBRIDGE
The Pitt Building, Trumpington Street, Cambridge CB2 1RP, United Kingdom

CAMBRIDGE UNIVERSITY PRESS
The Edinburgh Building, Cambridge, CB2 2RU, UK
  http://www.cup.cam.ac.uk
40 West 20th Street, New York, NY 10011–4211, USA
  http://www.cup.org
10 Stamford Road, Oakleigh, Melbourne 3166, Australia

First published 1999

Printed in the United Kingdom at the University Press, Cambridge

Typeset in Plantin 10/12pt   [CE]

A catalogue record for this book is available from the British Library

Library of Congress Cataloguing in Publication data
Anderson, Jeffrey J.
German unification and the union of Europe: the domestic politics
of integration policy / Jeffrey Anderson.
      p.   cm.
Includes bibliographical references.
ISBN 0 521 64355 4 – ISBN 0 521 64390 2 (pbk.)
1. Germany – History – Unification, 1990.   2. Germany – Relations – Europe.
3. Europe – Relations – Germany.   4. European Union – Germany.
5. Germany – Commercial policy.   I. Title.
DD290.3.A537   1997
327.4304′09′049 – dc21   98–41171   CIP

ISBN 0 521 64355 4 hardback
ISBN 0 521 64390 2 paperback

to Celeste

Contents

Figures and tables

Figures

Tables

Acknowledgments

I spent June and part of July 1989 in the Federal Republic as a participant in the annual Fulbright–Hayes Summer Seminar on German Civilization (*Landeskunde*). This six-week program brings fifteen to twenty American college professors, mostly German literature specialists but also a smattering of social scientists, to the Federal Republic each year to meet scholars, journalists, business leaders, and politicians. The goal of the *Landeskundekonferenz* is to develop a deeper understanding of politics and history among area specialists in the United States, with an eye toward broadening the curriculum of German studies programs. At the time, national newspapers were filled with the Tiananmen Square massacre and Gorbachev's triumphant visit to Bonn. Our seminar dealt with a host of historical and contemporary issues – national socialism, the postwar *Wirtschaftswunder*, immigration, environmental politics – and included visits to a depressed industrial region (the Saarland) and to the divided capital of Berlin. We left in early July with a balanced portrait of the West German Republic of the late 1980s. In late December, long after the Wall had ceased to function and the prospect of unification had become very real, I received a certificate of participation from Fulbright-Hayes, along with a cover letter from the Foundation's Bonn office apologizing for the fact that the summer seminar had failed to prepare us for the extraordinary events of the last six weeks!

I was certainly no more prescient than my German hosts. In fact, unification and the ensuing end of the postwar divide in Europe took the world by surprise. And yet, looking back on this momentous event with the benefit of over nine years of hindsight, it is striking how familiar the continent of today looks. NATO and the European Union (then the Community) still exist. Britain remains a skeptical participant in European affairs, the recent turnover in government to the contrary notwithstanding. France is still searching for a leadership role on the world stage. And Germany is still anchored comfortably in the West.

This book explores the origins and consequences of continuity, as well as the hidden sources of change, in a key nexus of post-1989 Europe: the relationship between German unification and European integration. In its successive historical manifestations, the German Question has defined the basic parameters for European conflict and cooperation, and this is no less true today, in the aftermath of (re)unification, as it was after 1871. Unlike past occasions when the futures of Germany and Europe have become intertwined, the events of 1989–90 unfolded in a context shaped by four decades of stable German democracy embedded within a peaceful European multilateral framework. The uniqueness of this setting, embracing both the domestic and supranational levels, demands close attention in its own right.

I could not have completed this project without sustained institutional support. First and foremost, I would like to thank the German Marshall Fund of the United States for a Postdoctoral Fellowship for Younger US Scholars to Germany. This fellowship enabled me to spend calendar year 1992 in Bonn, where I carried out the bulk of the field research for this book. I would like to express my appreciation to the Deutsche Gesellschaft für Auswärtige Politik (DGAP) in Bonn, which appointed me as a Research Fellow for the duration of my stay in Germany. Finally, I would like to thank the Thomas J. Watson Institute for International Studies at Brown University for providing travel support for follow-up interviewing and archival research I initiated in 1994.

I could not have completed this volume without the advice and assistance of several colleagues, to each of whom I owe a debt of gratitude: Thomas Banchoff, Simon Bulmer, Karl Kaiser, Peter Katzenstein, Paulette Kurzer, Andrew Moravcsik, Wolfgang Wessels, and Alan Zuckerman. I would also like to thank the (anonymous) civil servants, politicians, and interest group representatives in Brussels and throughout Germany who gave generously of their time and insights in the course of over 150 open-ended interviews I conducted between 1992 and 1995.

This book is dedicated to my wife, Celeste Wallander. She was a source of priceless intellectual and emotional nurture during the long years I spent taking this project from the drawing board to final publication. I vow never to subject her to another such marathon again.

Abbreviations

AA	Auswärtiges Amt
BFB	Bund Freier Bürger
BGA	Bundesverband des Deutschen Groß- und Außenhandel
BMF	Bundesministerium der Finanzen
BMGB	Beteiligungs-Management-Gesellschaft Berlin
BML	Bundesministerium für Ernährung, Landwirtschaft, und Forsten
BMU	Bundesministerium für Umwelt, Naturschutz, und Reaktorsicherheit
BMWi	Bundesministerium für Wirtschaft
BvS	Bundesanstalt für vereinigungsbedingte Sonderaufgaben
CAP	Common Agricultural Policy
CDU	Christian Democratic Union
CIS	Commonwealth of Independent States
CMEA	Council for Mutual Economic Assistance
COPA	Committee of Professional Agricultural Organizations
CSF	Community Support Framework
CSU	Christian Socialist Union
DBV	Deutscher Bauernverband
DG	Directorate-General
DGB	Deutscher Gewerkschaftsbund
DIHT	Deutscher Industrie- und Handelstag
DM	Deutsche Mark
DMS	Deutscher Maschinen- und Schiffbau AG
EAGGF	European Agricultural Guidance and Guarantee Fund
EC	European Community
ECJ	European Court of Justice
ECSC	European Coal and Steel Community
ECU	European Currency Unit
EEC	European Economic Community
EFTA	European Free Trade Association
EMU	economic and monetary union

EP	European Parliament
ERDF	European Regional Development Fund
ERM	Exchange Rate Mechanism
ESF	European Social Fund
EU	European Union
FDP	Free Democratic Party
FRG	Federal Republic of Germany
GA	Gemeinschaftsaufgabe "Verbesserung der regionalen Wirt-schaftsstruktur"
GAK	Gemeinschaftsaufgabe "Verbesserung der Agrarstruktur und des Küstenschutzes"
GATT	General Agreement on Tariffs and Trade
GDP	gross domestic product
GDR	German Democratic Republic
GEMSU	German economic, monetary, and social union
IEM	internal energy market
IGBE	IG Bergbau und Energie
LPG	Landwirtschaftliche Produktionsgenossenschaften
MKG	Management-Kommanditgesellschaft
MWP	Mecklenburg-West Pomerania
OECD	Organization for Economic Cooperation and Development
PDS	Party of Democratic Socialism
PHARE	Pologne-Hongrie assistance à la restructuration des écono-mies
SEA	Single European Act
SED	Socialist Unity Party of Germany
SPD	Social Democratic Party of Germany
TACIS	Technical Assistance for the Commonwealth of Independent States
TEN	Trans-European Network
TEU	Treaty on European Union
THA	Treuhandanstalt
TPA	third party access
UK	United Kingdom
VEG	Volkseigene Güter
VW	Volkswagen
WS	Wirtschaftsvereinigung Stahl

1   A new Germany in Europe?

On October 3, 1990, the German Democratic Republic dissolved into West Germany accompanied by formal ceremony and joyous celebration. In the same moment, the new territories joined the European Community, an event that passed with little fanfare or controversy even though something extraordinary had taken place. German unification, experienced and observed with immense hope by some and visceral unease by others, had occurred not against but within Europe, indeed *for* Europe: The Community channeled the unification process as unification in turn imparted new impulses to integration. Unification and union combined to produce an equilibration of political momentum.

To many observers, these events confirmed elemental postwar continuities.[1] For forty-five years after the end of World War II, West Germany's relationship to Europe resembled a virtuous circle in stable equilibrium: the Federal Republic drew economic prosperity and political legitimacy from its membership in a larger European project, which in turn gained strength from Germany's constructive engagement on the continent. The contrast with prewar Europe could not have been more stark.

And yet there is good reason to peer more closely into this comfortable and still intact fit between Germany and Europe, if only because so much of the postwar landscape has changed since the collapse of the Berlin Wall on November 9, 1989. Internationally, Cold War constraints on German foreign policy vanished with astonishing rapidity. Where once the mighty Warsaw Pact alliance stood poised on West Germany's doorstep, the settling dust now revealed a collection of fledgling democracies seeking to free themselves from a mortally weakened Soviet empire. Domestically, unification brought an additional 17 million

---

[1] But by no means all; see John Mearsheimer, "Back to the Future: Instability in Europe after the Cold War," *International Security* 15 (Fall 1990), 5–56; Kenneth Waltz, "The Emerging Structure of International Politics," *International Security* 18 (Fall 1993), 44–79; Christopher Layne, "The Unipolar Illusion: Why New Great Powers Will Rise," *International Security* 17 (Spring 1993), 5–48.

citizens into the expanded Federal Republic. Although the West Germans dictated the terms of unification to their eastern cousins, they could not prevent new wine from mixing with the old in a 1949 vintage bottle.

Since 1990 a complex pattern of continuity *and* change in Germany's European policies has emerged. Beneath broadly consistent approaches to the larger goals of integration, post-unification German policies exhibit considerable variation, from seamless continuity in trade and internal market affairs to conscious breaks with pre-1989 positions on cohesion, agricultural, and even state aid policies. The goal of this volume is to explain why this has happened. Specifically, how has the domestic politics of unification, stemming from new actors, problems, and structures, influenced German policies toward Europe? Why has continuity reigned in some areas, whereas in others significant changes, some approaching complete reversals, have been registered? What are the implications of this checkered pattern of outcomes for Germany and for Europe?

Germany in Europe: a framework of analysis

The aim of this volume is to explain the impact of unification on Germany's European policies. As such, this volume falls in the category of "case-oriented investigations", which attempt "to account for significant historical outcomes ... by piecing evidence together in a manner sensitive to historical chronology and [by] offering limited historical generalizations which are sensitive to context."[2] This type of study requires an analytical framework, or what Boudon describes as a "conceptual paradigm" – an integrated system of theoretical concepts that structures complex phenomena, narrows the range of likely causes, and thereby provides a basis for constructing explanatory propositions.[3] The framework developed in the remainder of this chapter draws on theoretical debates in comparative and international political economy about the role of interests, institutions, and ideas.

Peter Hall observes that economic policy "is influenced most significantly, first, by what a government is *pressed* to do, and secondly, by

---

[2] Charles Ragin, *The Comparative Method: Moving Beyond Qualitative and Quantitative Strategies* (Berkeley: University of California Press, 1987), 35. For an excellent discussion of standards of explanation in comparative politics, see Alan Zuckerman, "Reformulating Explanatory Standards and Advancing Theory in Comparative Politics," in Mark Lichbach and Alan Zuckerman, eds., *Comparative Politics: Rationality, Culture, and Structure* (New York: Cambridge University Press, 1997), 277–310.

[3] Raymond Boudon, *The Crisis in Sociology* (New York: Columbia University Press, 1980), 159–69.

what it *can* do in the economic sphere."[4] In other words, interests and institutions matter. Interests directly shape policy responses by establishing a distribution of societal preferences that national officials take into account as they seek to build electoral coalitions capable of winning and then holding political power.[5] Institutions influence what governments do (or don't do) by allocating power to some actors but not others, structuring the content and sequence of policymaking, and providing opportunities for and constraints on the state as its officials seek societal support for their policy choices.[6]

To Hall's succinct formulation, one must add a third variable: shared beliefs about the way the world works and one's place within it. Put another way, ideas matter too.[7] They enable actors to manage uncertainty about the expected consequences of alternative choices. Ideas can also function as cognitive maps that specify the range of possible solutions to problems, and as "frames" that provide actors with a symbolic and conceptual language to advance their causes.[8] In the context of strategic interaction among numerous actors, ideas frequently serve as "focal points," helping the expectations and strategies of actors to converge when there exist several possible outcomes, each of which would improve the position of the parties involved.[9]

[4] Peter Hall, *Governing the Economy* (Oxford: Oxford University Press, 1986), 232. Emphasis in the original.

[5] Peter Gourevitch, *Politics in Hard Times* (Ithaca: Cornell University Press, 1986), 55–60.

[6] Hall, *Governing the Economy*, 233.

[7] Goldstein and Keohane identify three types of beliefs, ranging from the general-universal to the specific: world views, principled beliefs, and causal beliefs. To their typology, one should add a fourth category: identity beliefs, which are described by Katzenstein as "ideologies of collective distinctiveness and purpose." Identity beliefs appear to occupy the space between principled and causal beliefs, serving as a filter for the former and a set of normative reference points for the latter. See Judith Goldstein and Robert Keohane, "Ideas and Foreign Policy: An Analytical Framework," in Judith Goldstein and Robert Keohane, eds., *Ideas and Foreign Policy* (Ithaca: Cornell University Press, 1993), 8; and Peter Katzenstein, "Introduction: Alternative Perspectives on National Security," in Peter Katzenstein, ed., *The Culture of National Security: Norms and Identity in World Politics* (New York: Columbia University Press, 1996), 1–32 at 6. See also Peter Hall, ed., *The Political Power of Economic Ideas* (Princeton: Princeton University Press, 1989); Kathryn Sikkink, *Ideas and Institutions* (Ithaca: Cornell University Press, 1991); and Judith Goldstein, *Ideas, Interests, and American Trade Policy* (Ithaca: Cornell University Press, 1993). For a review and critique of the ideas literature, see John Kurt Jacobson, "Much Ado about Ideas: The Cognitive Factor in Economic Policy," *World Politics* 47 (January 1995), 283–310; and Mark Blyth, "'Any More Bright Ideas?' The Ideational Turn of Comparative Political Economy," *Comparative Politics* 29 (January 1997), 229–50.

[8] John Campbell, "Institutional Analysis and the Role of Ideas in Political Economy," paper presented to the Seminar on the State and Capitalism since 1800, Center for European Studies, Harvard University, October 13, 1995.

[9] Geoffrey Garrett and Barry Weingast, "Ideas, Interests, and Institutions: Constructing the European Community's Internal Market," in Goldstein and Keohane, *Ideas and Foreign Policy*, 173–206.

Interests, institutions, and ideas are not independent of one another. Interests are typically conceptualized in material terms – that is, they arise from the position of actors in the domestic and international economies.[10] However, interest formulation is shaped not only by the material world, but by the realm of the possible, which is itself a function of the institutional context in which actors operate.

Similarly, ideas are bound up with both interests and institutions. Ideas that achieve political ascendance almost always are intimately tied to the interests they serve. Over time, though, the belief system may begin to serve as an independent rationale for choice, and even to reshape the very interests that originally propelled it into prominence.[11] Moreover, once an ascendant idea emerges through political competition, it is very likely to become institutionalized, as adherents of the belief system enact laws and create agencies to secure the policy outputs consistent with the idea. Ideational effects, mediated by institutions, will often persist long past the point where the idea ceases to command broad support and legitimacy. In fact, the institutionalized idea continues to influence politics because it serves interests – specifically, those of the individuals charged with carrying out government activities based on its principles. Interests still matter, although they are not necessarily the same ones that gave rise to the idea in the first place.

Reflecting on the main empirical questions framed above, it is unlikely that a focus on the interaction of *national* interests, *national* institutions, and *national* ideas can explain patterns of change and continuity in German policies toward Europe since 1990. The reason: Germany is literally "in" Europe; that is, it belongs to an ongoing and in many ways unique supranational venture.[12] The government's policy choices are shaped by a national context that is itself embedded in a larger system of political and economic governance that embraces actors who (a) operate within institutions that are independent of the member states;[13] (b) hold

---

[10] See for example Ronald Rogowski, *Commerce and Coalitions* (Princeton: Princeton University Press, 1989); Helen Milner and Robert Keohane, "Internationalization and Domestic Politics," in Robert Keohane and Helen Milner, eds., *Internationalization and Domestic Politics* (New York: Cambridge University Press, 1996), 3–24.

[11] Thus, it is possible to think of ideas in much the same way as Downs conceived ideology in his work on spatial party competition: as intellectual shortcuts to choice – an efficient alternative to the cumbersome task of tallying up the costs and benefits of various strategic options. See Anthony Downs, *An Economic Theory of Democracy* (New York: Harper and Row, 1957).

[12] This is a point made forcefully and articulately by Peter Katzenstein, "United Germany in an Integrating Europe," in Peter Katzenstein, ed., *Tamed Power* (Ithaca: Cornell University Press, 1997), 1–48.

[13] Institutionalist accounts of European integration include Simon Bulmer, "The Governance of the European Union: A New Institutionalist Approach," *Journal of Public Policy* 13:4 (1993), 351–80; and Paul Pierson, "The Path to European

and pursue interests that are in no way purely derivative of the member states; and (c) are infused with ideas situated at the supranational level.[14]

In a phrase, membership in the EC/EU matters.[15] And as far as national policy choice is concerned, membership is most profitably conceptualized in terms of the multilayered interactions of interests, institutions, and ideas at both the national and supranational levels. This perspective expressly recognizes the permeability of national boundaries and the contingent nature of sovereignty, which is nowhere more apparent than in contemporary Europe.[16]

What does this mean in concrete terms? First and foremost, the analytical focus rests squarely on national decision-makers, who ultimately decide whether and how to respond to the mix of pressures, challenges, and opportunities presented to them by a multilevel environment consisting of overlapping constellations of ideas, interests, and institutions. National officials not only reflect, act, and react within this complex environment; they constitute a significant part of that environment. Consequently, they are better positioned than other actors to wield influence over process and outcomes at the level of domestic politics. So too are they positioned advantageously *vis-à-vis* domestic actors to shape the corresponding political context in Brussels.[17]

Integration: A Historical Institutionalist Analysis," *Comparative Political Studies* 29 (April 1996), 123–64.

[14] An example of an idea operating at the European level is the principle of "multi-lateralism"; see John Gerard Ruggie, "Multilateralism: The Anatomy of an Institution," in John Gerard Ruggie, ed., *Multilateralism Matters* (New York: Columbia University Press, 1993), 3–47. Another is the principle of "mutual recognition," which is based on a 1979 ruling by the European Court of Justice and basically stipulates that a product made and sold legally in one member state cannot be barred from another member state. A third example is the principle of "subsidiarity," which prescribes that "policy decisions ... be made on a level as close as possible to the one on which they are implemented while remaining consonant with the basic principles of social justice." Peter Lange, "The Politics of the Social Dimension," in Alberta Sbragia, ed., *Euro-Politics* (Washington, DC: Brookings Institution, 1991), 231. In addition to these more comprehensive principles, numerous internally coherent belief systems, attached to concrete policy areas administered by the EC/EU, permeate the supranational political process.

[15] Wayne Sandholtz, "Membership Matters: Limits of the Functional Approach to European Institutions," *Journal of Common Market Studies* 34 (September 1996), 403–30.

[16] An earlier formulation of this analytical approach can be found in Jeffrey Anderson and Celeste Wallander, "Interests and the Wall of Ideas: Germany's Eastern Trade Policy after Unification," *Comparative Political Studies* 30 (December 1997), 675–98. On sovereignty in contemporary Europe, see Thomas Biersteker, "Locating the Emerging European Polity: Beyond States or State?" in Jeffrey Anderson, ed., *Regional Integration and Democracy: Expanding on the European Experience* (Boulder: Rowman & Littlefield, 1998).

[17] The treaty foundations of the EC/EU privilege the member governments over domestic

Second, explaining national policy choice in an integrating Europe requires some basic assumptions about the integration process itself and the goals and motivations of national officials.

Assumption 1: There are two political dimensions to the European integration process: constitutive and regulative.

Constitutive politics involves processes and outcomes that establish or amend Community rules of the game, and is largely coextensive with the high politics surrounding periodic "grand bargains" like the Treaty of Rome, the Single European Act (SEA), and the Treaty on European Union (TEU). Regulative politics, on the other hand, takes place within established, routinized areas of Community activity, such as agricultural or technology policy.

Although rule-making and rule-applying are conceptually and procedurally distinct, constitutive and regulative politics are not independent phenomena; each influences the other in complex ways. For example, obtaining agreement on the SEA in 1986 necessitated an explicit side-payment that entailed a substantial budget increase and far-reaching procedural reforms enacted two years later to Community regional policies;[18] in this instance, constitutive politics drove regulative politics. In turn, the 1988 reforms encouraged a flowering of regionalist sentiments and political mobilization across the Community that ultimately contributed to the creation of a new European institution – the Committee of the Regions – in the Treaty on European Union; here, regulative politics influenced constitutive politics.

Unpacking integration into its component parts is essential not only because it more accurately depicts the complexities inherent in postwar European multilateralism. It also contributes to a more refined understanding of the motivations behind the European policies of member governments. This leads to the second assumption on which this study rests.

Assumption 2: National officials will pursue a particular kind of "milieu goal" in Brussels – namely, to ensure that government policy objectives are consistent, both within Europe *and* across the national and supranational levels.[19]

(*and* supranational) actors in many areas of Community policymaking, particularly those involving the treaty framework itself. See Alberta Sbragia, "Thinking about the European Future: The Uses of Comparison," in Sbragia, *Euro-Politics*, 257–91. Of related interest is Andrew Moravcsik, "Why the European Community Strengthens the State: Domestic Politics and International Cooperation," paper presented at the Conference of Europeanists, Chicago, March 31–April 2, 1994.

[18] Gary Marks, "Structural Policy in the European Community," in Sbragia, *Euro-Politics*, 191–224.

[19] On the concept of milieu goals, see Arnold Wolfers, "The Goals of Foreign Policy," in Arnold Wolfers, ed., *Discord and Collaboration* (Baltimore: Johns Hopkins University Press, 1962); and Simon Bulmer, Charlie Jeffery, and William Paterson, "Germany's

National officials will avoid persistent contradictions between the constitutive and regulative goals they pursue in Brussels. In other words, if member states are to derive benefits from membership, then national preferences concerning how the larger framework of Community rules should be constructed must be compatible with national preferences on substantive policy issues, and vice versa. Where enduring incompatibilities between constitutive and regulative policy objectives surface, national officials will try to reconcile inconsistencies by adjusting the government's constitutive agenda, its various regulative agendas, or both.

Furthermore, national officials will strive to replicate or, at a minimum, secure at the European level the constellation of ideas, interests, and institutions that they find (or would find) most advantageous at the domestic level. In so doing, they seek to preserve and/or create "comparative institutional advantage" for the national economy.[20] Each member government conducts its European foreign policy, which entails both constitutive and regulative politics, with an eye to surrounding the national political economy with a supranational environment that is facilitative, or at a minimum not hostile.

This is not to suggest that each member government succeeds in forging Europe in its own image; an obvious contrary example is the United Kingdom, which has fared abysmally in Brussels. Nor does it imply that influence is just a one-way street; as national officials pursue their supranational objectives, they open up their countries to the effects of European-level institutions, ideas, and interests.[21] Indeed, there are

European Diplomacy: Shaping the Regional Milieu," paper prepared for the Forschungsgruppe Europa of the Centrum für Angewandte Politikforschung, Munich, December 1996. This assumption is consistent with Putnam's characterization of international negotiations, where participants face strong pressures to bargain in ways that are consistent across both the international and domestic tables. See Robert Putnam, "Diplomacy and Domestic Politics: The Logic of Two-Level Games," *International Organization* 42 (Summer 1988), 427–60.

[20] For an extended discussion of comparative institutional advantage, a concept that originates in endogenous growth theories, see Peter Hall, "The Political Economy of Adjustment in Germany," in Frieder Naschold *et al.*, eds., *Ökonomische Leistungsfähigkeit und institutionelle Innovation. WZB-Jahrbuch 1997* (Berlin: Wissenschaftszentrum-Berlin, 1997), 293–317.

[21] This touches on a fierce debate in international relations over "constructivism." At issue is the causal role of institutions and norms: do they act as constraints on rational, self-interested actors (the central constructivist criticism of IR orthodoxy), or do they actually "constitute" the interests and even identities of actors (the constructivist challenge)? See i.a. Jeffrey Checkel, "The Constructivist Turn in International Relations Theory," *World Politics* 50 (January 1998), 324–48. This controversy is replicated within the Community studies literature; advocates of principal–agent theories like Moravcsik and Pollack come very close to ruling out the possibility that EC actors and institutions can influence the preferences and identities of domestic actors, a position hotly disputed by "diffusionists" like Marks and Hooghe. See for

many instances of national governments actively seeking to expose their countries to supranational influence; witness Italy's use of the European agenda of economic and monetary union in the 1990s as leverage to push through difficult and controversial economic reforms at home.

West Germany (1949–89)

The soundness of these two starting assumptions is borne out by the West German experience, an unparalleled success in the creation of a supportive supranational environment for the national political economy. In this section, I review the basic elements of the German model in Europe to establish this point, and furthermore to set the stage for the ensuing discussion of the possible effects of unification.

The West German model

The German model has been labeled a "coordinated market economy"[22] that embodies a number of distinctive attributes. On the market side, West Germany featured an "articulated industrial system"[23] based on close relationships among firms and between firms and universal banks; these institutional linkages led managers to adopt long-term planning and investment horizons, and they conferred on the private sector the capacity to undertake sectoral adjustment in the context of industrial crisis. West German industrial relations approximated the classic Scandinavian model of neocorporatism in which comprehensive, well-organized representatives of labor and capital engaged each other in an institutionalized process of negotiated adjustment; the primary locus of activity, in contrast to Scandinavia, was at

example Andrew Moravcsik, "Preferences and Power in the European Community: A Liberal Intergovernmentalist Approach," *Journal of Common Market Studies* 31 (December 1993), 473–524; Mark Pollack, "Obedient Servant or Runaway Eurocracy? Delegation, Agency, and Agenda Setting in the European Community," Working Paper No. 95–10, Center for International Affairs, Harvard University, 1995; and Gary Marks, Liesbet Hooghe, and Kermit Blank, "European Integration from the 1980s: State-Centric v. Multi-Level Governance," *Journal of Common Market Studies* 34 (September 1996), 341–78. What is fodder for scholarly conflict in international relations is more or less conventional wisdom in comparative politics, where scholars have long accepted the notion that institutions and ideas can influence and even "constitute" the preferences and identities of actors.

[22] David Soskice, "The Institutional Infrastructure for International Competitiveness: A Comparative Analysis of the UK and Germany," in A. B. Atkinson and R. Brunetta, eds., *Economics for the New Europe* (Basingstoke: Macmillan, 1991), 45–66.

[23] Andrew Shonfield, *Modern Capitalism: The Changing Balance of Public and Private Power* (Oxford: Oxford University Press, 1969), 247.

the sectoral and plant level, giving the German system a decentralized cast.[24]

The West German state was similarly decentralized. Territorially, this took the form of administrative federalism, in which the states (Länder) enjoyed significant autonomy in relation to the federal government, were responsible for implementing federal legislation, and participated directly in the national legislative process through the upper house, the Bundesrat. Functionally, decentralization flowed from the independence of the Bundesbank,[25] as well as the autonomy of individual national ministries, which was anchored in the constitution and enhanced by the recurrence of coalition government in the Federal Republic. The tendency of the West German constitutional order to generate many centers of authority and power contributed to several trademark characteristics of the German policy process – specifically, concertation, consultation, and power-sharing.[26]

These institutional arrangements rested on a broad and deep ideational consensus about the relationship between state and market. Agreement over fundamentals manifested itself in numerous ways, including the high level of policy continuity despite frequent partisan turnover in government, as well as the generally depoliticized manner in which policy was carried out. The consensus was permissive in that it granted policymakers considerable leeway to formulate concrete policy alternatives and to debate their relative merits with vigor, but at the same time it imposed well-understood and accepted limits on both public and private actors.

At the core of this belief system, dubbed the "social market economy,"[27] was a set of consistent yet flexible principles that assigned primacy to the market, defined not as the perfect competition lionized in economics textbooks or in American political discourse, but in terms compatible with Germany's distinctive brand of "organized

---

[24] Kathleen Thelen, *Union of Parts: Labor Politics in Postwar Germany* (Ithaca: Cornell University Press, 1991), 43; Andrei Markovits, *The Politics of the West German Trade Unions* (New York: Cambridge University Press, 1986); Fritz Scharpf, *Crisis and Choice in European Social Democracy* (Ithaca: Cornell University Press, 1991), 119.

[25] For a study of the Bundesbank in comparative perspective, see John Goodman, *Monetary Sovereignty: The Politics of Central Banking in Western Europe* (Ithaca: Cornell University Press, 1992).

[26] This clearly impressed Shonfield, who notes the coherence of German economic policymaking despite the large number of competing centers of power generated by the constitution. His explanation – coherence results from an "irrepressible administrative instinct to centralize authority" – is unsatisfactory, conjuring up tired cultural stereotypes. Shonfield, *Modern Capitalism*, 271.

[27] The phrase was coined by Alfred Müller-Armack, *Wirtschaftslenkung und Marktwirtschaft* (Hamburg: Verlag für Wirtschaft und Sozialpolitik, 1948).

capitalism."[28] The primary task of the state was to uphold the self-regulating economic order by establishing a facilitative framework of rules and regulations (*Ordnungspolitik/Rahmenpolitik*). The state also bore a social responsibility to lessen the dislocation that inevitably accompanies the workings of the market. This entailed comprehensive welfare programs as well as a variety of industrial and regional policies designed to ease the hardship visited on individuals and regions by sectoral adjustment.[29]

To say that West Germany sustained a market-oriented political economy is to make a relative statement. Like its EC neighbors, the Federal Republic subsidized industry.[30] Like its neighbors, it engaged in sectoral policies that were difficult to justify on anything other than political grounds; aid to the coal industry and agriculture stand out as prime examples. But unlike its EC neighbors, the Federal Republic subsidized less, in a less interventionist manner, and with conscious orientation to market principles.[31]

Thus, the ideology of the social market economy entailed much more than *laissez-faire* in *Lederhosen*. The state was assigned responsibilities and tasks that took it well beyond the nightwatchman state lionized by neoclassical economists and American business. Nevertheless, the postwar German state fell short of its interventionist and at times

---

[28] Christopher Allen, "The Underdevelopment of Keynesianism in the Federal Republic of Germany," in Peter Hall, ed., *The Political Power of Economic Ideas* (Princeton: Princeton University Press, 1989), 263–89.

[29] For a comprehensive overview of German industrial policy, see Roland Sturm, *Die Industriepolitik der Bundesländer und die europäische Integration* (Baden-Baden: Nomos Verlagsgesellschaft, 1991). Brief but insightful discussions can also be found in Peter Katzenstein, *Policy and Politics in West Germany: The Growth of a Semi-Sovereign State* (Philadelphia: Temple University Press, 1987), 101–04; and Josef Esser and Wolfgang Fach (with Kenneth Dyson), "'Social Market' and Modernization Policy: West Germany," in Kenneth Dyson and Stephen Wilks, eds., *Industrial Crisis: A Comparative Study of the State and Industry* (New York: St. Martin's Press, 1983), 125.

[30] For a comprehensive, comparative overview of West German subsidy and non-tariff barrier practices, see Herbert Giersch, Karl-Heinz Paqué, and Holger Schmieding, *The Fading Miracle: Four Decades of Social Market Economy in Germany* (New York: Cambridge University Press, 1992), 227–36.

[31] Giersch, Paqué, and Schmieding argue that despite the aggregate level of subsidies doled out by the government, most of which is directed at sunset industries on the basis of social rationales, Germany belonged to the liberal camp in the EC. Giersch, Paqué, and Schmieding, *The Fading Miracle*, 227 and 235. Other scholars have remarked on the high level of consistency between economic ideology and practice in West Germany; see Kenneth Dyson and Stephen Wilks, "Conclusions," in Dyson and Wilks, *Industrial Crisis*, 252; Michael Porter, *The Competitive Advantage of Nations* (New York: The Free Press, 1990), 378; Kenneth Dyson, "West Germany: The Search for a Rationalist Consensus," in Jeremy Richardson, ed., *Policy Styles in Western Europe* (London: George Allen and Unwin, 1982), 24.

omnipresent counterparts in Japan and France. Streeck aptly describes it as an "enabling state."[32]

Of course, these interlocking frameworks of institutions and ideas did not emerge full blown from the ruins of the Third Reich, nor once established did they preclude divisive conflicts between left and right over foreign policy and social and economic priorities. However, political debates unfolded within clear parameters. Although left and right disagreed vehemently over the limits of state intervention or the extent of worker co-determination, at no time during the postwar period were core institutional and ideational features of the West German political economy at stake politically. The Bonn model served the interests of a cross-class coalition centered in the export sectors of the economy, and could draw on the unswerving support of the state bureaucracy responsible for economic policy.[33]

The West German model in Europe

Often overlooked in discussions of the German national model is the degree to which it was embedded in Europe. This resulted from a series of conscious choices by German elites after 1945. Hanrieder has described the fifteen years after "zero hour" (*Stunde Null*) alternately as a time when, for German policymakers, "necessity overwhelmed choice" and "choice coincided with necessity."[34] There is truth in both formulations. Military defeat led not to a truncated, embittered version of prewar Germany, but to a new polity with tender democratic roots and uncertain economic prospects. Based on hard-nosed instrumental calculations, German elites embraced western multilateralism and in particular European integration. Achieving an "equality of rights" with its European neighbors via integration was viewed in Bonn as the *sine qua non* for the international rehabilitation of the new German republic and the domestic objective of reunification.[35] It also was seen as essential to economic recovery and reconstruction.

[32] Wolfgang Streeck, "German Capitalism: Does It Exist? Can It Survive?", in Colin Crouch and Wolfgang Streeck, eds., *Political Economy of Modern Capitalism: Mapping Convergence and Diversity* (London: Sage Publications, 1997).

[33] These include the Federal Ministry of Finance (Bundesministerium der Finanzen, or BMF) and the Federal Ministry of Economics (Bundesministerium für Wirtschaft, or BMWi). The latter, dominated by ministers from the liberal Free Democratic Party (FDP), has been described as "the political spokesman for the doctrine of the social market economy." Dyson, "West Germany," 35. See also H. Richard Friman, *Patchwork Protectionism* (Ithaca: Cornell University Press, 1990), 49.

[34] Wolfram Hanrieder, *Germany, America, Europe* (New Haven: Yale University Press, 1989), 2 and 7 respectively.

[35] Alan Milward, *The European Rescue of the Nation-State* (Berkeley: University of

Material and political interests infused Germany's foreign policy choices during this period, but as causal agents they can only take one so far. To fully account for many aspects of Bonn's external behavior, including its pacifist military security policy, its approach to national sovereignty, and its aversion to unilateralism, one must look beyond interests to the politics of identity in postwar Germany, which unfolded in searing domestic political debates over rearmament, reunification, and European integration carried out by a new mix of German political actors under the watchful eyes of neighboring countries and allies.[36]

Initially, the new collective identity defined itself as the antithesis of the expansionist, predatory, undemocratic, eastward-looking state that terrorized the European continent between 1933 and 1945. It also reflected foreign expectations about acceptable German behavior.[37] As such, joining Europe followed almost inexorably from the country's reconstituted national identity. The multilateral frameworks created by the Paris and Rome treaties provided welcome constraints: a liberal-democratic hood for a fledgling democracy. They also allowed political elites to signal to each other, to the German public, to Europe, and to the world beyond, a changed, benign identity.

As the Federal Republic established a reputation for economic prowess, new dimensions appeared in its identity, ones characterized more by what the country embodied in the present – e.g. "the trading state" – than by the negation of what it once was.[38] The coincidence of European integration and democratic consolidation in Germany also meant that over time, integration insinuated itself into the national matrix of economic and political values.[39] Along the way, Germany

---

California Press, 1992), 197–98. See also Simon Bulmer and William Paterson, *The Federal Republic of Germany and the European Community* (London: Allen & Unwin, 1987), 5–6.

[36] On this topic, which has been described variously as "the politics of collective memory" and "identity politics," see Andrei Markovits and Simon Reich, *The German Predicament: Memory and Power in the New Europe* (Ithaca: Cornell University Press, 1997); Thomas Banchoff, "Germany's European Policy: A Constructivist Perspective," Working Paper Series #8.1, Program for the Study of Germany and Europe, Minda de Gunzberg Center for European Studies, Harvard University, 1998; and Thomas Berger, "Norms, Identity, and National Security in Germany and Japan," in Katzenstein, ed., *The Culture of National Security*, 317–56.

[37] Scholars working in this tradition emphasize the extent to which identity is shaped by the broader environment, including the expectations of other actors. See Ron Jepperson, Alexander Wendt, and Peter Katzenstein, "Norms, Identity, Culture, and National Security," in Katzenstein, ed., *The Culture of National Security*, 33–75.

[38] See for example Berger, "Norms, Identity, and National Security in Germany and Japan." Others disagree, arguing that the Germans to this day retain an identity of negation rather than affirmation. See Marc Fisher, *After the Wall: Germany, the Germans, and the Burdens of History* (New York: Simon and Schuster, 1995), 288.

[39] Bulmer and Paterson, *The Federal Republic of Germany and the European Community*, 8.

experienced a "Europeanization of state identity."[40] Political elites and average citizens increasingly viewed the Community not just as a source of concrete economic and political benefits, but as an integral part of the national model of political economy.

Bonn's general goal in Europe was to erect institutional and normative frameworks at the supranational level that would nurture its successful domestic economic formula. Within specific policy areas, the government sought to preserve these overarching frameworks and adapt them to changing domestic and international circumstances. West Germany's political objectives in Europe were quite likely unique. Neither British nor French governments projected the kind of integrated national model of political economy, resting on a broad political consensus, that required a supportive supranational framework of institutions and policy regimes.[41]

European flying buttresses for the German model took many forms. Maintaining a barrier-free internal market and a free trade position *vis-à-vis* the rest of the world were essential to the Federal Republic's "apolitical 'politics of productivity'."[42] German policymakers consistently backed proposals for EC-wide harmonization in the areas of economic and monetary cooperation, industrial policy, and regional assistance programs, all to preserve a level field of competition for German firms and to reduce the negative consequences of other countries' policy decisions, such as imported inflation. The social dimension of the social market economy found expression and support in EC environmental policy, the Common Agricultural Policy (CAP), competition and regional policies, and social policy.

By the end of the 1980s, a high level of congruence had emerged between the Federal Republic and the European Community.[43] Institutionally, both were characterized by cooperative federal arrangements in which authority and competencies were shared among political

---

[40] Katzenstein, "United Germany in an Integrating Europe," 29.

[41] When Hanrieder identifies a persistent theme in postwar German history – "the Germans' stubborn determination to retain a measure of economic and monetary independence, the freedom to organize their national economic life according to the principles and values they cherish ..." – he is surely right at some level, but his statement tends to overlook the fact that German governments, in their relations with the EC, consistently sought and obtained more from Brussels than "freedom from." Hanrieder, *Germany, America, Europe*, 228.

[42] Joann Gowa, "Bipolarity and the Postwar International Economic Order," in Peter Katzenstein, ed., *Industry and Politics in Germany* (Ithaca: Cornell University Press, 1989), 34.

[43] The following analysis is based on Simon Bulmer, "Shaping the Rules? The Constitutive Politics of the European Union and German Power," in Katzenstein, *Tamed Power*, 49–79. See also the more general discussion in Katzenstein, "United Germany in an Integrating Europe," 33–44.

executives at multiple levels.[44] In West Germany and the EC, the policy process was organized in a highly segmented or sectorized manner. Similar ideational principles upheld the rules of the game in each system. Political and economic actors in the Federal Republic and the Community laid great emphasis on consensualism. Similarly, the norm of subsidiarity was firmly established in each system. In the economic sphere, the two systems cast the relationship between public authority and the market in comparable terms; that is, many elements of the West German doctrine of the social market economy found ready counterparts in the social-liberal orientation of the EC's common market. Finally, the content of German and EC policies dovetailed sufficiently to suggest broad areas of common interest between Bonn policymakers and Community officials; these included liberal external trade and internal market policies, price and structural support for agriculture, the social compensation principles underlying regional economic policy, and the price stability orientation of economic and monetary union (EMU).[45]

This national–supranational congruence was the product of reciprocal influence and convergence, not the outcome of Germany's forceful projection of its model onto the rest of Europe. That said, West Germany continually sought to intensify and expand the multilateralism on which the European project rested. The result was a splendid irony of postwar European history: German political elites originally embraced the Community as a means of establishing an equality of sovereign rights between Germany and its neighbors, but then used membership to diffuse a markedly different conception of those rights onto their European partners.[46]

The goal of maintaining domestic system requirements at the supranational level, combined with what I have described elsewhere as "reflexive support for an exaggerated multilateralism,"[47] carried weighty implications for Germany's approach to regulative policy questions. For

---

[44] In Germany, cooperative federalism embraces the federal government (Bund) and the states (Länder), whereas at the EC level, parallel institutions bring together the member governments and supranational actors like the Commission. See Fritz Scharpf, "The Joint-Decision Trap; Lessons from German Federalism and European Integration," *Public Administration* 66 (Autumn 1988), 239–78; and Sbragia, "Thinking about the European Future," 257–91.

[45] An up-to-date discussion of these EU policies can be found in Helen Wallace and William Wallace, eds., *Politics and Policy in the EU: The Challenge of Governance* (Oxford: Oxford University Press, 1996).

[46] See, among others, Bulmer and Paterson, *The Federal Republic of Germany and the European Community*, 9–11.

[47] Jeffrey Anderson, "Hard Interests, Soft Power, and Germany's Changing Role in Europe," in Katzenstein, *Tamed Power*, 85.

one, it meant that Bonn rarely adopted the accountant's yardstick in Brussels. In fact, more often than not it bankrolled expensive European initiatives like the promotion of economic and social cohesion, even though domestic actors stood to receive few material benefits. Up until 1989, Germany's constitutive and regulative policy agendas stood in lagged harmony with respect to one another, with the former setting parameters for the latter, and the latter reinforcing the former. In key respects, the relationship between West Germany and Europe took on elements of a stable equilibrium. Politically, this equilibrium remained operative throughout the postwar period because it satisfied the expectations of other Community members as to the acceptable face of German power in Europe, while drawing on a firm yet permissive domestic consensus about the German model and the country's place in Europe, a consensus that was nurtured by economic prosperity.

Unification and union: interests, institutions, and ideas

Having built a successful model of political economy and, furthermore, having achieved a remarkably stable, even symbiotic relationship to Europe, (West) German officials had every reason to try to sustain the national–supranational equilibrium in its pre-unification form after 1990. Yet the intricacies of this equilibrium were exposed to the full force of events after the collapse of the Berlin Wall in November 1989. Unification altered the national mix of interests, institutions, and ideas within a remarkably brief period.

By far the most visible changes occurred in the realm of interests. The former GDR encompassed actors with territorial and sectoral interests markedly different from the west across a broad range of policy areas. In most cases, these interests were opposed to long-established national government policies, which upon unification retained their basic orientation to western German constituencies and to West German national priorities. Given the strong congruence between national and supranational governance structures, eastern German interests by extension were likely to clash with many EC regulative policies too.

Institutional alterations wrought by unification – some of a permanent nature, others provisional – occurred as well. For the most part, these entailed the mere extension of West German parliamentary-electoral and administrative frameworks to the east. In some instances, however, more substantial changes followed, raising the possibility that the Bonn policymaking process itself, finely tuned after four decades of operation, would undergo a transformation. This post-unification institutional landscape must be seen in conjunction with the new actors and interests outlined above. Specifically, by virtue of unification, eastern German actors gained access to many national and EC policy regimes, which created obvious opportunities to exercise influence. More broadly, it meant that a major force for policy continuity – a stable institutional environment – was no longer a given after 1990.

It is less evident that unification altered the competition between ideas in the federal policy process. The discrediting of "real existing socialism," which began well before the collapse of the wall, left intact few if any viable eastern alternatives to the reigning capitalist model in the west. Still, many eastern German individuals, groups, and agencies brought to national political debates an outlook rooted in forty years of state socialism. Socialist and post-socialist conceptions of citizen–state and state–market relations, to name just two, challenged basic elements and assumptions of the social market economy.

By transforming the domestic mix of ideas, interests, and institutions, unification propelled Germany's complex, coherent relationship with the EC into a state of *potential* disorder. The central empirical question posed in this volume is whether and how the interaction of unification and union is contributing, either directly or indirectly, to shifts in long-standing German policies toward Europe, as well as to Germany's place in Europe writ large. To provide structure for the analysis that follows, it is appropriate here to formulate a handful of testable hypotheses.

Alas, the scholarly literature reviewed earlier offers few concrete prescriptions. One learns that interests, institutions, and ideas matter, and moreover one can obtain a sense of how each matters – that is, the causal mechanisms these factors set in motion. Less clear is under what circumstances and how much in relation to other factors each matters. In fact, the literature is often driven by causal one-upmanship: interest-based theories are criticized for ignoring institutions; institutionalist accounts are condemned in turn for disregarding the role of ideas; and so on. One can only lament the fact that so little attention has been devoted to theoretical synthesis.

That said, the political economy literature can be mined profitably for raw materials with which to formulate specific hypotheses that address the pattern of change and continuity in German policies toward Europe since 1990. Since the range of candidate hypotheses is vast, the analysis will concentrate on a restricted subset. Each is selected for its relevance to broader theoretical issues, and is framed according to *ceteris paribus* conditions in the clearest and strongest possible terms to facilitate empirical testing.

In any study of policy choice in a democracy, the search for the sources of change and continuity should begin with domestic interest politics. This premise is especially apropos for German unification, which resulted in the geographical extension of an established politico-economic system to previously "foreign" actors.

H1: If eastern German actors do not press for change in government policy toward Europe, government policy will not change. Conversely, if eastern German actors press for change in government policy toward Europe, national officials will adjust policy to meet their expressed needs.

H2: Regardless of the interests of eastern German actors, national officials will administer policy in a way that meets the expressed needs of western German actors. When western groups demand policy continuity, continuity will ensue. When they demand policy change, change will ensue.

H1 focuses attention on the effects of eastern German opposition to standing Bonn policies toward Europe. Empirical support for this hypothesis would sustain a central proposition derived from classical pluralist theory: interests agitate (or do not); democratically elected governments react (or do not). Even if H1 is not borne out, explanations consistent with the causal primacy of interests are still possible and perhaps even plausible. H2 addresses an especially important set of scenarios. In deciding whether to respond to pressures for policy change, national officials will have to balance any demands for change emanating from the new territories against the interests of domestic actors who have been served by existing policy. Eastern German pressure for policy change could spark a countermobilization among western German actors who support policy continuity, leading ultimately to no change in government policy. Similarly, even in the absence of eastern German pressures for change, national officials could adjust policy in response to the demands of western constituencies who are coping with new circumstances after unification.

Should either of these two hypotheses be confirmed, then explanations granting pride of place to domestic interests and the politics of unification are likely to suffice. That is, irrespective of an unchanged institutional and ideational landscape, alterations in the mix of domestic interests produces adjustments in national policy positions on EC matters. To echo the language of classical pluralism, changes in the vector of societal interests are both necessary and sufficient to alter the direction of public policy. If an irregular pattern of change and continuity materializes, however, the search for causes in the domestic politics of unification will have to expand beyond interests.

Politics unfolds within varied institutional contexts at the national level, which influence outcomes just as surely as interests do.

H3: Where unification results in a modification of national policy institutions, eastern German actors opposed to government policy toward Europe will enjoy greater success in effecting change.

H4: Where eastern German actors opposed to government policy toward Europe are included in the national policymaking process, national officials will adjust policy to meet their expressed needs.

H3 seeks to test a truism of the institutionalist literature: established institutional frameworks impede change and transformation, whereas institutional discontinuities create openings for change.[48] H4 takes a somewhat different tack, implying that certain kinds of institutional continuities are conducive to policy shifts. Specifically, it suggests that activated interests are necessary but not sufficient to produce policy change; eastern German opponents of government policy, however united and well organized, could be excluded from the decision-making process in the national capital, and thus fail. If they are entitled to participate directly in the policy process, on the other hand, they will enjoy more effective opportunities to shape the definition of national and/or European priorities, and may be able to enlist the support of western German groups and federal officials in their cause. As such, favorable terms of institutional access for mobilized eastern German groups will produce policy change.

The domestic politics of unification also takes place within variegated ideational contexts.

H5: Where unification results in a modification of the national belief system attached to a particular policy area, eastern German actors opposed to government policy toward Europe will enjoy greater success in effecting change.

With that in mind, H5 parallels the first of the institutional hypotheses outlined above: an established national belief system, particularly during times of great uncertainty, is a force for policy continuity, whereas a collapsed or even weakened ideational system can create a window for change.

The first five hypotheses are cast in terms of domestic interests and national institutions and ideas. There is of course another level, populated with independent actors, institutions, and ideas, that cannot be ignored in attempts to explain change and continuity in German policies toward Europe. Specifically, European actors will seek to advance their interests and policy models when confronting the challenges and opportunities generated by unification. Where their objectives dovetail with Bonn's positions, policy continuity is the likely result. Indeed, the

---

[48] Chapter 2 will present evidence that the German government's unification policy of rapid institutional transfer led to very few "discontinuities" of the type described in this hypothesis.

stronger the overlap in interests and ideas between national officials and Brussels, the more resistant the former will be to demands for policy change. Alternatively, where national-supranational congruence is lacking, political alliances between supranational and subnational actors may develop in opposition to federal policy, intensifying the pressures for change on Bonn.

H6: Where eastern German actors opposed to government policy toward Europe are excluded from the national policymaking process but enjoy access at the European level, they will have greater success in effecting a change in their government's policy.

H7: Where eastern German actors confront a situation in which the prevailing national policy model they oppose does not correspond to the prevailing European policy model, they will have greater success in effecting change.

H6 treats the European level as an alternative access point for stymied eastern German opponents of Bonn policy. In short, failure at home can be overcome by success in Brussels. H7 is designed to test the notion that eastern actors, when confronted with political obstacles in their national capital, may under certain circumstances be able to appeal successfully to larger European principles in pressing the case for change on their national government.[49]

Case selection

To test these seven working hypotheses, I compare national responses across several European regulative policy areas in the post-unification period. The focus on the regulative dimension of Germany's approach to integration is justified for two reasons. First, it is where the empirical puzzle lies; German continuity in constitutive politics has been accompanied by a much more diverse pattern at the level of regulative politics. Second, the focus on specific EC/EU regulative policy areas dovetails with what we know about the European policy process in Germany; it is highly "sectorized,"[50] and, as such, any policy shifts will flow not from a single, coherent government position, but rather will trickle in separately and in many cases independently from the various domestic policy communities involved with Community affairs.

I examine seven regulative cases in this volume: agriculture, structural

---

[49] The fact that distinct ideas underpin or inform individual policy areas opens up the possibility that they may play a highly variegated causal role in EC/EU–member state interactions. In short, ideas may have stronger effects in some policy areas, and weaker ones in others, due to differences in their degree of institutionalization or their level of coherence.

[50] Bulmer and Paterson, *The Federal Republic of Germany and the European Community*, 25–31.

funds, internal market, energy, environment, trade, and competition policy. Each is an intrinsically important issue area. As a case in point, together the Common Agricultural Policy (CAP) and the structural funds account for just over three-quarters of the annual EU budget, thereby establishing in practical terms the Union as an entity that "commands resources, distributes benefits, allocates markets, and adjudicates between conflicting interests."[51]

More importantly, there are compelling methodological reasons to select this set of cases. As subsequent chapters will document, the seven regulative policy areas examined encompass a range of policy outcomes; in trade and the internal market, German policies exhibit negligible signs of change since 1990, whereas significant shifts have occurred in the structural funds and agriculture.

Moreover, the cases incorporate variation in explanatory variables that are central to hypothesis testing (see table 1.1). In some policy areas, eastern German actors mobilized in opposition to government policy, whereas in others, domestic challenges from the east did not materialize. The seven cases also encompass variation at the intersection of two key institutional variables critical to the institution-based hypotheses: the organization of the domestic policy process in Bonn; and the organization of the supranational policy process in Brussels. Each regulative policy falls into one of two categories in Bonn; it is either the exclusive province of the federal government, or it is shared more or less equally between the federal and state governments. In Brussels, the policy areas delineate a range of shared and exclusive competencies between supranational and national actors.[52] Finally, the cases embrace significant variation in the degree of congruence between the EC/EU policy model and its German counterpart, which will be central to the idea-based hypotheses.

Unified Germany has not gone "back to the future." The country's basic postwar orientation toward Europe remains unaltered despite the upheavals associated with the end of the Cold War. Those who expected more radical departures from the world of post-1945 Europe failed to anticipate the extent to which a stable mix of (West) German identity

---

[51] William Wallace, "Europe as a Confederation," *Journal of Common Market Studies* 20 (September–December 1982), 61.

[52] This discussion follows the lead of Philippe Schmitter, "Interests, Powers, and Functions: Emergent Properties and Unintended Consequences in the European Polity," Stanford University, April 1992. For a similar classification exercise, see J. Goodman, "Do All Roads Lead to Brussels?" in Norman Ornstein and Mark Perlman, eds., *Political Power and Social Change* (Washington, DC: American Enterprise Institute, 1991), 24–45.

Table 1.1. *European regulative policy areas: explanatory variables*

EC/EU policy	Opposition in new Länder? (1)	Counter-opposition in western Germany? (2)	Organization of policy: Germany (3)	Organization of policy: EC/EU (4)	Policy model congruence? (5)
Trade	Yes	No	Federal	All supranational	Yes
Internal market	No	No	Federal	Mostly supranational	Yes
CAP	Yes	Yes	Shared	Mostly supranational	Yes
State aid	Yes	Yes	Federal	Shared	Yes
Structural funds	Yes	No	Shared	Shared	No
Environment	No	No	Federal	Shared	No
Energy	No	No	Federal	Some supranational	No

and interests, shaped and supported by an interlocking network of domestic institutions linked firmly to the European integration project, would survive this critical juncture in history.

To consign neorealist scripture to the dustbin of history is not to suggest that the recent past will simply continue reproducing itself into the post-millennium future. The German–European relationship is subject to tensions and dynamics that are capable of reconstituting that relationship. Indeed, subtle yet tangible changes are already occurring. And the prospect of *any* change in German–European relations raises a host of genuine but often contradictory concerns. Some worry about disengagement and the resulting impact of an inward, eastward-looking Germany on European integration. Others fret about the opposite problem – a Europe that cannot withstand an ineluctable hegemony of German values and priorities.[53]

What is the future trajectory of relations between Germany and Europe? The answer can be found in the evolution of Germany's complex place in Europe since 1990. And that, in a nutshell, is the focus of this volume. The next chapter presents an analysis of German unification and its impact on the constitutive dimensions of European integration, with special emphasis on EMU, EC/EU budgetary politics, and enlargement. Chapters 3–6 examine specific European policy areas; chapters 3 and 4 deal with those areas in which continuity is largely the order of the day, whereas the latter two take up the policies in which palpable changes can be observed. Chapter 7 provides an explanation of these patterns, and explores the broader substantive and theoretical questions raised by the findings.

---

[53] For an excellent overview of these various and often contradictory concerns, see Markovits and Reich, *The German Predicament*.

2 Unification and "Germany in Europe"

Man weiß, wie man aus Kapitalismus Sozialismus macht, aber nicht wie aus Sozialismus soziale Marktwirtschaft wird.
Bernhard Vogel (Christian Democratic Union), Prime Minister of Thuringia[1]

Observers followed the twists and turns of reform communism in Moscow and in Eastern Europe during the 1980s with keen interest, but no one, least of all in West Germany, thought to connect them with the imminent demise of the Berlin Wall. Yet within three weeks of November 9, 1989, unification – an existential goal transformed by *Ostpolitik* into a heartfelt but largely barren mantra of West German politics – vaulted to the top of the national agenda. The Bonn government, motivated largely by a belief system built around the social market economy and European multilateralism, adopted a unification policy of rapid institutional transfer.[2] However, by aiming at nothing less than the wholesale extension of the West German model and its supranational linkages to East German soil, the government's policies produced severe hardship in eastern Germany, which eventually resulted in a significant political challenge to the passive consensus in Germany about the domestic model of political economy and the larger goals of European integration.

[1] "We know how to create socialism out of capitalism, but not how a social market economy develops out of socialism." As quoted in "Fundsache," *Frankfurter Allgemeine Zeitung*, December 5, 1992, 3.

[2] Gerhard Lehmbruch, "Institutionentransfer: Zur politischen Logik der Verwaltungsintegration in Deutschland," in Wolfgang Seibel, Arthur Benz, and Heinrich Mäding, eds., *Verwaltungsreform und Verwaltungspolitik im Prozeß der deutschen Einigung* (Baden-Baden: Nomos Verlagsgesellschaft, 1993), 41–42; Wolfgang Seibel, "Innovation, Imitation, Persistenz: Muster staatlicher Institutionenbildung in Ostdeutschland seit 1990," unpublished paper, Universität Konstanz, 1995; and Christopher Allen, "From Social Market to Mesocorporatism to European Integration: The Politics of German Economic Policy," in Michael Huelshoff, Andrei Markovits, and Simon Reich, eds., *From Bundesrepublik to Deutschland: German Politics After Unification* (Ann Arbor: University of Michigan Press, 1993), 61–76.

Formal unification, November 1989 to October 1990

The story of the how the Berlin Wall came tumbling down is well known. The near-term origins of this bizarre tale of civil courage and official myopia, leavened with a dash of farce,[3] lie for the most part in Kremlin politics. Although the regime in East Berlin possessed the wherewithal to replicate the Chinese government's response to the Tiananmen Square democracy movement, which had been carried out with deadly force only five months prior, it chose carrots and sticks over tanks when the scale of its isolation within the international socialist order became apparent.

Yet to appreciate the profound disaffection of East German citizens with their self-appointed leaders – in short, to explain why they ultimately rejected socialist carrots in favor of capitalist bananas – one must look to domestic factors. By the end of the 1980s, the Eastern bloc's flagship economy was on the verge of collapse, its reputation as "a world-ranking industrial country"[4] notwithstanding. Four decades of socialist economics had created a catalogue of crippling socioeconomic ills that would plague the region long after the political superstructure had been forced from the scene: outdated capital stock and production techniques; overstaffing in both industry and administration; sectoral imbalances;[5] deficient public infrastructure, particularly in transportation and telecommunications; dysfunctional incentives for managers of state-owned enterprises, would-be entrepreneurs, and workers; a severely degraded environment; and a mountain of foreign debt.[6]

Unlike many of its allies, which had embarked on the arduous path of

---

[3] Owing to miscommunication among Politburo members, a senior Communist party official announced during an evening press conference on November 9 that the GDR had opened its borders, including those in Berlin, and within hours, "the peaceful storming of the wall" was on. Manfred Görtemaker, *Unifying Germany, 1989–90* (New York: St. Martin's Press, 1994), 88. See also Elizabeth Pond, *Beyond the Wall: Germany's Road to Unification* (Washington, DC: Brookings Institution, 1993).

[4] Ian Jeffries, "The GDR in Historical and International Perspective," in Ian Jeffries and Manfred Melzer, eds., *The East German Economy* (London: Croom Helm, 1987), 1.

[5] This included an underdeveloped service sector, an oversized agricultural sector, and an industrial sector dominated by huge state monopolies (*Kombinate*), with small- and medium-sized firms notable by their absence. On the GDR economic system, see Gert Leptin and Manfred Melzer, *Economic Reform in East German Industry* (Oxford: Oxford University Press, 1978), and Mike Dennis, *German Democratic Republic: Politics, Economics, and Society* (London: Pinter Publishers, 1988), chs. 4–5.

[6] Jarausch estimates the GDR's total foreign debt at 34.7 billion Ostmark in 1987, which represented a fifteen-fold increase over the level obtaining in 1970. Merely servicing the debt by the end of the 1980s took two-thirds of annual hard currency earnings, and further distorted planning, investment, and export decisions taken by the SED regime. Konrad Jarausch, *The Rush to German Unity* (New York: Oxford University Press, 1994), 99.

reform earlier in the decade, the GDR remained true to socialist orthodoxy right up until the bitter end. The dismissive attitude toward Gorbachev's reform program was captured by Kurt Hager, Socialist Unity Party (SED) Central Committee Secretary for Science and Culture, who quipped, "If your neighbor chooses to rewallpaper . . . his house, would you feel obliged to do the same?"[7] East German elites were lulled into a false sense of security, in part by their own success in demoralizing and demobilizing citizens with a highly effective internal security apparatus, the Staatssicherheitsdienst (Stasi), and an official policy of exporting dissidents to the Federal Republic.[8] Thus, the tepid calls from below for reform up through the late 1980s were inaudible to the SED leadership, hunkered down in the posh, insulated residence compound at Wandlitz just outside East Berlin. Their comfort and complacency were shattered by the swelling ranks of peaceful protesters, who took to the streets in earnest in the fall of 1989.

The view from the West

Over the course of 1989, West Germans observed the great drama unfolding across the Elbe with interest and hope, but not much capacity to influence events. The building confrontation between the SED and its domestic opponents took on added urgency in Bonn as the number of East German refugees (not to mention ethnic Germans from Eastern Europe) entering the Federal Republic swelled into the hundreds of thousands, each entitled by law to citizenship.[9] In early November, Kohl issued an extraordinary appeal to East Germans to stay in their country and work for change: "We want them to lead their lives and find their happiness in their own traditional homes."[10]

Domestic externalities were less significant in concentrating the minds of Bonn politicians than emerging ramifications at the international level. Bonn had to walk a thin tightrope. On the one hand, the government could not sit in silence as demonstrators, chanting "We are

---

[7] As quoted in Görtemaker, *Unifying Germany, 1989–90*, 49.

[8] See Görtemaker, *Unifying Germany, 1989–90*, 53, 57; and Albert Hirschman, "Exit, Voice, and the Fate of the German Democratic Republic: An Essay in Conceptual History," *World Politics* 45 (January 1993), 173–202. Jarausch estimates that between 1961 and 1988, a total of 616,066 East German refugees left the country; of these, a little over 380,000 were granted official permits to leave, while 29,670 were "bought free" by the Federal Republic at about DM100,000 per head. The rest escaped, either over the inner-German border or via third countries. Jarausch, *The Rush to German Unity*, 17.

[9] During the calendar year 1989, just under 350,000 people left East Germany for the Federal Republic; they represented over 2 percent of the total GDR population.

[10] Jarausch, *The Rush to German Unity*, 23.

the people!" (Wir sind das Volk!) and demanding basic human rights, were set upon by GDR security forces armed with water cannon, truncheons, and police dogs. On the other hand, Kohl's government could ill afford to do anything that might provoke a lethal crackdown by the GDR regime. Nor could it openly raise the prospect of unification, even indirectly, since this would almost certainly undermine Gorbachev's already precarious political position in Moscow.

On November 8, in a state-of-the-nation address to parliament, Chancellor Kohl called for an all-German dialogue, and pledged a comprehensive assistance package if the SED relinquished its monopoly on power, allowed the formation of independent political parties and groups, and provided for free and fair elections. Bonn politicians on both the left and the right consistently framed any possible road to unification in terms of the self-determination of the East German people within a pan-European settlement of the Cold War.

The politics of unification: domestic imperatives

Although there was no doubt in anyone's mind after November 9 that unification was now firmly on the agenda, the time-frame was still measured in years, perhaps even decades. For the West Germans, a gradualist approach to unification seemed especially wise in light of the prevailing uncertainty about Moscow's reaction. For the SED, the attractions of gradualism were many: an extended lease on power and its perquisites; a continuation of the East German experiment with socialism; and time to manage and ultimately contain opponents of the regime, whose numbers were growing daily. Yet by the end of November, developments in East Germany unexpectedly began to push both governments off their preferred path.

Within two weeks of the wall's collapse, demonstrations in the GDR registered a marked change; chants and banners proclaiming "Wir sind das Volk!" were crowded out by those asserting "Wir sind ein Volk!" (We are one people!). Part of this can be traced to demographic changes in the composition of the demonstrators. As the original participants – young, university-educated, and idealistic – were joined by the GDR's previously silent working class, the demands on public display shifted to reflect more impatient, material concerns.[11]

---

[11] These had no doubt been strengthened by increased contact with the Federal Republic. Although the entire GDR population had enjoyed access to West German television, vicarious experiences of the West could hardly compare to being there. In the first week after the collapse of the Wall, 9 million East Germans visited the Federal Republic, taking back with them sights, sounds, and consumer purchases that for many only

The failure of gradualism lay ultimately in the almost preordained failure of GDR reformers both inside and outside the official apparatus to develop a socialist alternative to the Federal Republic. The abortive search for a "Third Way" – alternately described as socialism with a bottom line or capitalism with a human face – was intended to stave off unification by salvaging unique and valued components of the East German economic model and, it is no exaggeration to say, of East German identity: solidarity, community, security, equality.[12] In the end, the attempt to chart a path between western capitalism and eastern communism grossly overestimated the stamina and patience of average citizens, who were interested not in abstract critiques of capitalism but in tangible, rapid improvements in their standard of living. GDR reformers failed to win a West German commitment to underwrite what officials regarded as a play with no clear script, ending, or purpose.

The Bonn government, confronting an unremitting flow of East German refugees into the country and sensing that the international window of opportunity could slam shut at any moment, soon was compelled to adopt a more direct approach to the reopened German Question, an approach that gained in confidence and direction as the reform movement in East Germany faltered and the regime began to teeter on the brink of collapse. Kohl seized the political initiative on November 28 with his "Ten-Point Plan for German Unity," which outlined the short-term objective of a "treaty community" (*Vertragsgemeinschaft*) between the FRG and GDR. Kohl proposed the subsequent creation of "confederative structures" linking the two countries, which would later culminate in formal unity under a European umbrella. The Ten Points elicited worried statements from abroad, skepticism from important figures in the Social Democratic Party of Germany (SPD), and outright opposition from the Greens, who were especially enamored with post-Stalinist, socialist experimentation in the GDR.[13] Kohl's statement struck a chord with East German citizens, whetting their appetite for rapid change.

In early February 1990, Bonn received firm indications that Moscow would not necessarily insist upon neutrality as the price for German

---

strengthened their aversion to post-communist socialist experimentation. The most direct route to happiness was unification. And who can blame them?

[12] For a penetrating discussion of this exhilarating yet ultimately sterile discussion in East German intellectual circles, see Jarausch, *The Rush to German Unity*, ch. 4. As he concludes on p. 93, "Conceived as antipolitics rather than politics, the Third Way agenda was clearer on what it opposed than on how to reach positive goals." See also Phillip J. Bryson and Manfred Melzer, *The End of the East German Economy: From Honecker to Reunification* (New York: St. Martin's Press, 1991), 99–112.

[13] See Andrei Markovits and Philip Gorski, *The German Left: Red, Green, and Beyond* (Oxford: Oxford University Press, 1993).

unification, and immediately initiated consultations with the Bundes-bank over the technical requirements of currency union and complete economic integration; a basic framework for German economic, mone-tary, and social union (GEMSU) was in draft form by mid-February.[14] Meanwhile, Kohl threw himself into the task of forging a political mandate for unification, with his eye on the first ever democratic national elections in the GDR, held on March 18. Establishing formal links with newly reconstituted political parties in East Germany, many of which were tainted by prior collaboration with the old regime, the Chancellor and his ministers sought to transform the March 18 elections into a referendum on unification.[15] The Social Democrats, led by Oskar Lafontaine, struck a somber and oftentimes gloomy tone, warning of the dire economic and social consequences of unification for both West and East Germans, which left the field wide open for Kohl's upbeat (though ultimately illusory) vision of a painless path to a united, prosperous, and internally harmonious Germany.

The election results of March 18, in which the East German SPD suffered a stunning defeat at the hands of the Alliance for Germany (a coalition of parties linked to the Christian Democratic Union/Christian Socialist Union [CDU/CSU] in West Germany) and the Alliance of Free Democrats, sealed the fate of the German Democratic Republic. The East German electorate voted unambiguously for markets, democ-racy, and unification: "a ringing endorsement for the social market economy."[16] No longer was it a question of *whether* unification would take place, but when and how.

Clear differences of opinion within government and expert circles over the pace of economic unification were pushed to the background in the face of international and domestic pressures for rapid, decisive action. Those counseling gradualism, including the Bundesbank, finan-cial interest groups, and many leading economists, argued that a rush to economic and monetary union, particularly one built on a currency conversion rate of parity, would create insurmountable adjustment problems for East German industry, leading to mass regional unemploy-ment and a destabilization of the West German economy.[17]

[14] See David Marsh, *Germany and Europe: The Crisis of Unity* (London: Heinemann, 1994).
[15] West German political parties and interest associations moved quickly to establish an operating presence in the GDR. See Bernhard Boll, "Interest Organization and Intermediation in the New Länder," *German Politics* 3 (April 1994), 114–28.
[16] Jarausch, *The Rush to German Unity*, 127.
[17] For an excellent overview of the debate among economists over currency union and economic integration, see Michael Kreile, "The Political Economy of the New Germany," in Paul Stares, ed., *The New Germany and the New Europe* (Washington, DC: The Brookings Institution, 1992), 68–71.

Leading figures within the government, above all the Chancellor, believed that only a credible offer of economic hope could ease the flow of immigrants and avert a total collapse of the GDR. Government politicians were confident of the ability of the West German economy to play the role of regional "locomotive" for the east, and they believed that the transition to a market economy in the east, although certain to be accompanied by upheaval and dislocation, would be accomplished in a very short period of time. The government's "social market optimism" was encouraged by an unwillingness on the part of the West German public to accept tax increases to pay for unification; Kohl's message to the electorate throughout 1990 was that economic growth would generate increases in tax revenues sufficient to cover the costs.

The State Treaty (*Staatsvertrag*) establishing GEMSU, which came into effect on July 1, has been described as "a manifesto of the German ... social market economy."[18] The treaty stipulated that German economic, monetary, and social union would be established on the principles of "private property, competition, free prices, free movement of labor, capital, goods, and services, as well as labor legislation and a social security system in line with these principles."[19] The treaty text laid out the legal framework for currency union, including a lattice-work of conversion rates that bore the mark of the Bonn politicians, not the economists: 1:1 for wages, salaries, and pensions; a three-tier system of conversion rates for cash and savings;[20] and 2:1 for other financial assets and debts.

The *Staatsvertrag* provided for the retooling of GDR social services to conform to the West German model, and addressed myriad other areas, including trade, GDR fiscal reform, and West–East budgetary transfers. And at the heart of the treaty was a financing arrangement to cover the costs of unification: a DM115 billion German Unity Fund (*Fonds Deutscher Einheit*) for the period 1990–94. The federal government agreed to contribute DM20 billion, with the remainder financed by public sector borrowing. Debt servicing was to be shared between the federal government and the old Länder, with the latter picking up half the costs.

---

[18] Rolf Hasse, "German-German Monetary Union: Main Options, Costs, and Repercussions," in A. Ghanie Ghaussy and Wolf Schäfer, eds., *The Economics of German Unification* (New York: Routledge, 1993), 35.

[19] Otto Singer, "The Politics and Economics of German Unification: From Currency Union to Economic Dichotomy," *German Politics* 1 (April 1992), 82.

[20] Children up to the age of 14 were allowed to exchange 2,000 Ostmark at parity; people between 15 and 59 years of age could exchange 4,000 Ostmark at parity; and senior citizens (60 and above) could exchange 6,000 Ostmark at parity. Amounts above these limits could be exchanged at a 2:1 conversion rate.

Both sides viewed the *Staatsvertrag* as a precursor to formal political unification. The West German constitution (*Grundgesetz*, or Basic Law) offered two routes to unity. Article 23, after defining the territories to which the Basic Law applied as of the date of inauguration, stated: "In other parts of Germany it shall be put into force on their accession." This article had been used to bring the Saarland into the Federal Republic in 1959, and it represented the least cumbersome approach to unification in 1990; the GDR, either as a whole or as separate state (Land) entities, would request accession to the Federal Republic. Article 146, by contrast, provided for a fresh start: "This Basic Law shall cease to be in force on the day a constitution adopted by a free decision of the German people comes into force."[21]

Not surprisingly, Article 23 appealed above all to the government coalition in Bonn and to the civil servants charged with steering the process, who maintained that neither country could afford a time-consuming, contentious, and potentially indeterminate political outcome when one of the parties to the negotiations was on the verge of collapse and clouds were gathering on the international horizon. They also linked the success of GEMSU to rapid closure on the legal-political front; economic integration could not be expected to function in an unsupportive or uncertain legal-political environment. Furthermore, in their eyes the FRG's political system had proven its worth, not just in comparison to the GDR's moribund brand of socialism but in absolute terms, and was therefore worthy of complete and total extension to the east. Finally, Article 23 was consistent with the outcome of the March 18 elections in the GDR, which they interpreted as a mandate for the rapid importation of the West German model to eastern Germany.

Article 146, on the other hand, appealed to many (though by no means all) Social Democrats and trade union leaders on both sides of the border, as well as to GDR reformers. Their assertions that East German citizens were interested in a new constitutional arrangement that took the best from both systems were undercut by public opinion polls circulating in early 1990 and ultimately by the March election results.[22] The new coalition government formed in East Berlin after the

---

[21] See Press and Information Office of the Federal Government, *Basic Law of the Federal Republic of Germany, promulgated by the Parliamentary Council on 23 May 1949 as amended up to and including 21 December 1983* (Wolfenbüttel: Roco-Druck GmbH, 1989).

[22] Public opinion polls taken in late February showed that 89.9 percent of West Germans and 84.1 percent of East Germans favored the adoption of the Basic Law as the constitution for a united Germany. See Görtemaker, *Unifying Germany 1989–1990*, 200.

election issued a statement on April 12 endorsing unification based on Article 23.

The final text of the Unification Treaty (*Einigungsvertrag*) was signed on August 31, and with very few exceptions effected a wholesale replacement of the GDR system by the West German, with some provision for brief transition periods. GDR demands for concessions ranging from the symbolic (new flag and national anthem) to the structural (a federal ministry of reconstruction, mechanisms for direct democracy, a constitutional right to work) languished on the cutting-room floor. Decisions on several unresolved issues, like the location of the capital, were postponed. After October 1990, there would remain a single institutional holdover from the GDR political economy: the Treuhandanstalt (THA), responsible for privatizing the state-owned sector.

On October 2, the GDR dissolved, and the five new Länder – Brandenburg, Mecklenburg-West Pomerania, Saxony, Saxony-Anhalt, and Thuringia – plus East Berlin acceded to the FRG on the following day (figure 2.1). With unification, the national parliament expanded to include individual and Land representatives from the east; the number of seats in the lower house (Bundestag) increased from 518 to 656, while the upper house (Bundesrat) expanded from 45 to 69 votes, 24 of which are controlled by the new Länder and Berlin (see table 2.1). The eastward extension of West German governmental arrangements was completed with little or no change to the basic federal principles under-pinning the system.[23]

The diplomacy of unification: European parameters

Moscow held the key to unification.[24] Europe, however, was no irrele-vancy. The Bonn government confronted two challenges linked to its Community membership and associated obligations: first, to allay the concerns of its EC partners about unification and its implications for stability in Europe; and second – as rapid unification became a virtual certainty – to secure an EC accession for the soon-to-be former GDR in

---

[23] Klaus Goetz and Peter Cullen, "The Basic Law after Unification: Continued Centrality or Declining Force," *German Politics* 3 (December 1994), 5–46 at 33; and Heinrich Mäding, "Die föderativen Finanzbeziehungen im Prozeß der deutschen Einigung," in Seibel, Benz, and Mäding, eds., *Verwaltungsreform und Verwaltungspolitik im Prozeß der deutschen Einigung*, 319.

[24] There are several excellent accounts of the "2 + 4" negotiations, including Pond, *Beyond the Wall*, and Philip Zelikow and Condoleezza Rice, *Germany Unified and Europe Transformed: A Study in Statecraft* (Cambridge, MA: Harvard University Press, 1995).

Figure 2.1.   Germany after unification.

Table 2.1. *Distribution of seats in the Bundesrat*

German Länder	Population (million)	Seats after (before) unification	
North Rhine-Westphalia	16.7	6	(5)
Bavaria	10.9	6	(5)
Baden-Württemberg	9.3	6	(5)
Lower Saxony	7.2	6	(5)
Hesse	5.5	4	(4)
Saxony	5.0	4	(0)
Rhineland-Palatinate	3.6	4	(4)
Berlin	3.3	4	(4)[a]
Saxony-Anhalt	3.0	4	(0)
Brandenburg	2.7	4	(0)
Schleswig-Holstein	2.6	4	(4)
Thuringia	2.5	4	(0)
Mecklenburg-West Pomerania	2.1	4	(0)
Hamburg	1.6	3	(3)
Saarland	1.1	3	(3)
Bremen	0.7	3	(3)
Total	77.7	69	(45)

Note: [a] Observer status; non-voting delegation.

a timely and mutually acceptable manner. Both involved German–EC negotiations at the constitutive *and* regulative levels. In a manner that echoed its domestic agenda for unification, Bonn sought to signal and secure the maximum amount of continuity in its relationship to the EC.

West and East Germans alike could hardly be faulted for wondering why their Western European neighbors did not share their elation about the prospect of unification. British prime minister Margaret Thatcher cautioned against a "rash" resolution of the German Question, while French president François Mitterrand described German unification as "a legal and political impossibility."[25] European reactions were especially pointed after Kohl's surprise announcement of his Ten-Point Plan. Skeptical foreign actions and statements, which continued into 1990, were received with anger and consternation in Bonn. As the ghosts of Germany's past roamed the continent in late 1989 and early 1990, political elites both inside and outside the Federal Republic sought refuge in European integration.

Bonn's emphasis on the European dimension of unification resonated with the architectural designs of actors elsewhere on the continent: specifically, Jacques Delors, president of the EC Commission, and key

---

[25] Görtemaker, *Unifying Germany, 1989–90*, 155.

members like France, eager to secure from Germany an early and irreversible affirmation of integration. In March 1990, Kohl announced his government's unwavering support for the goal of economic and monetary union, and one month later, he and Mitterrand called for the convening of an intergovernmental conference on political union to run parallel to formal discussions over EMU, which would chart a course toward a stronger, more democratic Community and a common foreign and security policy.[26]

Thus, in the face of deep-seated domestic unease about the risks of economic and monetary union, the Chancellor committed his country to the twin objectives of economic and political union. Once again, Bonn asked for "the golden handcuffs," and its European partners obliged.[27] The reaffirmation – indeed, intensification – of Bonn's approach to EC constitutive politics in Brussels still left many questions about integration and the GDR unresolved.

The natural starting point for discussions after November 1989 was a formalization of relations between the EC and the GDR. Some of the groundwork was already in place. In trade relations, for example, the GDR had been a clandestine, "nth + 1" member of the European Community from the EC's inception.[28] Chancellor Kohl's Ten-Point Plan placed a formal association agreement between the GDR and the EC on the agenda. Delors, recognizing the importance of Germany to Europe, welcomed the long-term prospect of unification, and announced in his January 1990 address to the European Parliament that East Germany should be viewed as a special case, entitled to a place within the Community should it so desire.[29] The Commission President acted out of a concern that public handwringing by EC member governments over unification risked isolating Germany, possibly provoking the very behavior they so openly feared. His positive response to

---

[26] The result, of course, was the Treaty on European Union, negotiated at Maastricht in December 1991 and signed by the leaders of the twelve member governments in early February 1992. See Michael Baun, *An Imperfect Union* (Boulder: Westview, 1996); and Wayne Sandholtz, "Choosing Union: Monetary Politics and Maastricht," *International Organization* 47 (Winter 1993), 1–39.

[27] Timothy Garton Ash, *In Europe's Name* (New York: Random House, 1993), 358.

[28] On the basis of an agreement reached between Germany and the other five members in the late 1950s, inter-German economic exchange was not treated as foreign trade. Owing to stringent licensing systems subsequently put in place by France and the Benelux countries, the vast majority of GDR imports remained in West Germany. Eberhard Grabitz and Armin von Bogdandy, "Die Europäischen Gemeinschaften und die Einheit Deutschlands – die rechtliche Dimension," *Integration* 14 (April 1991), 49–50.

[29] George Ross, *Jacques Delors and European Integration* (New York: Oxford University Press, 1995), 49.

intra-German developments also flowed from self-interest: bringing East Germany into the EC, first as an associate and then as a full-fledged member, would give the Community – and within it, the Commission – the opportunity to influence the unification process.

Bonn officials had decided by February 1990 to discourage independent accession negotiations between East Berlin and Brussels.[30] Bilateral discussions risked unnecessary and even unwanted complications, among other things by providing the EC with additional leverage over the outcome, something that Bonn wished to avoid in light of the urgency of events and the "domestic" quality of the issues involved. As an Article 23 path to unification became a foregone conclusion in Germany, Bonn officials requested that the EC treat the incorporation of the GDR's territory not as a formal accession, but as the territorial expansion of an existing member. In effect, the Germans argued that unification via Article 23 would not affect the legal identity of the Federal Republic, and thus formal accession negotiations were not only unnecessary but inappropriate.[31]

The European Commission shared Bonn's reasoning, and worked assiduously to convince member governments and the European Parliament (EP) of the wisdom of treating East Germany as a special case. At the Dublin meeting of the European Council in April 1990, the member governments agreed to handle the incorporation of East Germany into the EC as a *de facto* but not *de jure* enlargement of the Community. Consensus formed around a Commission paper on unification, which was premised on very optimistic assessments of the East German economy's current health and future prospects.[32]

The Commission's paper proposed a step-wise integration of the GDR into the EC, accompanied by transitional arrangements to ease convergence to the *acquis communautaire*. It outlined several problems associated with the integration of eastern Germany; these reflected the

---

[30] Barbara Lippert, "Die EG als Mitgestalter der Erfolgsgeschichte: Der deutsche Einigungsprozess 1989/90," in Barbara Lippert et al., eds., *Die EG und die neuen Bundesländer* (Bonn: Europa Union Verlag, 1993), 72. See also Beate Kohler-Koch, "Die Politik der Integration der DDR in die EG," in Beate Kohler-Koch, ed., *Die Ostwerweiterung der EG: Die Einbeziehung der ehemaligen DDR in die Gemeinschaft* (Baden-Baden: Nomos Verlagsgesellschaft, 1991).

[31] This conclusion was based on their interpretation of the doctrine of moving treaty frontiers, taken from international law. See Grabitz and Bogdandy, "Die Europäischen Gemeinschaften und die Einheit Deutschlands," 53. See also David Spence, "The European Community and German Unification," in Charlie Jeffery and Roland Sturm, eds., *Federalism, Unification, and European Integration* (London: Frank Cass, 1993), 143.

[32] Commission of the European Communities, "The European Community and German Unification," *Bulletin of the European Communities* (Supplement 4/1990), 9.

anxieties of individual member governments as well as Commission officials, and served to shape the ensuing negotiations. For example, Spain, Portugal, and Greece, although supportive of East German integration in light of their own recent, undemocratic pasts, were concerned about losing scarce Community aid resources to the economically troubled region. Wealthier members, notably the UK and France, harbored suspicions that Bonn planned to construct a low-wage, deregulated economy in the former GDR. Overall, the Commission expressed a desire to limit the number and duration of transitional arrangements, while acknowledging that special measures to facilitate the incorporation of the new German territory would be necessary for economic and social reasons. In keeping with the deadline established by the Single European Act, the Commission recommended that wherever possible, transitional arrangements for the GDR should expire on December 31, 1992.

Kohl signaled his government's support of the Commission's position, and publicly ruled out any German demands for EC "co-financing" of the costs of adjustment in East Germany.[33] Combined, these actions allayed many fears of the other eleven members, and the European Council accepted the Commission's recommendations as a basis for proceeding with the EC's first eastern enlargement. In the aftermath of the Dublin summit, the Commission established a formal Task Force for German Unification, which conducted the ensuing discussions over the precise terms of incorporation, and even sent representatives to monitor inter-German negotiations over the *Staatsvertrag* and *Einigungsvertrag* to ensure that "the implications for Community law were correctly assessed" by the participants.[34]

Commission officials and representatives from the Bonn government hammered out the details of the actual incorporation package, policy area by policy area. Unification, which would increase the territorial and population size of Germany by a substantial amount, opened up a host of institutional questions – voting weights in the Council; number of Commissioners appointed by Germany; size of the German delegation in the European Parliament – that threatened to upset the delicate balance established for the twelve members by the existing treaty framework. To the relief of its partners and of the Commission, the Bonn government declined to raise any issues pertaining to the Council and Commission, although it pressed for an increase of eighteen in the size of the German EP delegation, a matter that was ultimately resolved at

[33] Lippert, "Die EG als Mitgestalter der Erfolgsgeschichte," 83.
[34] Spence, "The European Community and German Unification," 150.

Maastricht. Regarding the Community's secondary legislation, Bonn eschewed a Mediterranean strategy of long transition periods and significant derogations for the acceding region. Instead, Bonn sought a rapid convergence to EC standards, with few exceptions. In adopting this approach, West German officials built on the *Staatsvertrag*, which

had provided the basis for incorporating the GDR into the Community by ensuring equal treatment of Community and German firms in the GDR, establishing reciprocal free trade, the applicability of the common agricultural policy, Community rules on company law, freedom of establishment, competition, VAT and customs and excise.[35]

Much of the Community's secondary legislation posed few obstacles for the negotiating parties. The most contentious issues revolved around environmental policy, structural policy, the Common Agricultural Policy, and external relations.[36] In each case, Bonn and Brussels reached agreement on transitional arrangements that acknowledged the special needs of the *Beitrittsgebiet* (literally, "acceding area") while safeguarding the interests of the other member governments and Bonn's commitment to rapid institutional transfer of the German model in Europe.

After formal unification, 1990–96

October 3, 1990 brought the formal unification process to a breathless finish. It placed a second book-end on a period in which the goal of continuity, both in domestic politics and international affairs, reigned supreme within the Federal Republic. West Germans could hardly deny that unification would result in a larger and more populous country, but they resisted, in both word and deed, the notion that unity would represent a break with their postwar trajectory. Yet subsequent developments made the government's pledge of continuity the subject of intense domestic debate.

---

[35] Spence, "The European Community and German Unification," 153.
[36] Details of the agreements forged between Bonn and Brussels in these various policy areas will be presented in later chapters. For an account written by the lead German negotiator, see Hans-Dieter Kuschel, "Die Einbeziehung der ehemaligen DDR in die EG," *Wirtschaftsdienst* 71 (February 1991), 80–87.

Domestic debates and policies

Buoyed by a decisive federal election victory two months after formal unification,[37] the Kohl government, true to social market orthodoxy, put in place a package of economic programs for the eastern Länder – the so-called *Gemeinschaftswerk Aufschwung-Ost* – that was drawn straight out of the pre-unification playbook: tax incentives, investment credits, infrastructure grants, and the like. The emphasis was on small and medium-sized firms, and the main vehicle was federal regional economic policy. Privatization was entrusted to the Treuhandanstalt, an institutional carryover from the GDR; the sell-off of state-owned firms was to be rapid and profitable, according to government officials.

The coalition government rejected calls from the SPD and eastern German representatives for new taxes to finance restructuring and to hold down overall public debt, insisting that unification would be paid for by growth dividends and shifts in spending priorities; ministers identified approximately DM5 billion in subsidy programs for western German problem sectors (e.g. agriculture, coal, and regional aid to Berlin and border areas) that could be phased out and reallocated to the east. The federal government also rebuffed demands for new institutions to implement the government's policies, such as a federal ministry for reconstruction (Aufbauministerium).[38] Officials argued that the federal bureaucracy, coupled with the THA, was up to the task, and pointed out that Bonn ministries had already created internal task forces,

[37] The December 1990 Bundestag election results were as follows:

	(percentage of popular vote)		
	West	*East*	*Total*
CDU/CSU	44.1	43.4	43.8
SPD	35.9	23.6	33.5
FDP	10.6	13.4	11.0
Greens	4.7	0.0	3.9
Greens/Bündnis 90	0.0	5.9	1.2
PDS	0.3	9.9	2.4
Republikaner	2.3	1.3	2.1
Others	2.1	2.5	2.1

Source: "Bundestagswahl '90," *Süddeutsche Zeitung*, December 4, 1990, 11–16.

[38] In late 1990, the SPD pushed hard for the creation of a separate ministry for eastern affairs, on the grounds that institutional amplification of eastern demands was required if the traditional Bonn policy process was to meet the new challenges adequately and effectively. The initiative foundered on vehement opposition from within the Bonn ministerial establishment. The most vocal opponent was the BMWi, which stood to lose the most in terms of personnel and responsibilities. Among the government parties, the FDP was an active opponent of this proposal, since the ministries it controlled – specifically, the BMWi and the justice ministry – would be weakened.

divisions, and Berlin outposts (*Außenstellen*) to deal with the new challenges.[39]

The government's confident predictions of prosperity for all were quickly overtaken by events; economic performance indicators in eastern Germany soon rivaled those registered during the Great Depression.[40] GEMSU completely undermined the export competitiveness of eastern firms, already suffering from a host of internal ailments.[41] Over the course of 1990, industrial production fell by 53.9 percent in East Germany, which contributed to a 13.3 percent decline in GDP over the same period. Estimates of the real unemployment rate by the end of 1990 hovered around 33 percent.[42] By early 1992, the number of officially unemployed persons in the eastern region stood at just over 1 million, and the unemployment rate fluctuated between 13 and 17.5 percent over the next four years – a little under double the western average.

Meanwhile, the flow of new investment into the eastern economy was impeded by the framework of property rights established in the unification settlement. Investment projects invariably became mired in legal challenges, as previous owners filed claims for restitution against the current occupants. The economic downturn afflicting most of Europe at this time was also beginning to take its toll on the eastern Länder. Newspaper articles that only a few months previously had trumpeted the arrival of West Germany's elite firms in the new Länder – Volkswagen, Mercedes Benz, Deutsche Airbus – were now filled with stories of plant closures, rising unemployment, and a rash of canceled or

---

[39] For example, a "Leitungsstab neue Bundesländer" (Coordination Staff for the New Federal States) was created within the Federal Ministry of Economics in mid-1991 to coordinate policy for the new territories and to monitor ongoing economic developments there.

[40] Rudiger Dornbusch and Holger Wolf, "East German Economic Reconstruction," in Olivier Blanchard, Kenneth Froot, and Jeffrey Sachs, eds., *The Transition in Eastern Europe* (Chicago: Chicago University Press, 1994), 155; Hans-Werner Sinn and Gerlinde Sinn, *Kaltstart: Volkswirtschaftliche Aspekte der deutschen Vereinigung* (Tübingen: J. C. Mohr, 1991), 124.

[41] GEMSU caused an instantaneous revaluation of the Ostmark by over 400 percent, which initiated a virtual collapse of trade as GDR products were priced out of their markets. The ripple effects of GEMSU were soon felt in firm closures and rising unemployment. Although there can be little doubt that a less generous rate of exchange would have helped many firms, this would only have been a temporary reprieve, in view of the reference point set by prevailing West German wages coupled with the express commitment by the unions to seek rapid convergence to the western norm. See Ullrich Heilemann and Reimut Jochimsen, *Christmas in July? The Political Economy of German Unification Reconsidered* (Washington, DC: The Brookings Institution, 1993), 11.

[42] Dornbusch and Wolf, "East German Economic Reconstruction," 161.

postponed investments.[43] Economic data available at the beginning of 1992 revealed that the eastern German region, with 23.9 percent of the nation's population, accounted for a mere 6.9 percent of GDP.[44]

Thus, the fast track to unity accelerated the onset of economic crisis in the new Länder, and led to a deterioration in the performance of the western German economy. Inflation jumped from an annual rate of 3 percent in 1990 to 4.8 percent in 1992, evoking worried statements from research institutes and a policy of high interest rates from the Bundesbank, which created ripple effects throughout Europe.

For many observers, the fallout from Bonn's recipe of rapid unification came as no surprise. To others, particularly in the new territories, the cascade of bad news evoked despair and accusations of betrayal. Representatives from the eastern Länder complained bitterly of the risk-averseness of capital and the unwillingness of the western public to sacrifice. Between late February 1990 and July 1992, the percentage of eastern Germans expressing a good opinion of the social market economy dropped from 77 percent to 44 percent; support in the region for nationalization of industry doubled over the same period from 20 percent to 40 percent of the population. Public opinion polls conducted in mid-1992 revealed that only 36 percent of western Germans were pleased with unification.[45]

Growing disenchantment in both east and west, albeit for different reasons, provided fertile ground for a more determined assault on federal economic policies by the political opposition. The government's privatization program quickly developed into a ripe target, since the THA's efforts to restructure and sell off its holdings began to falter as industrial output fell dramatically in 1991. Social Democrats, Greens, members of the Party of Democratic Socialism (lineal successor to the SED), organized labor, coalition representatives from eastern constituencies, and the prime ministers of the new Länder (all but one of whom hailed from the CDU) warned of dire consequences – the deindustrialization or "Sicilianization" of eastern Germany – if the government failed to adopt a more activist approach.[46] More broadly, the government came under pressure to engage in systematic consultation with the unions and the opposition: a post-unification *Konzertierte Aktion*.

[43] For example, in November 1992, Mercedes Benz announced that it was postponing indefinitely plans to build a truck factory in Brandenburg; the project, at full capacity, would have employed 3,500 to 4,000 workers.

[44] "Ostanteil bei 6,9 Prozent," *Süddeutsche Zeitung*, January 16, 1992, 1.

[45] Renate Köcher, "Die Ostdeutschen frösteln in der Freiheit," *Frankfurter Allgemeine Zeitung*, September 9, 1992, 5; Renate Köcher, "Opfern fällt den Westdeutschen schwer," *Frankfurter Allgemeine Zeitung*, July 8, 1992, 5.

[46] See chapter 5 for a thorough discussion of this debate.

The government acknowledged that reconstruction was not following the original script, and enacted changes in property rights legislation and other laws to remove obstacles to investment in the east. Supplementary budgets were passed to provide additional funds for eastern German economic programs. However, government ministers consistently rejected calls for an overt industrial policy that focused on individual sectors; instead, new policy initiatives between 1993 and 1995 targeted the small- and medium-sized firm sector, which was seen as especially weak and vulnerable. Bonn officials leveled an unceasing stream of criticism at unions, which they accused of exacerbating unemployment and deindustrialization by pursuing wage convergence to the western mean for their new members in the east.[47]

Political pressure on the government intensified as unemployment in the former GDR climbed. For a time in 1992, efforts by leading figures in eastern Germany to create an "Ost-Partei" – a party devoted exclusively to the defense of eastern German interests – gained the support of several prominent eastern politicians with ties to the CDU, and although the initiative fizzled, it sent shock waves through the party leadership. Kohl's response was to establish a formal access point for eastern CDU Bundestag members in the Federal Chancellery, and to publicize the regular meetings between Chancellery officials and their counterparts in the new Länder.[48] The government also set up ten so-called "coalition working groups," on which both civil servants and CDU members of parliament from the east were represented, to draft policy proposals benefiting the new Länder. According to a civil servant in the economics ministry, the initiative, pressed on Kohl by eastern CDU members, was designed "to call the Bonn civil service on the carpet."[49] By bringing bureaucrats face-to-face with eastern elected representatives, advocates of the eastern region hoped to render the civil service more amenable to what it regarded as unorthodox or even objectionable ideas.

---

[47] For a complete discussion of this issue, see Kreile, "The Political Economy of the New Germany," 75. See also Reiner Hoffmann *et al.*, *German Industrial Relations under the Impact of Structural Change, Unification, and European Integration* (Düsseldorf: Hans-Böckler Stiftung, 1995), and more recently Lowell Turner, *Fighting for Partnership: Labor and Politics in United Germany* (Ithaca: Cornell University Press, 1998).

[48] Kohl's efforts to centralize economic policies for the eastern Länder in the Chancellery in the hands of a new state secretary (*Staatssekretär*) foundered on the opposition of the FDP, which feared that its power base in the BMWi would be weakened. Bowing to his junior coalition partner's wishes, Kohl appointed Johannes Ludewig to a new state secretary position in the economics ministry, with the official title of Federal Commissioner for Eastern Germany (*Bundesbeauftragter für Ostdeutschland*) in January 1995.

[49] Interview with BMWi official, Bonn, December 4, 1992.

While avoiding a formal change of course, Kohl bowed to pressure in November 1992, and stated publicly that his government supported the goal of preserving the so-called industrial cores of the eastern German economy. As chapter 5 will show, this had significant consequences for the THA's privatization program, and by extension Germany's position on state aid in Brussels. Kohl's announcement foreshadowed the contents of the "Solidarity Pact" of March 1993 – an initiative of the CDU-Ost parliamentary caucus – in which the government pledged to provide the THA with approximately DM10 billion in additional resources to preserve eastern Germany's industrial cores in exchange for a union commitment to exercise wage restraint. Hailed as a renaissance of the neocorporatist German model, the pact represented a large-scale package deal that, among other matters, settled financing issues between the federal and state governments and elicited pledges from German finance and industrial capital to increase the rate and level of investment in the eastern region.[50]

The government's response, which fell far short of the level of intervention demanded by its critics, nevertheless evoked growing consternation from business associations and research institutes. Beginning in 1992, these actors issued numerous reports and statements calling attention to the risk of locking in inefficient industrial structures. The tone and target of their complaints shifted as the country slipped into a general economic crisis brought on by the fiscal strains of unification, European-level constraints generated by the Maastricht convergence criteria (see below), and general worries about the health and competitiveness of the German model of political economy.

Fiscal debates sharpened during this period as the government coped with the mounting costs of unification, which translated into widening budget deficits and growing debt levels in light of the government's reluctance to increase taxes.[51] Plans to begin phasing out subsidy programs for western sectors initially fell afoul of parliamentary opposition and social protests. By 1993, when significant subsidy reductions had been achieved, transfer payments to the east gobbled up the savings.

The debate grew even more pointed in 1993, when for the first time the government proposed significant cuts in Germany's cradle-to-grave welfare system. After long, bitter struggles with the SPD opposition, which held a veto point through control of the Bundesrat, the government began to carve out a more austere fiscal path for the country. In

---

[50] Razeen Sally and Douglas Webber, "The German Solidarity Pact: A Case Study in the Politics of the Unified Germany," *German Politics* 3 (April 1994), 18–46.

[51] Public sector debt increased from a little over 40 percent of GDP in 1991 to over 60 percent of GDP in 1995.

1996, the government introduced a comprehensive austerity program to parliament, which included a public sector wage freeze and cuts in social expenditures. Welfare retrenchment was designed to save the government DM50 billion, or approximately $33 billion, in 1997. The proposals elicited swift and total condemnation from union representatives and the SPD, who accused the government of undermining the very foundations of the postwar German social contract at a time when national unemployment topped four million, a postwar record. Employer associations and conservative economists criticized the proposals for not going far enough. The government's austerity line cost it significantly in terms of popularity.[52]

Within the larger debate about fiscal austerity, tensions over economic policy for eastern Germany continued to simmer. Amid what would prove to be ephemeral signs of progress in the region – growth rates of over 9 percent for 1994 and 1995, the best in the EU[53] – the government began in early 1995 to lay the political groundwork for an eventual phase-out of eastern subsidies, which were running at DM150 billion a year. Responding to a fresh round of reports issued by Germany's leading economic research institutes and the Bundesbank, which called for a thoroughgoing reevaluation of assistance programs for the east,[54] ministers affirmed that the region would continue to require special treatment, but not in perpetuity and not as an undifferentiated entity. The government's change in tone reflected the deteriorating fiscal climate and growing skepticism in western Germany *and* in Brussels about the ability of the eastern region to put these considerable transfer sums to good use.[55]

---

[52] Between December 1990, the date of the national parliamentary elections, and February 1998, support for the government coalition parties dropped from 54.8 percent to 39.0 percent of the German electorate. The collapse of government support in eastern Germany was even more precipitous; the government parties could only claim the support of 30.1 percent of the regional electorate in early 1998, as compared to 56.8 percent of the regional vote in the 1990 Bundestag elections. Renate Köcher, "Opfern fällt den Westdeutschen schwer," *Frankfurter Allgemeine Zeitung*, July 8, 1992, 5; Elisabeth Noelle-Neumann, "Was ist anders als 1994?", *Frankfurter Allgemeine Zeitung*, February 25, 1998, 5.

[53] "Institute Sees East German Economy Growth Continuing," *Reuters*, September 20, 1994. In 1994, the eastern region's contribution to GNP had increased to 8.6 percent. "Facts on German Unification," *Associated Press*, September 23, 1995.

[54] The Bundesbank noted that between 1991 and the end of 1995, the eastern Länder received DM840 billion in public transfers, and warned of the emergence of a "subsidy mentality" in the region. Deutsche Bundesbank, *Monatsbericht Juli 1995* (Frankfurt, 1995).

[55] In early 1995, the Federal Audit Office (Bundesrechnungshof) released a study suggesting that 10 percent or higher of the billions of DM sent to eastern Germany since 1990 for economic and administrative restructuring may have been wasted through incompetence and even graft; the magazine *Der Spiegel* calculated the losses at

The national opposition parties, led by the SPD, which donned the official mantle of "Anwalt der ostdeutschen Interessen" (chief advocate of eastern German interests), were joined by a broad coalition of eastern political representatives that reached well into the heart of the governing coalition parties in an angry and defensive rejection of the government's proposals. Their case was helped considerably by a worsening economic situation in the eastern region; despite the outward signs of progress, the former GDR remained highly vulnerable to downturns in the national economy; GDP in the region grew by only 2 percent in 1996, as compared to a national growth rate of 1.3 percent.[56] This effectively stalled the rate of economic convergence between east and west,[57] and also caused official unemployment in eastern Germany to rise to just over 18 percent in 1997.[58] Opponents of the government's programs could point to ever gloomier public sentiments among eastern Germans about such basic values as democracy and the social market economy.[59] Bowing to these domestic pressures, the federal government decided in mid-1997 to extend special investment assistance programs for eastern German industry up through 2004, and only then begin to phase them out.

European debates and policies[60]

The Maastricht Treaty, formulated in part to further embed the Federal Republic in the west, represented, at least on paper, a significant deepening of political and especially economic integration for the twelve

---

DM65 billion. These announcements touched off a heated national debate over the costs and benefits of unification. Although both the government and eastern interests closed ranks on the issue, defending the rationale for and use of transfers to the east, the wounds opened by the debate were deep and left lasting effects on the climate of public opinion in both parts of the country. "Baggern statt Denken," *Der Spiegel*, February 13, 1995, 46–73.

[56] "Geringeres Wachstum in Ostdeutschland," *Frankfurter Allgemeine Zeitung*, February 20, 1997, 13.

[57] By 1997, per capita GDP in Germany had reached 57 percent of the western German level. Horst Siebert, "Model Under Strain," *Financial Times*, January 5, 1998, 22.

[58] Peter Norman, "E German Jobless Approaching 20%," *Financial Times*, October 29, 1997, 6.

[59] In 1997, the percentage of eastern Germans expressing a favorable opinion of the Federal Republic's economic system stood at 22 percent, down from a high of 69 percent in 1990. Between 1992 and 1997, the percentage of eastern Germans who believed that the country's problems could be solved by democracy dropped from 52 percent to 30 percent. Renate Köcher, "Die Zweifel wachsen in Ost und West," *Frankfurter Allgemeine Zeitung*, July 16, 1997, 5.

[60] For overviews of post-1989 German European policies, see Simon Bulmer and William Paterson, "Germany in the European Union: Gentle Giant or Emergent Leader?", *International Affairs* 72 (1996), 9–32.

member countries. In a marked departure from past grand bargains, however, the Treaty on European Union ignited a domestic politicization of integration that cast serious doubt on the ratification of the treaty. With the unexpected rejection of the treaty by Danish voters in a June 1992 referendum and the paper-thin "oui" voiced by the French electorate a few months later, pitched domestic debates over the future of integration blossomed throughout Europe.[61] In Germany, growing doubts about the Maastricht agreement coalesced principally around the issue of economic and monetary union (see below). The treaty also sparked a wide-ranging constitutional debate, which was eventually resolved in the form of a new Article 23 that provides, among other points, for a significant reordering of the formal relationships between the political executive and the legislature, notably the Bundesrat.[62]

In the turbulent post-Maastricht period, the German government's approach to the constitutive dimensions of European integration revealed strong elements of continuity with the pre-unification period. Both political elites and the general public maintained their bedrock commitment to the European project. A major reference point for German policymakers remained the perceptions and concerns of their neighbors; Kohl repeatedly declared that integration was irreversible, and rejected accusations that Germany was trying to dominate Europe. In concrete terms, this meant that the Bonn government expressed continuing support for EMU, a strengthened European Parliament, greater use of qualified majority voting in the Council, closer cooperation in the fields of foreign policy and internal security, and enlargement. With France, Germany also began to explore "flexibility" options designed to allow subsets of EU members to push ahead more rapidly with integration in certain areas, and succeeded in inserting favorable language into the Treaty of Amsterdam signed in October 1997.[63]

That said, Bonn's policies took on a harder edge in comparison to the

[61] See Baun, *An Imperfect Union*, for an excellent account.

[62] The Länder, which participate in the federal legislative process via the Bundesrat, argued that EC matters could no longer be considered foreign affairs but were in fact a form of "European domestic policy" and, as such, the Länder were entitled to represent the interests of Germany in Brussels on EC affairs that impinged on their powers and competencies. Since formal ratification of the treaty required Bundesrat approval, the demands of the Länder carried decisive weight in discussions with a skeptical coalition government and deeply concerned civil servants. See Charlie Jeffery, "The Länder Strike Back: Structures and Procedures of European Integration Policy-making in the German Federal System," Discussion Papers in Federal Studies FS94/4, University of Leicester, September 1994; and George Ress, "The Constitution and the Maastricht Treaty: Between Cooperation and Conflict," *German Politics* 3 (December 1994), 48–74.

[63] For an excellent overview of German integration policy after 1990, see Bulmer, Jeffery, and Paterson, "Germany's European Diplomacy," 76–99. A comprehensive overview

pre-1989 period, a direct result of domestic economic difficulties generated by unification and deepening skepticism at all levels of German
society about the wisdom of an open-ended political and especially
financial commitment to Europe.[64] In contrast to years past, German
leaders began to adopt a more sober outlook on the long-run goals of
integration. For example, Bavarian prime minister Edmund Stoiber was
quoted in November 1993 as saying that "We are no longer striving for a
federal state ... I want a simple confederation." Although government
officials distanced themselves from Stoiber's comments, grand talk of a
United States of Europe was no longer to be heard in official Bonn
circles. Chancellor Kohl, in prepared remarks on the occasion of his
receipt of the Schumpeter Prize in 1993, declared that the EU must not
develop into "a European superstate ... I find it understandable that
people ... want to be Europeans, but at the same time remain Germans,
Frenchmen, Italians or Spaniards ... The creation of a European Union
does not mean that still essential national and federal structures disap-
pear."[65]

Government officials also gave greater emphasis to short-term material benefits in their calculations, and stepped up their campaign for a
more democratic and transparent Union. What follows is a brief
account of these new accents in three policy areas central to Germany's
regulative politics: EMU, EC/EU finances, and enlargement.

Economic and monetary union

Over the objections of his advisors and particularly those of the Bundesbank, Chancellor Kohl agreed at Maastricht to a firm timetable for the
phased implementation of economic and monetary union by January 1,
1999.[66] In return, the German delegation insisted on an institutional

of the Treaty of Amsterdam can be found in Michel Petite, "The Treaty of
Amsterdam," Harvard Jean Monnet Chair Working Paper Series No. 2/98, 1998.

[64] An avowedly anti-European political party, the Bund Freier Bürger (League of Free
Citizens) campaigned against Maastricht in the 1994 EP elections. Although the BFB
fared quite poorly, its emergence can be viewed as a sign of the changing times in
Germany. The mantle of Euro-skepticism in Germany has since been picked up by the
Party of Democratic Socialism (PDS), which openly opposes the introduction of EMU
on the grounds that monetary integration will intensify neoliberal deregulation and its
attendant effects on society.

[65] All quotes from Quentin Peel, "Bavaria's PM Exposes Split on European Union,"
Financial Times, November 3, 1993, 1; "Kohl spricht sich gegen 'europäischen
Superstaat' aus," *Frankfurter Allgemeine Zeitung*, May 19, 1993, 2.

[66] For insightful analyses of the role of the Bundesbank in EMU, see David Cameron,
"British Exit, German Voice, French Loyalty: Defection, Domination, and Coopera-
tion in the 1992–93 ERM Crisis," paper for the Annual Meeting of the American
Political Science Review, Washington, DC, September 1993; and Dorothy Heisenberg,
"The Mark of the Bundesbank: Germany's Role in European Monetary Cooperation,"
unpublished Ph.D. dissertation, Yale University, 1996.

framework modeled closely on the German system, and moreover a set of strict economic convergence criteria that aspiring members of the monetary club would have to meet prior to joining. These include (1) a rate of inflation not exceeding that of the best performing member countries by more than 1.5 percentage points; (2) a budget deficit not exceeding 3 percent of GDP; (3) an accumulated public debt not exceeding 60 percent of GDP; (4) a national currency that has remained within the narrow band of the Exchange Rate Mechanism (ERM) for at least two years prior to entry into the final stage of economic and monetary union (EMU); and (5) an average nominal interest rate on long-term government bonds not exceeding that of the three best-performing member states by more than two percentage points. The German delegation agreed to a flexible interpretation of some of the convergence criteria, allowing trends in budgetary and fiscal performance to be taken into consideration for countries failing to meet the specific thresholds.

Reaction to the Maastricht agreement in Germany was decidedly cool – critics accused the government of giving away too much on EMU in exchange for too little on political union. Public unease, reflected in opinion polls, was fed by the German press; the day after the conclusion of the Maastricht summit, many German newspapers printed screaming headlines that trumpeted the imminent demise of the D-Mark. The European exchange rate crises of 1992 and 1993, combined with growing worries about domestic economic fundamentals and the lack of progress on the European agenda, fed the public's skepticism about EMU.[67] Polls conducted between 1995 and 1998 revealed that fully two-thirds of the German public expressed concerns about a loss in monetary stability arising from EMU, and fluctuating majorities flatly opposed the introduction of a single currency. At the same time, the public retained basically positive feelings about Europe and Germany's place within it; only one in three Germans expressed a desire to see the integration process slow. Just under 80 percent expressed support for currency union if it excluded the poorer Mediterranean members. And even among strict opponents of EMU, a large majority (68 percent) thought that Germany should join if the single currency were introduced.[68]

---

[67] See Cameron, "British Exit, German Voice, French Loyalty."

[68] Data taken from: Renate Köcher, "Kühle Realisten," *Frankfurter Allgemeine Zeitung*, November 15, 1996, 5; "Most Germans Doubt Euro Currency Stable – Poll," *Reuters*, December 1, 1995; "Germans Wary of South Europeans Joining EMU," *Reuters*, December 14, 1995; "Most Germans Oppose Single Currency Plan for 1999," *Reuters*, 31 January 1996; "Europeans Increasingly Divided on Euro, Poll Shows," *Agence France-Presse*, March 3, 1998.

The heightened domestic politicization of European issues was reflected in the sharpness of the attacks leveled by the SPD against the government over EMU. Looking for an issue with bite, Social Democratic leaders criticized Kohl both for failing to secure Germany's fundamental economic interests in the EMU framework negotiated at Maastricht and for leading an assault on the national welfare state in the name of neoliberal and Europeanist ideologies.[69] Gerhard Schröder, the SPD's chancellor candidate for the Fall 1998 federal elections, sought to make Europe an overt campaign issue by demanding both a postponement of the EMU timetable if Germany or other key members failed to meet the convergence criteria, and a greater emphasis on employment creation by the EU. Similar concerns about EMU were expressed from within the governing coalition itself, such as those of maverick Bavarian prime minister Stoiber.[70]

In response to domestic criticism and to genuine concerns about glaring loopholes in the TEU, the federal government, in conjunction with the Bundesbank, held to a strict interpretation of the admission criteria, and in 1995 began to advocate a "stability pact for Europe," the purpose of which was to ensure that EMU members continued to pursue fiscal policies consistent with the convergence criteria after the introduction of the single currency in 1999. In a dramatic address to the CDU annual party congress in October 1995, Kohl underscored the importance of a stringent EMU framework both to Germans and to Europe.

So, dear friends in Europe, it is not some German hysteria if we stress again and again ... that the Maastricht Treaty stability criteria must be maintained and not questioned. This is a question of the very destiny of German democracy, (as we can see) from the experiences of the century now drawing to a close ... We want a European community of stability. Anything else would put into question the great successes we have achieved in integrating Europe in the past. It could

---

[69] In October 1995, the chairperson of the SPD, Rudolf Scharping, stated: "To give up the D-mark for some idea or other, which even then in the end does not bring economic stability and also monetary stability, is wrong." His remarks and those of other figures in the SPD caused a stir inside the party as well. Klaus Hensch, an SPD member and president of the EP, warned his party not to "try to use nationalist populism to win votes which will in any case go somewhere else." Former Foreign Minister Genscher accused the SPD of "gambling with its great European tradition." "Die SPD-Führung sieht sich in der Rolle des Mahners," *Frankfurter Allgemeine Zeitung*, October 31, 1995, 3; David Crossland, "German SPD Under Fire Over Maastricht Doubts," *Reuters*, November 5, 1995.

[70] Stoiber promised "fierce resistance" by the CSU and the Bavarian state government if Kohl in any way backed away from a literal interpretation of the convergence criteria. "Stoiber fordert punktgenaue Erfüllung der Maastricht-Kriterien," *Frankfurter Allgemeine Zeitung*, June 25, 1997, 1.

be worse: the citizens' mistrust could very quickly turn against the idea of Europe itself.[71]

Although all fifteen members supported in principle the aims of a stability pact, serious differences arose between Germany and the rest of the EU, led by France, which advocated a less rigid approach to fiscal policy that took into account employment and growth performance. The final agreement, reached in December 1996, allows an EMU member to run a budget deficit of greater than 3 percent of GDP if overspending is caused by circumstances beyond its control or if it is suffering from a severe recession, which is defined as a 2 percent contraction in annual GDP. Members with a smaller fall in growth may plead special circumstances to the EMU members, which would decide on the basis of a two-thirds majority whether the member should be exempted from fines reaching a maximum of 0.5 percent of GDP. The move away from automatic penalties represented a concession on the part of Germany.[72]

Back home, government officials, including Chancellor Kohl himself, repeatedly rejected calls to postpone the implementation of EMU, which would have dire consequences for the integration process and Germany's interests. Nevertheless, political debates in the nation's capital began to focus on the EMU convergence criteria and Germany's fragile bid to meet them on schedule.[73] The issue of Europe began to intrude on domestic budget debates; the government frequently justified general budget austerity, overhaul of the welfare system, and deferral of long-promised tax cuts with reference to EMU-related goals and obligations.

One does not have to look far to find evidence of the government's intense desire to see a timely EMU departure with Germany on board. Two instances are worth highlighting. In late May 1997, a bitter row between the finance minister and the Bundesbank erupted over the former's ultimately unsuccessful attempt to revalue the central bank's gold reserves and use the resulting profits to retire debts accumulated since unification, thereby ensuring that Germany would meet the EMU public debt criterion. The initiative bordered on ill-considered folly,

---

[71] "Kohl – Weak EMU Would Hurt German Democracy," *Reuters*, October 16, 1995.

[72] Otmar Issing, a senior member of the Bundesbank, commented sarcastically, "Unrestrained automaticity would not have been possible, but one cannot be satisfied with a decision mechanism in which potential sinners pass judgment on actual sinners." "EU Warned Over Policing EMU," *Financial Times*, December 17, 1996, 1.

[73] After failing to meet all the convergence criteria in 1995 and 1996, Germany appeared to be back on track by 1997, according to a report issued by the Commission in March 1998. Germany's performance on public debt, at 61.3 percent of GDP, was the only weak spot, and the government issued statements that it expected leniency on this criterion because of the unique problems generated by unification.

since it undermined the government's stability pact agenda and further-more exposed it to the charge of engaging in precisely the kind of budgetary sleights-of-hand that it directed regularly against the Italians and other soft aspirants to EMU membership.

And in May 1998 at the Brussels summit, Kohl agreed to a last-minute compromise on the head of the European Central Bank that many newspapers described as his political death warrant. Bowing to French desires to see a Frenchman head up the key monetary agency, Kohl and the other heads of state appointed Wim Duisenberg of the Netherlands to an eight-year term on the express understanding that he would step down after four years in favor of Jean-Claude Trichet. Roundly denounced by journalists, bankers, and the political opposition in Germany (to name just three groups) as undermining the credibility of the euro before it had even begun the circulate, the compromise stemmed from the German Chancellor's strong reflex for consensus, particularly with France, on this critical matter for Europe's future.

Budgeting and finance

The SEA was purchased with a substantial side-payment to members likely to be disadvantaged by the completion of the internal market.[74] Maastricht followed the same script; the treaty's price tag included a general commitment on the part of the Union to increase cohesion payments to the poorer member countries, whose leaders argued that such assistance was essential to help their countries meet the stringent entry criteria for EMU. In 1992, the Commission published the so-called Delors II budget proposals for the period 1994–97, recommending among other things a large increase in the structural funds budget coupled with an expansion of the EC/EU's global budget ceiling from 1.2 to 1.37 percent of Community GDP.

Bonn, joined by other wealthy member governments, was true to its pre-unification form, and voiced strong dissatisfaction with what it viewed as an unacceptable increase in the EC budget ceiling. The Germans also rejected any linkage between convergence and cohesion, arguing that the former was for each individual member to achieve under its own power.[75] At the Edinburgh summit in December 1992, after long and arduous negotiations, the Community resolved most of these seemingly intractable budgetary issues on the basis of a compro-

---

[74] Marks, "Structural Policy in the European Community."

[75] This was consistent with the German notion that member states had to develop a domestically anchored "stability culture" if EMU was to work as advertised. Achieving convergence through massive EU subsidies would be counterproductive to the emergence of such a culture.

mise hammered out by Spain and Germany. The member governments decided to extend the budget plan by two years (to the period 1994–99), to fix the EC budget ceiling at 1.2 percent of Community GDP in 1993 and 1994, but to allow the ceiling to reach 1.27 percent by 1999.[76] A substantial increase in structural funding (a portion of which was destined for the new Länder), combined with a decision that the poorer members would pay less into the EU budget in future years, accompanied agreement on the larger budgetary parameters.[77]

After Edinburgh, German statements about the EC budget hardened still further. The domestic discussion about Germany's role as EU "paymaster" (*Zahlmeister*) was galvanized by a November 1993 Bundesbank report that was highly critical of EU spending practices, and that forecast a dramatic rise in German contributions to the EU budget, currently at 30 percent of the total, if spending discipline was not imposed. The report predicted that Germany's aggregate contributions would increase from DM38 billion in 1993 to DM52 billion by 1998. Annual net contributions, which were more than double the combined payments of the other net contributors (Britain, France, the Netherlands, and Italy), were expected to rise to DM30 billion over the same period. The central bank described the situation as untenable.[78]

The SPD used the report as an occasion to criticize Kohl's management of the country's European policies, marking the emergence of the *Zahlmeister* issue in German national electoral politics. Government officials began to question the formula for financing the EC/EU budget – in particular, the reliance on aggregate GDP (as opposed to per capita GDP) for calculating a member's contribution, which had caused the German contribution to jump with unification. Germany's 1991 check to Brussels totaled DM33 billion, a 46.7 percent increase over the previous year.[79] Germany's annual net contribution (payments minus receipts) almost doubled to DM22 billion between 1989 and 1997, representing a situation that, according to German officials, did not take into account the deterioration in the country's economic circumstances since 1990.[80]

[76] See Michael Shackleton, "Keynote Article: The Delors II Budget Package," *Journal of Common Market Studies* 31 (August 1993), 11–25.

[77] See chapter 6 for a complete discussion of the issues relating to the structural funds.

[78] Deutsche Bundesbank, *Monatsbericht November 1993* (Frankfurt: 1993).

[79] "DIHT sieht keinen Anlaß zur Kritik an Nettozahler-Position," *Frankfurter Allgemeine Zeitung*, May 18, 1994, 15.

[80] "Germany's Kinkel Wants Rethink on EU Financing," *Reuters*, July 20, 1997. Germany ranked first in GDP among EC members in 1993; measured in terms of GDP per capita, Germany ranked fifth, at 5.6 percent above the EC average. R. Messal and A. Klein, "Finanzlasten und Eigenmittelstruktur der Europäischen Gemeinschaft," *Wirtschaftsdienst* (July 1993), 377.

In 1996, the Commission released figures showing that Germany contributed 29.2 percent of the EU's budget but received only 14.8 percent of total spending.[81] As this information ricocheted around Bonn political circles, the BMF began work on a proposal to place a ceiling on Germany's financial contributions to the EU, and warned that if the Commission and other member governments failed to take up the issue, it could jeopardize public acceptance of European integration in Germany. The following year, Foreign Minister Kinkel described Bonn's contributions as "out of proportion," and called for an overhaul of the EU's financing system that would result in a more just distribution of burdens among the member governments.[82] German demands for an abolition of the British rebate grew louder over this period. Paradoxically, at the same time the Bonn finance ministry began to circulate a proposal under which countries would receive an automatic rebate when their annual net contribution to the EU rises above 0.4 percent of GDP; for Germany, this would have resulted in a DM7 billion repayment in 1997.[83]

In the day-to-day budget battles in Brussels, Bonn expressed a much keener interest in a fair return to Germany through various EU programs, and consistently blocked efforts by the Commission and the Mediterranean members to increase various spending programs.[84] By 1996, Bonn could claim some measure of success in its efforts to rein in the EU budget; applying the logic of the EMU convergence criteria, Germany, engaged like France and other member governments in difficult austerity politics at home, forced through a "zero growth" EU budget for 1997 and a modest increase of 1.4 percent in 1998. Commission officials expressed concern that the direction of the larger EU budget debate risked creating insurmountable obstacles to further integration, as well as to the goal of enlargement.

Enlargement

By 1990–91, the economic pull generated by the EC's single market initiative, combined with the dissolution of Cold War geopolitical

---

[81] "Commission Fires Back at Dutch, Germans in EU Budget Row," *Agence France-Presse*, October 10, 1997.

[82] "Germany's Kinkel Wants Rethink on EU financing."

[83] "Germany Savages Brussels in EU Budget Row," *Agence France-Presse*, October 13, 1997.

[84] For example, the Commission sought repeatedly to allocate large sums of money to its Trans-European Networks program (TEN), particularly as unemployment became a dominant theme of the Commission's program after Maastricht. German officials referred to these designs derisively as "Trans-European Nonsense." Interview with BMWi official, Bonn, May 18, 1994. The German government, in the face of domestic opposition from the SPD and pressure from EU members led by France, remained fiercely opposed to European employment creation schemes on budgetary grounds.

constraints, had produced a lengthy queue of applicants for membership in the EC/EU.[85] Germany, "the most consistent advocate of enlargement" in the 1970s and 1980s,[86] gave enthusiastic support to the wave of European Free Trade Association (EFTA) applicants in the early 1990s, which eventually resulted in the "northern" accession of Sweden, Finland, and Austria on January 1, 1995.

Germany also pushed for enlargement to the east; a general consensus among political elites held that the prospect of EU membership for Central and Eastern European countries would undergird their path to democracy and markets, thereby contributing to political stability and economic prosperity in the region.[87] The German government spearheaded the creation of EC assistance programs like PHARE (Pologne-Hongrie assistance à la restructuration des économies) and TACIS (Technical Assistance for the Commonwealth of Independent States). It also provided much of the impetus for the string of "Europe Agreements" negotiated with Poland, Hungary, the Czech and Slovak Republics, Bulgaria, Romania, the Baltic republics, and Slovenia, which were viewed as precursors to formal membership in the EU.[88]

As the anticipated costs of eastern enlargement began to weigh more heavily on member governments like France, Germany helped to sustain political momentum behind the initiative, most notably at the Essen summit in December 1994. However, the Kohl government's ostensibly unbounded enthusiasm for eastern enlargement began to ebb, albeit subtly and gradually, as the *Zahlmeister* debate hit its stride in Bonn.

In July 1997, the Commission published "Agenda 2000," which set out its vision of the Union's enlargement process.[89] The report

---

[85] For general overviews of the "widening" issue and its manifold implications, see Neill Nugent, "The Deepening and Widening of the European Community: Recent Evolution, Maastricht, and Beyond," *Journal of Common Market Studies* 30 (September 1992), 311–28; and Anna Michalski and Helen Wallace, *The European Community: The Challenge of Enlargement* (London: Royal Institute for International Affairs, 1992).

[86] Simon Bulmer, "European Integration and Germany: The Constitutive Politics of the EU and the Institutional Mediation of German Power," paper presented at the Conference on "The Influence of Germany and the European Union on the Smaller European States," Budapest, Hungary, May 31–June 3 1995, 24.

[87] Here, German elites extrapolated from their own experiences with national democratic consolidation and supranational integration in the 1950s. As chapter 3 will show, the German government also believed that eastern Germany would benefit from closer economic and political ties between the EC and the former Soviet satellites.

[88] See Heinz Kramer, "The European Community's Response to the 'New Eastern Europe'," *Journal of Common Market Studies* 31 (June 1993), 213–44.

[89] Commission of the European Communities, *Agenda 2000*, vol. I: *For a Stronger and Wider Union* (Brussels: Office for Official Publications of the European Communities, 1997); Commission of the European Communities, *Agenda 2000*, vol. II: *The Challenge of Enlargement* (Brussels: Office for Official Publications of the European Communities,

recommended that accession negotiations commence immediately with six countries deemed best qualified to join: Cyprus, the Czech Republic, Estonia, Hungary, Poland, and Slovenia. The Commission identified a second group of applicants – Bulgaria, Latvia, Lithuania, Romania, the Slovak Republic, and Turkey – which would have to demonstrate further progress on economic and political liberalization before negotiations with the EU could commence. Acknowledging the budgetary concerns of many current members, principally Germany, the Commission maintained that enlargement could be financed without increasing the overall budget ceiling of 1.27 percent of EU GDP established by the Delors II agreement. Agenda 2000 proposed an extension of the current financing arrangements up through the year 2006, with reform of the Common Agricultural Policy and the structural funds – specifically, tighter eligibility requirements for aid recipients – generating the necessary savings.

The Commission's budgetary proposals were greeted with open skepticism by poorer members of the EU, led by Spain. Their reactions turned angry when, in September, the Germans and the Dutch stepped up demands for a new financing formula that would reduce their countries' net contributions to the EU. In March 1998, German officials openly threatened to derail the package of policy reforms contained in Agenda 2000 if a commitment to "substantial and permanent" cuts in Germany's net contributions to the EU was not forthcoming.[90]

Their furor was compounded when the Bonn government expressed reservations about reform of the CAP and structural funds, since this could end up increasing Germany's net contributions to the EU and would almost certainly harm eastern German interests in the process.[91] The Spanish government stated categorically that the accession of poor, farm-intensive members from Central and Eastern Europe could not be financed on the backs of those in the EU most vulnerable to enlargement and least able to afford it. Amid the growing row over the costs of enlargement, France, Belgium, and Italy demanded that unresolved questions pertaining to institutional reform of the EU be taken up and settled *prior* to commencing accession talks with the first wave of applicants. Thus, in an ironic twist, Germany's budget goals began to conflict with its widening objectives; the end result was an almost certain and lengthy delay in the prospects for eastern enlargement.

1997); Commission of the European Communities, *Agenda 2000*, vol. III: The Opinions of the European Commission on the Applications for Accession (Brussels: Office for Official Publications of the European Communities, 1997).

[90] Angus MacKinnon, "EU Faces Bruising Battle Over Enlargement Costs," *Agence France-Presse*, March 23, 1998.

[91] See chapter 6 for more details.

Interests, institutions, ideas, and the unification process

As the prospect of unification took concrete form, the federal government set out to reproduce West Germany in eastern Germany, and to maintain the country's place in the multilateral web of European institutions formed around the nucleus of the EC and NATO. Not only did Bonn automatically reaffirm EC membership, but it chose rapid, often instantaneous convergence to Community rules and norms. Matching rhetoric to action, the German government treated unification and Europe as two sides of the same coin.

This reflexive policy of rapid institutional transfer was driven primarily by the power of ideas. The government's chosen path to constitutional unification (Article 23) as well as to EC "accession" for the former GDR (the doctrine of moving treaty frontiers) suggests the powerful effects of continuity in (West) German identity. In a context of incomplete information on the economic situation in East Germany and acute uncertainty about the GDR's stability, the perceptions of neighboring countries, and the duration of a favorable geopolitical context, the Bonn leadership reached explicitly for principles and historical analogies bound up with the social market economy and Germany's European vocation to lend orientation and direction to its policy choices.

Almost immediately upon implementation, however, institutional transfer generated significant social and economic problems for the new Länder and for unified Germany. Eastern German actors, emboldened by the faltering performance of social market orthodoxy, teamed up with skeptics in the west to question many of the established truths of postwar political economy in West Germany, forcing the government into a mode that one scholar has described as "improvisation".[92] Together (and often for different reasons), they challenged the passive consensus in Germany surrounding the domestic model of political economy, which in turn fed into a larger debate about the goals of European integration. This changed political context would play an important role in the various regulative agendas Germany pursued in Brussels after 1990.

[92] Gerhard Lehmbruch, "Die deutsche Vereinigung: Strukturen und Strategien," *Politische Vierteljahresschrift* 32 (December 1991), 585–604.

3   Continuity in trade and internal market

In the aftermath of unification, Germany's trade and internal market policies continued on much as before, despite the fact that domestic debates in these issue areas were vigorous, and in some instances, specifically relating to trade, challenged core government assumptions. The analytical task here is to explain the absence of policy change.

Trade policy

West Germany's postwar trade policy was Western-oriented and liberal. The strategy of export-led growth presumed an expanding, barrier-free European market, which enabled German firms to achieve scale economies and successfully penetrate foreign markets. The EC also helped the German economy by creating a zone of monetary stability and contributing to open international trade. Within this basic trade orientation, a complex mixture of security interests and domestic politics drove West Germany's foreign economic policy toward the Soviet Union and its Eastern bloc satellites. *Ostpolitik*, launched by the Brandt-Scheel government in 1970, sought to establish a sturdy regional *détente* capable of withstanding the vicissitudes of superpower relations, and to promote the cause of unification by drawing East Germany into ever-deepening ties (*Wandel durch Annäherung*).[1]

Trade and the unification settlement, 1989–90

External trade proved to be one of the few truly contentious issues to occupy West German and Community negotiators during talks over the terms of the GDR's accession. The issue revolved around the question of *Vertrauensschutz* – in other words, meeting the "legitimate expectations" of the German Democratic Republic's trading partners, which were concentrated for the most part in the Soviet Union and Eastern

---

[1] Hanrieder, *Germany, America, Europe*, and more recently Garton Ash, *In Europe's Name.*

Europe.[2] Without some kind of transitional arrangement, the accession of the GDR meant raising the common external tariff around East German territory, which would have choked off its trade with Eastern bloc members of the Council for Mutual Economic Assistance (CMEA) overnight.

In the period immediately following the wall's collapse, the Germans were motivated exclusively by foreign policy considerations. Moscow demanded that unification leave untouched the tariff-free status of exports to the GDR that were covered by multi-year contractual arrangements. This request carried considerable weight in Bonn, since the Soviet position on unification was still ambiguous. Similarly, Chancellor Kohl and his government were anxious to demonstrate that unification would generate no immediate economic disadvantages for Germany's neighbors in Central and Eastern Europe, who linked the fate of their liberalization programs to the tariff-free issue.

In Brussels, the Germans argued that Eastern bloc goods currently under contract should be allowed in under the terms requested by the Soviets and, furthermore, that the goods should be allowed to circulate freely within the Common Market. Bonn maintained that these goods met prevailing EC standards, and thus posed no undue health or safety risks to consumers. Furthermore, government officials were convinced that the goods in question stood absolutely no chance of competing with Western products, and so allowing these goods to circumvent the common external tariff represented a costless but politically significant gesture.

In the words of a BMWi official closely involved with the negotiations in Brussels, "by this point in time our thinking had advanced somewhat farther than those of our fellow EC members."[3] The German position was accepted, after some hesitation, by the Commission and by the member governments of Denmark, Spain, and Portugal. However, Bonn's proposal encountered strong objections from Italy, France, and the UK, which feared that Germany was planning to erect a new Hong Kong in the soon-to-be former GDR, replete with low taxes, low wages, and minimal regulatory frameworks. German officials reacted with disbelief; according to the official quoted above, "if you had traveled around the GDR during this time, the notion of a Hong Kong in East Germany would have been met with derision."[4]

[2] Spence, "The European Community and German Unification," 145.
[3] Interview with BMWi official, Bonn, July 9, 1992.
[4] As documented in chapter 2, German goals for the new Länder, which presumed a rapid equalization of living standards, ruled out a "Hong Kong" strategy from the start. In fact, concern in the Federal Republic revolved much more around preventing a

Thus commenced long and arduous discussions over the treatment of goods from Eastern bloc countries. France, the UK, and Italy were willing to accept a compromise, and allow the goods into East Germany tariff-free, but on the condition that Bonn establish procedures to ensure that they be consumed on site in the former GDR. The Germans insisted that this was simply not feasible, both for technical and political reasons. In effect, the Community would be asking Germany to erect a new economic wall on the ruins of the old political one. As a counter-proposal, Bonn offered to create less obtrusive administrative mechanisms to contain imports from CMEA countries into eastern Germany, to which the Council eventually agreed.

In a directive issued on December 4, 1990, the Council lifted the common external tariff for products covered by existing trade agreements between the GDR and individual CMEA countries as well as the Republic of Yugoslavia until December 31, 1992. The directive applied to both manufactured goods and agricultural products; a subsequent Council decision extended the provisions to goods governed by the European Coal and Steel Community Treaty, specifically coal and steel.

East German actors were not involved in negotiations over the terms of incorporation. It is important to recall that during this period, a pervasive optimism reigned in Bonn about the economics of unification. Thus, the government approached the regulation of the GDR's external trade links almost exclusively from the vantage point of foreign policy. After 1990, and in particular after eastern German economic performance began to deteriorate, the provisions relating to the former GDR's external trade relations took on a more pronounced domestic economic dimension. As we shall see in a later section, eastern German industrial interests began to mobilize around the issue, requesting among other things an extension of the derogation to the EC's common external tariff.

Trade policy after unification, 1990–95

General trade policy

Germany's liberal trade orientation came through the unification process intact. Political elites from all points on the party spectrum asserted that Germany's commitment to free trade intensified after 1990, since the mounting costs of unification could only be financed through increased exports, which presupposed international trade liberalization. This manifested itself in strong, public support for a successful

German Mezzogiorno from taking root. See Sinn and Sinn, *Kaltstart*, 49; and Singer, "The Politics and Economics of German Unification," 85.

conclusion to the Uruguay Round of the General Agreement on Tariffs and Trade (GATT),[5] and in opposition to attempts by the European Commission to expand its competencies in the trade field, which the German government feared would benefit protectionist members in the Council like France.

The consensus on free trade among political elites was mirrored by equally strong agreement among the country's leading economic institutes, as well as organized labor and business in the united Germany. The heavenly chorus, to paraphrase Schattschneider, sang with a strong western German accent,[6] although the few eastern German groups, principally sectoral industry associations, that participated in the discussion over free trade affirmed the government's general stance. An official in the BMWi's Berlin *Außenstelle* stated emphatically that there were no significant protectionist voices to be heard in the new Länder; "firms in the east are aware that they cannot close off the home market and still hope to survive."[7]

As in the pre-unification period, however, the government's stated position on international trade liberalization did not always translate into resolute action. The clearest instance of a gap between German rhetoric and action on trade issues involved the Uruguay Round, which almost foundered on agricultural subsidies. This sensitive issue – a new item on the GATT agenda – generated a bitter controversy between the United States, which sought a significant decrease in the EC's capacity to subsidize production and especially exports, and France, which vigorously opposed the American initiative.[8] The Kohl government's stated desire to see the Uruguay Round succeed was counterbalanced by (a) its commitment to protect the interests of Germany's small-scale farming sector located in the western parts of the country, and (b) its reluctance to isolate the French government, which repeatedly declared the issue a matter of national importance in the face of mounting and increasingly violent protests by French farmers.

Germany's domestic constraints softened in mid-1992, when EC members approved a sweeping reform of the CAP, thereby opening the way to a resolution of the outstanding disagreements on GATT.

---

[5] In the words of Norbert Wieczorek, SPD spokesperson on trade issues, "The more liberalization is achieved in Geneva, the more favorable the implications for the new Länder." Deutscher Bundestag, debate on the Große Anfrage "GATT-Welthandelssystem," 67th Session, 12 December 1991, 5753.

[6] E. E. Schattschneider, *The Semi-Sovereign People* (New York: Holt, Rinehart, and Winston, 1960), 35.

[7] Interview with BMWi (*Außenstelle* Berlin) official, Berlin, October 29, 1992.

[8] This issue will be discussed at greater length in chapter 6, where German agricultural policy is evaluated.

However, French objections persisted. Although Bonn officials let it be known through press channels that Germany would vote against France in the Council on any up or down vote on GATT, the government was determined to prevent this unhappy choice from materializing. Chancellor Kohl worked tirelessly behind the scenes to bring about an acceptable compromise between the American and French negotiating teams, which they achieved in December 1993. The Chancellor's actions revealed a continuing sensitivity to Germany's capacity for influence, which historically has been constrained by fear of political backlash from EC partners.[9]

On a related issue, the German government resisted Commission efforts to acquire the power unilaterally to activate protection clauses or to levy countervailing duties and restrictive import quotas against countries deemed to be employing unfair trading practices, and to receive the complaints of individual firms directly, instead of through intermediaries like sectoral associations or national governments. The Commission's reform proposals struck at the heart of Article 113 of the Rome Treaty, which stipulates that all trade policy recommendations of the Commission must be approved by a qualified majority of the member governments. By affirming the status quo, Bonn hoped to preserve the strength of a liberal blocking minority in the Council, consisting of Germany, the UK, the Netherlands, Luxembourg, and Denmark.

The Commission's proposals were strongly supported by a coalition of southern members led by France. In the end, the two sides agreed to a compromise package that made it easier for the European Union to retaliate against the unfair trading practices of non-member countries, but still fell short of the original Commission proposals. The outcome became bound up with the GATT negotiations; as the price for a GATT deal, France insisted on some strengthening of the Commission's authority in this policy area, and Germany declined to block the request. Once again, the health of the Franco-German partnership took precedence.

Eastern trade policy[10]
If the united Germany's stance on general trade issues remained true to its pre-unification heritage, the matter of Eastern trade, which was

---

[9] Interview with Bundesministerium für Ernährung, Landwirtschaft, und Forsten (BML) official, Bonn, December 4, 1992. Heinrich Weiß, president of the BDI, characterized the situation in the following terms: "Germany is accepted by its neighbors only as an economic power, not as a schoolmaster." "Die besten Köpfe befassen sich mit der Erfindung neuer Barrieren," *Frankfurter Allgemeine Zeitung*, April 27, 1992, 17.

[10] This section is based closely on Anderson and Wallander, "Interests and the Wall of Ideas."

intimately bound up with the larger issue of German *Ostpolitik*, presented more complex challenges. In the words of a BMWi official interviewed in 1992, "the fact that Germany now has a piece of the former CMEA system within its borders has created additional nuances in *Ostpolitik*."[11] German elites believed that the promotion of economic and political liberalization in the former Eastern bloc, culminating in EU membership for many Central and Eastern European countries, would contribute not just to regional stability, but to the rejuvenation of the eastern German economy. Thus, German *Ostpolitik*, in the words of a civil servant in the Federal Ministry of Economics, experienced "an extremely strong shift" in favor of domestic considerations after unification.[12]

To advance these interrelated objectives, Bonn concluded separate treaties with the principal countries in the region, the purpose of which was to signal Germany's peaceful intentions and to promote cooperation in the areas of cultural exchange, the environment, and trade. In mid-1991, as domestic budgetary constraints began to tighten, the federal government shifted from bilateral to multilateral aid packages and trade agreements organized through EC and G-24 frameworks. By 1992, German aid to the USSR/CIS alone had reached DM70 billion, or fully half of all international aid to the former Eastern bloc.

Relations with its Community partners as well as domestic politics drove Germany's diplomatic initiatives, resulting in a string of "Europe Agreements" that, while establishing the long-term goal of a free trade zone between the EC and the signatory countries, shielded so-called sensitive sectors in the Community – steel, textiles, coal, and agriculture – from Eastern European competitors with tariff barriers and import quotas. Over the course of the next several years and occasionally at Bonn's insistence, the Commission activated protection clauses of the Europe Agreements covering i.a. steel, aluminum, and livestock imports.

Beginning in 1993, the Commission, reacting to the bitter complaints of Eastern European leaders, tried to convince the member governments to accelerate trade liberalization with these countries across the board, including some of the sensitive areas. Bonn reacted unenthusiastically; although the Foreign Ministry approved of the initiative and its underlying rationale, both the BMWi and the agriculture ministry opposed the Commission's proposals, fearing the consequences for steel, textiles, and farmers. In the end, the Commission's proposals were approved largely intact at the Copenhagen summit in June 1993.

[11] Interview with BMWi official, Bonn, October 2, 1992.
[12] Interview with BMWi official, Bonn, October 5, 1992.

Domestically, this was old politics, however, with little connection to unification. Powerful western German sectoral associations like the Wirtschaftsvereinigung Stahl (WS) made the running on these issues. Western groups were not averse to using unification to increase their leverage over government officials; for example, WS raised the possibility that continued low-price steel imports from Czechoslovakia could complicate the difficult restructuring and privatization process under way at Eko Stahl, the main steel production site in eastern Germany.[13] According to BMWi officials, however, this did not weigh heavily in the final decision to activate the protection clause.

Bonn civil servants sought to explain these and other decisions with reference to the broader principle of trade liberalization with the East. For example, an official in the economics ministry said that such decisions flowed from a concern that the Eastern European countries "do not get too successful"; otherwise, the fragile support for the accords could begin to disintegrate within the Council, particularly in a recessionary environment.[14] Another official in the BMWi wryly noted that the Europe Agreements, no small thanks to Germany, function as both "a bridge and a bulwark."[15] Commitment to free trade, as to any abstract principle, is always relative, and it should be noted that these protectionist reflexes notwithstanding, Germany as always remained far more committed to comprehensive trade liberalization *vis-à-vis* Eastern Europe and the CIS than its fellow European partners.

Domestically, Bonn confronted the extreme dependence of eastern German export industry on Eastern bloc markets. East German foreign trade, two-thirds of it conducted with its CMEA partners, contributed 28.9 percent of GDP in 1989.[16] One in ten eastern German jobs depended on exports to Comecon markets, the bulk of which were capital goods; in its heyday, GDR industry exported 76 percent of its fishing vessels, 68 percent of its passenger rail-cars, and 84 percent of its

---

[13] As chapter 5 will show, WS simultaneously was pressing the government to adopt a very strict line on the subsidization of Eko through the THA. Interviews with BMWi officials in 1992 revealed that the Czech steel issue quickly became a matter of personal concern to the minister, Jürgen Möllemann, who overrode the vigorous objections of his officials responsible for Community affairs and for economic relations with the former Eastern bloc and lodged the formal request for protection with the Commission. Officials in these departments variously described the decision as "a real clanger" and "an unfortunate case." Civil servants responsible for steel policy supported the minister's decision. Interviews with BMWi officials, Bonn, October 2, 1992 and October 5, 1992.

[14] Interview with BMWi official, Bonn, October 2, 1992.

[15] Interview with BMWi (*Außenstelle* Berlin) official, Berlin, October 29, 1992.

[16] The figure had already dropped to 26.8 percent in 1990. Klaus Werner, "Der Außenhandel der neuen deutschen Bundesländer mit Osteuropa," *Wirtschaftsdienst* (April 1992), 207.

cranes to the USSR.[17] Most of the production was substandard and, thanks to Soviet subsidies, priced well above their world market value.[18]

To shore up GDR–USSR trade while negotiators hammered out the terms of unification, the federal government responded on several fronts. In addition to negotiating the derogations to the common external tariff described above, Bonn agreed to maintain the CMEA's "transfer ruble" mechanism in 1990, and deferred claims for payment on the pre-1990 transfer ruble account balance of DM1.7 billion owed the GDR by the Soviet Union.[19] The government also provided DM2 billion in subsidies to eastern German firms in 1990, much of it prior to formal unification, to enable them to meet contractual obligations to CMEA purchasers. These measures had the effect of actually increasing GDR exports to its Comecon partners by 7.9 percent in the second half of 1990.[20]

The fundamental assumption underlying these early government responses was that the economic adjustment problems at home and abroad were essentially transitory. Consequently, after unification Bonn opted for a veteran instrument to support trade between the USSR and the new Länder: Hermes, the federal export credit insurance program in operation since 1949. The original goal of this program was to help West German firms gain a foothold in world markets. It was expressly designed *not* to serve as a general export subsidy; indeed, coverage is legally proscribed if there is a high probability of default. In comparison to other state-run programs in Europe, Hermes operated "more on the principles of *laissez-faire* and subsidiarity."[21]

The decision to apply an old trade instrument to new challenges was preceded by hard-fought ministerial debates in the BMWi and BMF between late 1990 and early 1991. Those in favor of Hermes stressed three arguments. First, the instrument had an established, proven track

---

[17] Sinn and Sinn, *Kaltstart*, 135; Deutscher Bundestag, *Antwort der Bundesregierung auf die Kleine Anfrage "Zur Situation des Handels der DDR mit den RGW-Ländern nach Einführung der D-Mark in der DDR,"* 11. Wahlperiode, Drucksache 11/8289, October 24, 1990, 2.

[18] On *de facto* Soviet trade subsidies to Eastern Europe, see Paul Marer, "The Political Economy of Soviet Relations with Eastern Europe," in Sarah M. Terry, ed., *Soviet Policy in Eastern Europe* (New Haven: Yale University Press, 1984), 155–88; and Valerie Bunce, "The Empire Strikes Back: The Evolution of the Eastern Bloc from a Soviet Asset to a Soviet Liability," *International Organization* 39 (Winter 1985), 1–46.

[19] The transfer ruble provided a means of clearing trade payments in the CMEA's nonconvertible member currencies. In the CMEA system, 1 transfer ruble = DM2.34.

[20] Werner, "Der Außenhandel der neuen deutschen Bundesländer mit Osteuropa," 208.

[21] Ingo Hichert, *Staatliche Exportabsicherung* (Cologne: Deutscher Instituts-Verlag, 1986), 139. Hermes is administered by a state-backed agency, Hermes Kreditversicherungs-AG (Hamburg), which pledges to reimburse commercial loans for exports in the event the purchasers default on payment.

record. Second, it could sustain trade with the USSR during what officials believed would be a brief transition period, since the USSR did not yet possess the requisite hard currency reserves to finance trade without assistance. Finally, it would stabilize export-dependent jobs in the new Länder and provide firms located there with a stable source of revenue that could be used to support their eventual shift into western markets – all without adding to government budget outlays.

Officials opposed to Hermes rejected the fiscal argument, pointing out that in the event of the USSR's inability to pay, budget costs were sure to rise, perhaps sooner rather than later. Opponents also maintained that Hermes would lock in pre-1990 trade linkages between the former GDR and the CMEA region, which would retard structural economic transformation both at home and abroad. Reliance on Hermes would foster the illusion among eastern German firms that they could continue to sell their outmoded products in perpetuity, thereby reinforcing the huge gap between the eastern and western regional economies.

Opponents of Hermes proposed a package of tied export credits, but were rebuffed on the basis of the projected budgetary costs and the need for EC and OECD permission, which was considered highly unlikely. In fact, according to a BMWi official, subsidy-based programs were never in contention, since they would never have been approved by Germany's trading partners and would have seriously undermined Germany's international credibility as a long-standing opponent of export subsidies.[22] Confronted with Hermes as the only available option, opponents countered that it would be better to abandon an approach based on export credit guarantees, and instead pump resources directly into eastern German firms to ease their liquidity problems and provide them with desperately needed investment capital. The sectoral approach to the *Osthandel* question also met with unyielding opposition in Bonn ministerial circles, since this would have required the government to abandon its approach to privatization (see chapter 6). In the final analysis, opponents were placed in the untenable position of advocating a do-nothing policy, which "would have delivered an unacceptable shock to the system, with catastrophic economic and social consequences in the new Länder."[23]

Hermes was subsequently modified to suit the needs of eastern German firms and their customers in the USSR. After formal negotiations with the OECD and informal consultations with the Commission, Bonn secured permission to implement a set of special conditions, for which only those applications submitted by eastern German firms to

[22] Interview with BMWi official, Bonn, October 2, 1992.
[23] Interview with BMWi (*Außenstelle* Berlin) official, Berlin, October 29, 1992.

cover export contracts with Soviet purchasers during the 1991 calendar year were eligible. The conditions consisted of generally easier insurance terms, including a waiver of the deposit requirements for Soviet purchasers and longer amortization deadlines. Bonn expressly declined to ask for a geographical extension of the conditions to cover trade with Eastern European countries, for fear of unleashing a chain reaction of demands from excluded countries in the developing world that could have undermined the prevailing OECD regime governing export subsidies.[24] The Bonn government was quite happy with the outcome as it appeared both to rescue eastern firms and establish a long-term basis for trade with Russia; according to a BMWi official, "no one at the time assumed that the special conditions would need to be a multi-year affair."[25] Of the Hermes budget of DM165 billion in 1991, DM20 billion was set aside for trade with the CIS under the special conditions.

From 1991 to 1992, the total value of exports to Eastern Europe and the USSR/CIS guaranteed by Hermes rose by over 160 percent to DM11.2 billion, or 29.6 percent of total Hermes coverage in 1991.[26] At the same time, however, the flawed assumptions underpinning the approach based on Hermes became increasingly apparent. First, export markets in the former Eastern bloc deteriorated rapidly, especially in the Soviet Union, leaving many eastern German firms floundering. Between October 1990 and October 1991, total exports from eastern Germany fell by 60 percent; exports to the USSR dropped by 49 percent – in some product categories, the decline approached total collapse.[27] Second, the assumption that the Soviets would continue to rely on trade with eastern German suppliers proved unfounded. Since Hermes offered no subsidies or grants to Russian importers, there were few incentives for them to rely on established trade relations with the former GDR in the absence of more generous or subsidized terms. Commenting on the USSR's new-found access to imports from anywhere in the world, an economics ministry official remarked, "The Russians simply don't want this junk any more."[28] Third, economic adjustment

[24] Deutscher Bundestag, *Antwort der Bundesregierung auf die Kleine Anfrage* ... *"Situation des Handels Ostdeutschlands mit den ehemaligen RGW-Ländern,"* 12. Wahlperiode, Drucksache 12/2116, February 19, 1992, 8.

[25] Interview with BMWi official, Bonn, October 22, 1992.

[26] DM5.9 billion in exports came from eastern German firms, the bulk of which was destined for Russia. Thus, not all of the DM20 billion in 1991 Hermes guarantees slated for eastern German firms was disbursed; the remaining funds were carried over into the next fiscal year. Bundesregierung, *Ausfuhrgarantien und Ausfuhrbürgschaften der Bundesrepublik Deutschland: Bericht über das Jahr 1991* (Bonn, 1992), 7–8.

[27] Deutscher Bundestag, *Antwort der Bundesregierung* ... *"Situation des Handels Ostdeutschlands,"* 2.

[28] Interview with BMWi official, Bonn, October 5, 1992.

in the new Länder was proving far more costly, slow, and wrenching than originally anticipated.

In the midst of these changing parameters, Bonn ministries considered suspending Hermes assistance for CIS trade. They rejected this option in January 1992 and, instead, decided to place a DM5 billion cap on export guarantees for the year, with each individual credit guarantee limited to DM100 million. At the same time, the government strengthened the domestic rationale for its approach; 95 percent of the credits were reserved exclusively for eastern firms.[29] The final decision represented a compromise between the BMF, which advocated a temporary suspension of the program, and the BMWi, supported by the Foreign Ministry, which pushed for an open-ended budgetary commitment to Hermes.

The federal economics ministry could point to a solid coalition of support for Hermes among public and private actors in the eastern Länder, comprised of management, trade unions, the THA, and local and state governments. This coalition stressed the dire consequences of a breakdown in German–CIS trade, which was estimated to support up to 850,000 eastern German jobs directly, and an additional half a million or so indirectly.[30] Eastern German demands for increased export insurance assistance were echoed by national business interest associations, principally the Bundesverband der Deutschen Industrie (BDI) and the Bundesverband des Deutschen Groß- und Außenhandels (BGA). West German firms remained silent on the issue.

The DM5 billion budgeted for Hermes in 1992 did not become available until well into the calendar year, largely because Russia was unwilling to provide the necessary state guarantees. Even after Moscow relented, Hermes assistance failed to flow owing to administrative bottlenecks at the receiving end in Russia.[31] Additional complications

---

[29] Only those eastern firms with solid, long-term economic prospects were to be considered, and any western German firms applying for assistance had to document that their supplier firms hailed predominantly from the eastern provinces.

[30] At this juncture, the THA had in its possession over 5,000 firms, many of them large employers almost wholly dependent on CIS contracts in the short term. For example, the Magdeburg machine tool manufacturer Sket announced it would be forced to lay off 80 percent of its 5,100 member workforce if contracts from CIS buyers were not forthcoming in the near future. Ralf Neubauer, "Am seidenen Faden," *Die Zeit*, April 10, 1992, 25.

[31] By the end of July, only DM713 million of the DM5 billion had been claimed, mostly for exports to Kazakhstan, Ukraine, and Byelorussia. In a situation of rampant inflation, few if any Russian firms were in a position to initiate a Hermes-supported deal with an eastern German supplier, owing to stringent financing conditions imposed by the Vnesheconombank (VEB), the Soviet (and now Russian) foreign trade bank. "Die guten Geschäfte mit der Sowjetunion sind vorbei," *Frankfurter Allgemeine Zeitung*, October 17, 1992, 14.

surfaced when the Russians published a list of priority goods for Hermes assistance: medical supplies and consumer products like pantyhose and cigarettes held the top positions. This caused much consternation in Bonn, where policymakers were preoccupied with the needs of capital goods producers in the new Länder.

In response to the precipitous decline in exports to the former Soviet republics and related complications in the privatization of eastern German industry, the federal government announced in mid-year that it would undertake a review of trade policy toward the East, and consider alternatives to Hermes. A final decision would be taken in September. The need for action was all the more pressing as eastern German firms, despite the blockage of Hermes guarantees, continued to produce goods on the assumption that trade with the CIS would eventually resume; for many factories, inventories by early September had reached a level equivalent to half a year's production.

The government's announcement elicited a blizzard of proposals to replace Hermes, many of which would have taken German trade policy into uncharted waters. The vast majority came from outside ministerial circles: the THA, the BDI, the BGA, the Ost-Ausschuß der Deutschen Wirtschaft, elected state governments in the new Länder, and the SPD opposition in Bonn. Proposals included: (a) debt–equity swaps, in which the CIS countries would mortgage raw materials like oil and natural gas against immediate deliveries of manufactured goods from eastern German firms; (b) liquidity assistance from the THA to cover exports by its firms to the CIS for which payment was promised but not received; (c) a ruble fund, into which CIS purchasers would deposit payments for eastern German exports – Bonn would then use this fund to finance German direct investment or joint ventures in these countries, and compensate eastern German firms in Deutschmarks via indirect federal payments; (d) state-supported "clearing houses," which would purchase inventory stocks from eastern firms and sell them on CIS markets for best offer; (e) the classification of some or all of the members of the CIS as developing countries, which would enable Bonn to access budgetary sources heretofore off-limits.

Hermes was also on the agenda. Proposals submitted for review included the reinstatement of the 1991 special conditions, the extension of coverage to include eastern German exports to western markets, and the introduction of greater flexibility into the Hermes instrument, for example by making barter exchange agreements eligible for export credit guarantees. The ministerial review also took up the more straight-forward option of simply increasing the existing program's budget.

The finance ministry played the role of devil's advocate. According to a high-ranking BMF civil servant, the ministry dismissed out-of-hand the various unorthodox proposals described above. In general, such ideas were viewed as too expensive and inconsistent with current German law and the country's international trade obligations. Emphasizing the latter point, the same official explained that consultations with the EC and OECD over the Hermes special conditions in 1991 had reinforced the ministry's determination to take into account the prevailing international norms in this policy area.[32] Moreover, he continued, Bonn wished to avoid a decision that would then require Germany to go hat in hand to Brussels for approval – "The EC always demands something in return."

The BMF also took a very skeptical view of Hermes, one that was colored by mounting evidence of severe Russian financial problems as well as in-house estimates of CIS defaults on Hermes credits in 1992, which totaled DM1.25 billion.[33] Ministry spokespersons maintained that in light of the current budgetary situation, no additional public funds for Hermes would be considered. They went on to suggest that Hermes was being misused, since conditions in the CIS did not meet the program's legal guidelines – namely, that there should be only a remote chance of default.

Within the BMWi, officials acknowledged that Hermes in its present incarnation was incapable of reviving and stabilizing exports to the CIS. They stressed that many of the problems were beyond the program's control, i.e. they resided in Russia. A sober realism had settled in among officials responsible for economic relations with the former Eastern bloc; as one official confessed, "our capacity to influence matters in the Eastern countries is highly circumscribed ... We face huge constraints in what we can hope to influence and to achieve."[34] Moreover, evidence that western German exports to the reform states of Poland, Czechoslovakia, and Hungary had risen by 10.9 percent between 1990 and 1991 while eastern German exports to the same markets had slumped suggested that Hermes was not only ineffective, but – as feared back in 1990–91 – was also locking in inefficient production structures in the new Länder.[35] An official in the Berlin *Außenstelle* of the BMWi

[32] This official remarked that on the written list of proposals, a check-mark in a small box next to each item signified whether the measure would require notification of and approval by the European Community or OECD. Interview with BMF official, Bonn, November 11, 1992.

[33] In fact, CIS defaults in 1992 reached DM1 billion, which contributed substantially to the 20.5 percent increase in the Hermes deficit that year. Bundesregierung, *Ausfuhrgarantien und Ausfuhrbürgschaften der Bundesrepublik Deutschland: Bericht über das Jahr 1992* (Bonn, 1993), 8.

[34] Interview with BMWi official, Bonn, October 2, 1992.

[35] Werner, "Der Außenhandel der neuen deutschen Bundesländer mit Osteuropa," 209.

remarked that the former GDR was "oriented downward ... chained to a developing country – the former USSR."[36]

The discussion of alternatives, however, revealed significant differences between the political leadership of the ministry and the BMWi's civil service. In a series of official press briefings, Minister Jürgen Möllemann suggested that unorthodox and, in all likelihood, expensive new instruments would be required to address the situation. At times, he appeared to openly support the more radical proposals pushed by the THA and the eastern Länder. Among civil servants, the approach was decidedly agnostic, resembling a neutral problem-solving exercise. According to one official, "We took a more nuanced view [than the finance ministry]. We did not adopt a fixed line. Rather, it was more in the way of 'If you want to achieve the following goal, here is the full range of options.'"[37]

BMWi civil servants adopted this seemingly noncommittal stance because of the crushing political pressures for a government response to the mounting crisis in the former GDR; in late August, Kohl had declared the issue of Eastern trade and the eastern German economy to be a matter of the utmost priority for the government. However, agnosticism should not be mistaken for indifference about the final outcome. BMWi officials described the interministerial decision-making process as verging on pro forma; the more unorthodox proposals carried so many strikes against them going into the review that the final outcome was never in doubt. A BMWi official responsible for economic relations with the CIS dismissed the ruble-fund scheme as "completely frivolous," while another described any proposal based on the ruble as "lost money."[38] An economics ministry official characterized the debt–equity swap proposal as "a suggestion originating in the old cadres in the east."[39]

BMWi concerns about these various proposals mirrored those expressed by the finance ministry. Each scheme represented an open-ended financial commitment from Bonn to subsidize trade with the Eastern bloc, which was unacceptable for several reasons: first, it meant a clear departure from social market orthodoxy in the trade policy area;

These trends were to continue; between 1993 and 1995, German exports to Central and Eastern Europe, 90 percent of which hailed from western firms, grew by 30 percent to around DM60 billion, or 8.2 percent of total German exports. "Osteuropa ist als Handelspartner inzwischen wichtiger als Amerika," *Frankfurter Allgemeine Zeitung*, July 19, 1996, 15.

[36] Interview with BMWi (*Außenstelle* Berlin) official, Berlin, October 29, 1992.
[37] Interview with BMWi official, Bonn, October 2, 1992.
[38] Interviews with BMWi officials, Bonn, October 2, 1992 and December 8, 1992.
[39] Interview with BMWi official, Bonn, October 2, 1992.

second, it threatened to exacerbate an already difficult budgetary situation; and third, it entailed problematical international ramifications. In fact, officials in the economics ministry made a point of consulting with the EC Commission in July 1992, prior to finalizing a set of recommendations for the interministerial review. Commenting on this fact, a civil servant explained, "There is not a single policy area in the EC in which one can act without considering the effects on other members' interests. This has nothing to do with unification; rather, it is simply the EC."[40]

During the review, officials within the Foreign Ministry (Auswärtiges Amt: AA) emphasized the foreign policy and security advantages of an active *Ostpolitik*. However, support within the AA for an open-ended commitment to Hermes had dissipated, since the mounting crisis in Russia made it clear to ministry officials that fashioning an Eastern trade policy to serve Bonn's larger security interests in the region would require instruments more typical of foreign aid and development policy. Foreign Ministry officials were increasingly concerned that the Hermes program for trade with Russia was becoming a export promotion program based on subsidies, which officials noted was in violation of international obligations.[41]

The outcome of the review revealed the extent to which the larger debate over Eastern trade policy had come full circle since 1990. The first item mentioned in both the government's formal written announcement of the decision and Minister Möllemann's ensuing address to parliament was not trade, but the Treuhandanstalt. The government called on firms in the former GDR to seek their fortunes and futures in Western markets; the task of the THA was to identify firms under its control that were capable of adopting an export strategy targeted at Western markets, and to develop restructuring plans, including, whenever possible, accelerated privatization timetables, to assist them in this transition. In contrast to the unsuccessful attempt in 1990–91 to address the needs of the eastern German export sector through the THA, proponents of a sectoral (as opposed to trade) approach were able to link the September trade review to the incremental reorientation of the privatization program under way (see chapter 2).

Trade did not go unmentioned in the final decision, to be sure. Bonn announced that there would be no increase in the Hermes budget for the time being, since DM1.8 billion of the original DM5 billion remained unspent. Officials left open the option to raise the Hermes budget ceiling in the future. Existing Hermes guidelines were modified

---

[40] Interview with BMWi official, Bonn, October 7, 1992.
[41] Interviews with Foreign Ministry officials, Bonn, September 25, 1992 and November 20, 1992.

to include barter-exchange, and certain guarantee deadlines for the CIS countries were extended into 1993. The government also encouraged private trading or clearing houses to get involved in moving the growing inventories of eastern firms. Finally, several small-scale measures, including public procurement programs and foreign marketing assistance, were announced.[42] The government advertised the entire package as revenue-neutral, and officials privately expressed confidence that it would generate no controversy in Brussels or Paris.

Eastern Germans reacted bitterly to the September decision. The manager of an Erfurt-based THA holding described the decision as "a catastrophe and a sign of impotence."[43] And although the THA had acknowledged from the beginning the need for its firms to reorient toward Western markets, its president, Birgit Breuel, expressed dismay at the pace set by Bonn, the lack of concrete financial assistance to ease the transition, and the implication that the THA had so far done too little to reorient its firms westward. A few days after the decision, she mused in public about the obstacles confronting THA-firms as they sought to break into Western markets: "If necessary, our firms will have to conquer new markets in the West with aggressive pricing policies (*Kampfpreise*). I can only hope that those who have encouraged us to look to the west will draw the necessary conclusions." Her agency, she added, would "support" its firms if they adopted such strategies.[44] German manufacturing associations, all with large western memberships, reacted swiftly; a spokesperson for the mechanical engineering industry accused the THA president of advocating a policy of dumping.[45] Breuel's remarks were noted with concern in the European Commission, and caused reactions ranging from bemused indifference to consternation within federal and Land policymaking circles.[46]

The bitter reactions to the September decision provide insights into the overall strength of the eastern lobby. Supporters of a more interventionist eastern trade policy had agitated in the Bundestag to no avail.

[42] The government eventually repackaged these programs into the "Einkaufsinitiative Ost," which was intended to facilitate the development of marketing concepts and participation in trade and industry shows by eastern firms.

[43] "Die Maschinen für die GUS sammeln sich auf dem Werksgelände," *Frankfurter Allgemeine Zeitung*, September 29, 1992, 17.

[44] "Breuel: Harter Kampf um neue Märkte im Westen," *Frankfurter Allgemeine Zeitung*, October 1, 1992, 13.

[45] Ralf Neubauer, "Kampfpreise im Visier," *Die Zeit*, October 9, 1992, 27.

[46] A Commission official responsible for competition policy noted that his office had received numerous complaints from western German firms about the pricing policies of THA-owned firms, and he expected the number of complaints to increase if Breuel followed through on her thinly veiled threat. Interview with Commission (DG-IV) official, Brussels, December 1, 1992.

Eastern German efforts to crack the insularity of the ministerial apparatus proved similarly unsuccessful. The various intraministerial bodies assigned responsibility for eastern German affairs participated in the policy process, but did not develop into bureaucratic sponsors of the new region. For example, the Berlin *Außenstelle* of the Federal Ministry of Economics, although generally sympathetic to the plight of eastern firms, possessed neither the inclination nor the decision-making authority to push the more radical demands within Bonn policymaking circles. According to one of the ranking officials there, "Such proposals tend to come from people who are standing in water up to their necks ... But in the end, these ideas are nothing more than crutches. We argued for no special conditions, no subsidies."[47]

In fact, there is but a single instance of eastern German influence over trade policy, and it involved the derogations to the EC's common external tariff. As the expiration deadline of December 31, 1991 approached, a coalition of eastern German manufacturing firms, backed by their respective Land governments, began to pressure the Bonn government for an extension of the derogation, since its terms were decidedly more advantageous than those prevailing under the various Europe Agreements with these former Eastern bloc countries.[48] Bonn officials supported the initiative, agreeing that the overnight increase in tariffs would be extremely disruptive and in some instances potentially fatal for a handful of eastern German manufacturers, including the major steel producer, Eko Stahl.[49] Officials were generally confident of eventual EC approval, in light of the small volume of goods covered by

[47] Interview with BMWi (*Außenstelle* Berlin) official, Berlin, October 29, 1992. Interestingly, these attitudes were also prevalent among civil servants and industry representatives in the eastern Länder. Unlike their political masters, who frequently expressed public support for the more radical proposals considered during the review, these officials viewed the final outcome with equanimity and even understanding. According to a bureaucrat in Mecklenburg-West Pomerania, "Export subsidies are simply not an issue. They would not work, and they would only get us into trouble with the OECD and the EC." A Berlin civil servant, referring with sarcasm to the original decision to go with Hermes, said the government would have been more effective and more honest politically if it had simply paid firms like Deutsche Waggonbau for its rail-cars, and then taken these cars over to Eko Stahl and simply dropped them back in the blast furnaces and started all over. An official with the Verband der Wirtschaft Thüringens, a regional industry association, described proposals like the ruble fund as products of a command economy mentality, and stressed that a basic reorientation of eastern German firms to world markets was essential. Interviews with Land officials in Mecklenburg-West Pomerania, Schwerin, October 27, 1992 and in Berlin, October 29, 1992; interview with industry representative in Thuringia, Erfurt, November 25, 1992.
[48] Typically, these were firms that relied on duty-free imports of raw materials or half-finished products from former CMEA trading partners to remain profitable. In contrast, eastern German agriculture opposed an extension of the derogation. Interview with BMWi official, Bonn, July 9, 1992.
[49] On the Eko case, see chapter 5.

the derogation and the marginal threat to EC competitors. They were even more certain that an extension would have little ameliorative impact on the overall economic situation in eastern Germany.[50] The EC granted the request. Bonn filed a similar request for a second, one-year extension of the derogation toward the end of 1992, which the Commission also approved.

The September 1992 decision established parameters for the federal government's Eastern trade policy that remain operative to the present day. Although it elicited immediate calls from eastern German industry and the SPD for export credit programs and variations on some of the unorthodox proposals considered during the review, the debate over trade instruments quickly died out. Indeed, the principal changes in Eastern trade instruments occurred subsequently in the private sector. For example, an industry-supported "clearing house" was set up in 1994 to facilitate barter exchange between German firms and producers in the former Soviet Union. In the eastern Länder, the state governments, well aware of the international and national-level constraints operating in this policy area, followed the government's lead by establishing or increasing support for Land-financed agencies and programs to assist their firms in developing export marketing strategies oriented toward the West. The results of these combined actions have so far been meager; the eastern Länder's share of total German exports has hovered around 1.8 percent since 1992.[51]

After 1992 the share of the annual Hermes budget for the CIS declined steadily. The government budgeted DM4 billion in 1993 and DM3.5 billion in 1994 (DM2.5 billion for Russia, and DM1 billion for the rest of the CIS). By 1996, the total was down to DM2.3 billion. The government adopted a more cautious approach to applications for Hermes assistance from eastern German firms in light of the mounting defaults by CIS purchasers and the overall level of federal liability for insured contracts with this region, both of which reached levels unprecedented in the forty-year history of the program.[52] In 1993, the BMWi announced that henceforth, Hermes guarantees for Russian trade would be issued only in exceptional circumstances, such as when the very

---

[50] Interview with BMWi (Außenstelle Berlin) official, Berlin, October 29, 1992 and with BMWi official, Bonn, October 5, 1992.

[51] Lucy Smy, "Strangers Bearing Gifts Fail to Boost East German Fortunes," *Financial Times*, January 8, 1997, 6.

[52] In 1993, federal liabilities for contracts with CIS purchasers reached DM39.6 billion, or nearly one-fifth of total liabilities. In the same year, CIS defaults on Hermes guarantees reached DM4.5 billion, a figure that contributed mightily to the 121 percent increase in the Hermes deficit for the year. All figures from Bundesregierung, *Ausfuhrgarantien und Ausfuhrbürgschaften der Bundesrepublik Deutschland: Bericht über das Jahr 1993* (Bonn, 1994).

existence of a significant eastern German employer hung in the balance.[53] To be eligible, firms also had to show that their medium- to long-term marketing strategies envisioned a decline in their reliance on CIS markets below 50 percent. Each decision to extend Hermes guarantees to an eastern German firm required formal approval at the state secretary level in the BMWi. Owing to these stringent procedures, the volume of exports to the region covered by Hermes dropped by approximately one-third to DM8.1 billion in 1993.[54]

With Hermes awash in red ink, the BMF used the opportunity to push through a sweeping reform of the program's premium structure. The reforms, which took effect in mid-1994, drew intense opposition from national industry associations like the BDI, which objected to any measures that might squeeze exports in a time of national recession, and from eastern German firms, which voiced fears that the reforms would hasten their demise.[55] The changes introduced differentiated premiums calculated to reflect the risks involved in trading with various regions of the world; this entailed placing CIS countries in the highest risk category, which effectively doubled insurance premiums for export contracts to these markets.[56] The BMF hoped to contain the mounting costs of Hermes and to keep pace with the efforts of the European Commission to harmonize export insurance programs across the European Union. According to BMWi officials, the reforms would enable the program to pay for itself over the medium term, and furthermore would address the lingering concerns of Germany's European partners that Hermes was evolving into a *de facto* trade subsidy program.[57] Thus, up through 1997, Germany's trade policy toward the East had main-

---

[53] One such exception was the Deutsche Waggonbau AG (DWA) plant in Annendorf, which relied on CIS markets for 75 percent of its annual production of railway carriages. In May 1994, the BMWi announced that DM500 million in Hermes guarantees would be extended to DWA to insure a contract with Russia. DWA management described Hermes guarantees as "absolutely essential to our survival," and asserted that the firm would require Hermes support for several more years. "Waggonbau Ost von Überkapazitäten und Exportrisiken belastet," *Frankfurter Allgemeine Zeitung*, September 17, 1992, 18.

[54] Bundesregierung, *Ausfuhrgarantien und Ausfuhrbürgschaften . . . 1993*, 11.

[55] It is interesting to note that the public statements of national industry associations, however, did not mention the darkened export prospects of eastern German firms. The BDI, for example, expressly counseled the government to abandon any export credit insurance policy that incorporated political or sectoral objectives, with specific reference to the large Hermes deficits run up by eastern German firms trading with the CIS countries.

[56] In mid-1996, the BMWi moved Russia into the next lower risk category, which meant an average premiums reduction of 25 percent. Officials justified this step by pointing to positive economic developments in Russia.

[57] Interviews with two BMWi officials, Bonn, May 17, 1994.

tained its liberal cast – indeed, judged by the 1994 Hermes reforms, it had moved even further away from interventionist principles.

Internal market policy

At the core of the European project is the common market. And so, in its most expansive guise, internal market policy touches on virtually every activity engaged in by Community members, either individually or collectively. Institutionally self-contained policy areas such as competition, the environment, agriculture, or energy deal in whole or in part with issues relevant to the free flow of goods, capital, people, and services across the boundaries of member governments. Narrowly conceived, the internal market embraces the myriad responsibilities of Directorate-General III (Internal Market and Industrial Affairs) in the European Commission; these include (but are not limited to) the harmonization of product safety and technical standards, taxation frameworks, intellectual property rights, company law, and customs legislation.

The same principles and objectives that underpinned West German trade policy applied to the internal market, leading national policymakers consistently to support the dismantling of potential and actual market barriers to internal trade in the EC. Just as in trade, Germany's liberalism on internal market matters was relative; although Bonn harbored a deep ambivalence about pushing the logic of a barrier-free market to its limits in areas like telecommunications, financial services, and insurance, its general orientation and specific preferences were distinctly liberal in comparison to protectionist members like France and Italy.

West Germany's liberal orientation to internal market policy can be seen clearly in its contribution to the single market initiative. Although the impetus for the SEA originated elsewhere,[58] the Kohl government provided crucial weight behind the act's two main components, teaming with Britain to strengthen the case for the completion of the internal market and with France to push through a key package of procedural reforms. In the aftermath of formal SEA ratification in 1987, Germany

---

[58] For contrasting accounts of the SEA's origins, see Wayne Sandholtz and John Zysman, "1992: Recasting the European Bargain," *World Politics* 42 (October 1989), 95–128; Andrew Moravcsik, "Negotiating the Single European Act: National Interests and Conventional Statecraft in the European Community," *International Organization* 45 (Winter 1991), 651–88; and David Cameron, "The 1992 Initiative: Causes and Consequences," in Alberta Sbragia, ed., *Euro-Politics: Institutions and Policymaking in the "New" European Community* (Washington, DC.: The Brookings Institution, 1992), 23–74.

helped advance implementation of the act during its Council presidency in the first half of 1988, an arduous task due to the sheer number of directives and their oftentimes controversial nature.[59]

The German government's support for the SEA was echoed by the main business interest associations and large, export-oriented firms. The BDI, which had pushed for the completion of the internal market since the 1960s, was an early and enthusiastic proponent of Project 1992. Joined by other major peak and sectoral associations, the BDI expressed confidence that German firms were well prepared to succeed in a barrier-free market.[60] Skepticism about the SEA came mainly from organized labor, which warned of "social dumping," as well as small- and medium-sized firms concerned about heightened competition. Producer groups across the board acknowledged the far-reaching market adjustment imperatives that would follow from completion of the internal market, and drew attention to the need to consider ways of improving the attractiveness of Germany as a location for production (*Standort Deutschland*). The tone of the debate remained somewhat muted, however, and would intensify only after unification.

Internal market policy and the unification settlement, 1989–90

Unlike trade, the internal market generated few disagreements during negotiations over the terms of the GDR's incorporation into the European Community. Of the approximately 600 harmonization directives governing the design, composition, labeling, and marketing of products (technical norms and standards) that were in effect at the EC level in 1990, only 10 percent could not be adopted in eastern Germany immediately upon accession. The problem areas centered on the processing and labeling of foodstuffs, pharmaceuticals, cosmetics, and chemical products, as well as the general area of veterinary and plant health.[61]

The politics in this area mimicked the patterns established in the trade area. Several member governments expressed deep concerns about the health and safety implications of allowing substandard East German goods to circulate freely within the common market. The

---

[59] W. A. Smyser, *The German Economy: Colossus at the Crossroads* (New York: St. Martin's Press, 1993), 245.

[60] Exceptions included the information processing and telecommunications industries. A. Herrmann, W. Ochel, and M. Wegner, *Bundesrepublik und Binnenmarkt '92: Perspektiven für Wirtschaft und Wirtschaftspolitik* (Berlin, 1990).

[61] Kuschel, "Die Einbeziehung der ehemaligen DDR in die EG," 83; Commission of the European Communities, "The European Community and German Unification," 67–69.

Commission and the German government were able to allay these fears by seeking a limited number of derogations, and by demonstrating that the products in question posed no substantial dangers to European consumers.

The Commission sought to balance the concerns of member governments against its desire to maintain momentum on the completion of the single market, which was due to take effect on January 1, 1993; in its opinion, erecting protective barriers around eastern Germany could establish an awkward precedent that could slow implementation of the SEA and the Schengen agreement, designed to open up EC frontiers to the free movement of people.[62] Bonn shared the Commission's interpretation, and remained convinced that a rapid transfer of European policy frameworks was good policy. Bonn was also unwilling to push hard on internal market derogations for fear of complicating the far more contentious problems thrown up by external trade and the environment.[63]

Internal market policy after unification, 1990–95

The terms of accession neither laid the groundwork for an eventual politicization of this issue area, nor ushered in shifts in Bonn's established position on the issues. More broadly, German support for the completion of the internal market did not diminish after or because of unification. In early 1992, the German government was sufficiently concerned about the status of the 1992 deadline that it pushed for a formal, binding commitment by the Council to issue the remaining fifty or so directives still requiring approval by year's end. A majority of member states rejected the proposal. The government also expressed deep regret at the lack of progress on VAT harmonization as 1992 drew to a close, and continued to push for a so-called "definitive" taxation regime, in which VAT on goods and services is levied in the country of origin. As Council deadlock on the issue threatened the proposed 1997 implementation deadline, a tax expert was quoted as declaring that "Germany is the only country which has seriously discussed the issue and is really pushing for the definitive regime."[64]

By 1997 Germany had slipped to the worst record of implementing the 217 SEA measures approved by the Council, but officials attributed

---

[62] Spence, "The European Community and German Unification," 155.

[63] Interview with BMWi official, Bonn, July 9, 1992.

[64] Press and Information Office of the Federal Government, "Das Program zur Vollendung des EG-Binnenmarktes: Ein Ziel gewinnt Kontur," *Aktuelle Beiträge zur Wirtschafts- und Finanzpolitik*, November 17, 1992, 3; Amelia Torres, "EU to Miss Deadline for New VAT Regime," *Reuters*, March 3, 1995.

the slowdown to the rapid pace set by Brussels – in January 1992 alone, fifteen approved directives arrived in Bonn – and to long-standing (i.e. pre-unification) concerns in politically sensitive areas like financial services, insurance, and public procurement, each of which sported well-entrenched domestic lobbies, anchored in the west and anxious to inhibit change. A BMWi official, commenting on the government's implementation record, maintained that intraministerial discussions focused invariably on technical and/or legal reasons for delays in implementation, and that these were unrelated to unification, except insofar as the crush of unification-related business in the legislature slowed down the translation of SEA obligations into domestic law.[65] Responding to criticism by the Commission and other member governments, Germany made a concerted push toward the end of 1997, sharply reducing the backlog of SEA directives awaiting action in Bonn.

In the new Länder, the common market was a non-issue, in spite of expert studies conducted in 1992 that concluded the five new Länder were poorly prepared for the launching of the single market.[66] According to the official quoted above, "For the most part, it doesn't concern them. They have more pressing issues to occupy their attention." Land officials in the east noted that, in contrast to the trade area, eastern German firms and their political representatives had not formulated requests for extensions of the various derogations to the EC's internal market regulations negotiated in 1990.[67] Business and government officials struck an optimistic tone; any problems encountered by eastern German firms in a barrier-free market, they argued, would be temporary and linked primarily to inefficiencies and incapacities in local and regional administration (i.e. not to firm- or market-specific factors).[68]

In fact, the momentum behind the internal market program created opportunities for German officials to push through contentious domestic legislation. In 1992, the Kohl government sought to justify an increase in Germany's base value-added-tax rate from 14 to 15 percent

---

[65] Interview with BMWi official, Bonn, March 23, 1992.

[66] "DIW: Neue Länder schlecht vorbereitet," *Frankfurter Allgemeine Zeitung*, September 2, 1992, 11.

[67] Interview with Thuringia economics ministry official, Erfurt, November 24, 1992.

[68] Bundesverband der Deutschen Industrie, "Öffentliche Anhörungssitzung des EG-Ausschusses (18. Sitzung) zum Thema 'Binnenmarkt' am Donnerstag 7. Mai 1992: Antworten des BDI auf den Fragenkatalog," Cologne, April 1992, 36–37. This position was rejected by organized labor, which blamed the government's policy of rapid institutional transfer for many of the eastern region's economic difficulties. See Deutscher Gewerkschaftsbund (DGB), "Stellungnahme des DGB zur öffentlichen Anhörung des EG-Ausschusses des Deutschen Bundestages am 7. Mai 1992 zum Thema 'Binnenmarkt'," Düsseldorf, April 21, 1992, 11–12.

by emphasizing EC-level commitments to harmonize VAT. The SPD and organized labor, which bitterly contested the measure, accused the government of "scapegoating" Brussels to achieve something that it desired on purely domestic grounds: the tax increase would generate much needed revenues that could be used to defray a portion of the mounting costs of unification as well as Germany's financial pledges to the Gulf War effort. Similarly, Bonn used the European commitment to liberalize the flow of persons – embodied first and foremost in the so-called Schengen agreement – to push through a tightening of the country's asylum laws in 1993.

Unification produced no apparent shift in Germany's internal market policy; rather, it provided a backdrop for a new edition of an old debate: Germany's status as an attractive location for manufacturing industry. This discussion focused on the qualities of the macroeconomy, not on the eastern German region *per se*. The impetus was provided by the business community, which, while remaining firmly committed to the goals of the internal market program,[69] began to question whether the country, which for many years has qualified as a high-cost production location, could continue to conduct business-as-usual under radically changed domestic and international circumstances. Industry peak associations and individual firm management blamed the unions and government policies for weakening *Standort Deutschland* to the point where Germany ranked number one in Europe (and in many instances the world) on a variety of cost factors: the highest wages, the shortest work week, the most vacation days, the most burdensome business taxation system, and the most stringent environmental standards.[70] To buttress their claims, industry groups pointed to a worrisome trend: Germany's share of world exports dropped from 12.1 percent to 10.3 percent between 1990 and 1995.[71]

According to business interests, unification and Europe interacted synergistically to bring Germany to the brink of a *Standort* crisis. The constant in this equation post-1990 was Europe – specifically, the looming prospect of the barrier-free internal market. The BDI, joined by the other major peak associations, maintained that the SEA would

[69] A spokesman for the Verband Deutscher Maschinen- und Anlagenbau e.V. (VDMA), the sectoral association representing mechanical engineering firms, commented in 1992, "We cannot put our firms under a cheese glass to protect them from the outside world – we see the consequences of that in the new Länder and Eastern Europe." Interview with VDMA official, Frankfurt, July 16, 1992.

[70] See, for example, the press release by the Institut der deutschen Wirtschaft, "Arbeitskosten nach Branchen: Deutsche fast überall Spitze," November 18, 1996, Nr. 48.

[71] Franz Bertsch, "Wie gut ist der Wirtschaftsstandort Deutschland?," Inter Nationes, Basis-Info Working Paper Series, 3–1997, 2.

generate intensified competition not just between firms, but also between national production locations in the EC. It noted that Germany, with the most stringent regulatory standards in Europe, could easily place its own firms at a competitive disadvantage if market integration proceeded as planned according to mutual recognition.

Thus, industry associations called upon the government to converge unilaterally to the European norm, whether it be in the area of business taxation or environmental standards. In short, they argued, the completion of the internal market placed a new onus on Bonn: to take account of current practice in other member countries, and to reconcile the competitive needs of industry with these practices when legislating. The BDI prophesied that national "solos" (*Alleingänge*) in these critical areas would be met with an export of jobs and investment; a spate of highly publicized decisions to relocate production facilities by firms in the automotive, electronics, and chemical sectors appeared to underscore this point.[72] Commenting on the increased availability of low-cost production sites in Eastern Europe after 1989, a BDI official remarked, "These changes in location incentives are potentially very interesting for individual firms, but they are dangerous for the economy as a whole . . ."[73]

Unification brought these long-standing concerns into sharp focus. To finance the rising costs of German unification, the government found it necessary to postpone reform of the business taxation system. Moreover, Bonn's faltering economic performance after unification led to growing worries within the business community that many of the parameters associated with German economic prowess – sound fiscal and monetary policies, a strong currency, a low inflation rate – were beginning to soften.[74] Business associations hoped to use unification as

---

[72] German foreign direct investment reached DM50 billion in 1995, the highest level ever and an 80 percent increase over the preceding year. Bertsch, "Wie gut ist der Wirtschaftsstandort Deutschland?," 5.

[73] Interview with BDI official, Cologne, July 10, 1992. A spokesperson for the Deutscher Industrie- und Handelstag (DIHT) stressed the need to distinguish rhetoric from reality in the *Standort* debate. Many German BIAs and firms are exaggerating the situation to generate political pressure for change, which he described as "standard fare" in a democracy, although perhaps somewhat "insincere" in light of the stridency of their claims. This official expressed concern over the danger of generating a self-fulfilling prophecy. A structural advantage that offsets many of the weaknesses identified by the business community, he added, is the constant pressure on Germany's European competitors to orient their products to the tastes and preferences of the EC's largest market, Germany. This advantage has only been strengthened by unification. Interview with DIHT official, Bonn, July 8, 1992.

[74] For a general discussion, see Michael Krakowski, Dirk Lau, and Andreas Lux, "Auswirkungen der Wiedervereinigung auf die Standortqualität Westdeutschlands," *Wirtschaftsdienst* (September 1992), 464–71.

an occasion to force policymakers to conduct a thorough overhaul of domestic regulatory, taxation, and social policy.

In mid-1992, business concerns elicited a formal response from the Bonn coalition; Kohl claimed emphatically that he intended to build his party's 1994 national election campaign around the motto "Standort Deutschland." Government officials were keen to emphasize the enduring strengths of the German economy, which included highly skilled labor, technical and managerial expertise, well-developed infrastructure, basic research, and sophisticated production methods. However, they pointed to serious warning signs that largely corresponded to the catalogue of concerns presented by the business community. A high-ranking member of the CDU parliamentary caucus commented, "Germany can no longer afford to be indifferent to the gap in economic and regulatory policy praxis between it and its neighbors."[75]

The debate led directly to passage of a law in 1993 to secure the German production location (*Standortsicherungsgesetz*), at the heart of which were a set of business tax reforms. The legislative response, however, did little to quell business worries. Noting a marked increase in German foreign direct investment coupled with continued decline in inward investment, the Bundesbank added its voice to the chorus of concern over the German production *Standort* in mid-1993, and the CDU parliamentary caucus issued a set of policy principles to guide a formal government review of the issue around the same time. The result, a hundred-page paper entitled "Zukunftssicherung des Wirtschaftsstandortes Deutschland" issued by the BMWi minister Günter Rexrodt, proposed sweeping reforms in the areas of taxation, budgetary consolidation, labor market policy, pensions, and health. The government also stepped up efforts at deregulation, which affected two policy areas taken up in the next chapter: energy and the environment.

Conclusion

In trade and internal market affairs, unification led not to far-reaching changes in German policies, but instead provided the occasion for a reaffirmation of pre-unification objectives. This is not to suggest that nothing happened after 1990; both Eastern trade policy and the health of Germany as a production location in a barrier-free market vaulted onto the domestic agenda, and received sustained and oftentimes heated attention from political and economic elites. These case studies demonstrate conclusively that policy continuity should be seen not as the

---

[75] Interview with CDU member of the Bundestag, Bonn, December 10, 1992.

absence of change, but as a dynamic process involving the political reproduction of choices made in the past. A complete discussion of the causes of continuity will be postponed until the final chapter, when they can be assessed in relation to the other case studies. In both instances, however, eastern German interests were represented largely by producer groups and members of parliament, who confronted an insulated federal civil service apparatus operating according to established principles and within strong supranational policy frameworks.

4   Mixed outcomes in energy and environment

The domestic politics of environment and energy were extremely intense after unification, and resulted in discernible shifts in national policy objectives, unlike the two cases reviewed in the preceding chapter. Yet these regulative policy areas were characterized by strong elements of continuity in basic German objectives at the EU level. That said, subtle changes in Bonn's European policies did in fact materialize during this period; the government's approach to EC/EU environmental policy grew more cautious, while its internal energy market policies took on a more determined cast.

Environmental policy

The Treaty of Rome makes no mention of the environment, let alone a common EC environmental policy. Nevertheless, the topic surfaced repeatedly during the 1960s, specifically in the context of the internal market. The Commission quickly discovered the importance of coordinating and where necessary harmonizing the environmental regulations of the member governments, in order to ensure that national governments did not erect green barriers, such as the classification and packaging of dangerous substances or auto emission standards, to the free flow of goods and services in the common market. At the Paris summit in 1972, the EC heads of state, drawing on this Community regulatory experience in environmental matters as well as on Article 2 of the Treaty of Rome, which defined the tasks of the EC in terms of "a continued and balanced expansion" and "an accelerated raising of the standard of living," expressly identified the protection of the environment as a Community objective, and established a new Directorate General in the Commission to handle these matters (DG-XI).[1]

Between 1972 and 1990, the EC approved four successive environ-

---

[1] See Dennis Swann, "The Social Charter and other Issues," in Dennis Swann, ed., *The Single European Market and Beyond* (London: Routledge, 1992), 224–28, and David Vogel, "Environmental Policy in the European Community," in Sheldon Kamieniecki,

mental action programs, each of which expanded the scope and ambitions of the Community's environmental policy. By the end of the 1980s, approximately 200 individual regulations and directives had been issued by the Community, covering almost every conceivable aspect of environmental policy: air, water, and noise pollution, waste disposal, environmental impact assessment, wildlife and habitat protection, nuclear safety, and toxic waste. The Community's policy actions on the environment were given a formal treaty basis with ratification of the SEA in 1987. Among other things, the SEA granted member governments the right to retain environmental standards that were more stringent than those approved at the EC level, providing this did not constitute a form of "hidden protectionism."[2]

Among EC member governments, West Germany, along with Denmark, staked out a position as an ardent advocate of strict and comprehensive environmental regulation at the supranational level. On issues ranging from auto emissions standards to the protection of the ozone layer, Germany repeatedly adopted a hard line, insisting on ambitious and exacting targets supported by policy instruments with teeth.[3] Frequently, the West Germans resorted to threats of unilateral action to force their EC partners to adopt a stricter approach, as in the case of auto emission standards in the 1980s.[4] Bonn also strongly advocated insertion of the environmental passages into the SEA, in particular the opt-out clause, of which it made frequent use – West German environmental standards were often more demanding than their EC regulatory counterparts. Commission statistics document that at the end of the 1980s, Germany led the EC in various expenditure categories: total environmental expenditure as a percentage of gross domestic product (1.6%); total environmental expenditure as a percen-

ed., *Environmental Politics in the International Arena* (Albany: State University of New York Press, 1993), 181–91.

[2] Vogel, "Environmental Policy in the European Community," 187.

[3] See, for example, Markus Jachtenfus, "The European Community and the Protection of the Ozone Layer," *Journal of Common Market Studies* 28(March 1990), 261–77; Ernst U. von Weizsäcker, "Environmental Policy," in Carl-Christoph Schweitzer and Detlev Karsten, eds., *The Federal Republic of Germany and EC Membership Evaluated* (London: Pinter Publishers, 1990), 49–50; Vogel, "Environmental Policy in the European Community," 185; J. Duncan Liefferink, Philip Lowe, and Arthur P. J. Mol, "The Environment and the European Community: The Analysis of Political Integration," in J. Duncan Liefferink, Philip Lowe, and Arthur P. J. Mol, eds., *European Integration and Environmental Policy* (New York: Belhaven Press, 1993), 6; Henning Arp, "Technical Regulation and Politics: The Interplay between Economic Interests and Environmental Policy Goals in EC Car Emission Standards," in Liefferink, Lowe, and Mol, eds., *European Integration and Environmental Policy*, 163, 169.

[4] Vogel, "Environmental Policy in the European Community," 191–96.

tage of total investment (3.8%); and business environmental expenditure as a percentage of total business investment (7.7%).[5]

West Germany's self-appointed role as the EC's environmental "golden boy" (*Musterknabe*) stemmed from two sources. First, environmental issues were especially salient in domestic politics. The rise of the Green Party (*Die Grünen*), which entered the Bundestag in the 1983 federal elections, was both cause and symptom of this phenomenon. The resonance of environmental issues extended well beyond the electoral constituency of the Greens, however; natural disasters played a part in sensitizing the broader German public to ecological issues, such as the dying of the forests (*Waldsterben*), which achieved visibility in the early 1980s, and the Chernobyl nuclear accident and Sandoz chemical spill on the Rhine, both of which occurred in 1986.[6]

Second, the export orientation of the German economy, coupled with the country's wealth, enabled political elites to marry a stringent, supranational environmentalism to economic growth and competitiveness, a situation that stood in marked contrast to southern and predominantly poorer EC members. German industry's opposition to exacting environmental standards was blunted by the following arguments: (1) environmental action is necessary on both substantive and political-electoral grounds; (2) ignoring the EC field of environmental regulation is misguided, since this would allow other EC members to lag behind Germany's strict standards, thereby placing German firms at a competitive disadvantage in the barrier-free market; and (3) German firms are best positioned to compete and to succeed in an EC characterized by the most stringent environmental standards possible. German politicians on both the center-right and the center-left argued that environmentalism promoted growth, competitiveness, and jobs by creating demand for new technologies and products.

Environmental policy and the unification settlement, 1989–90

Soon after the collapse of the Berlin Wall, the catastrophic state of the GDR's environment came to light as the veil of official secrecy was stripped away by citizen initiatives, many of which had their origins in the underground ecology movements of the late 1970s.[7] Forty years of

---

[5] Commission of the European Communities, *Der Zustand der Umwelt in der Europäischen Gemeinschaft: Überblick* (Luxembourg: Office for Official Publications of the European Communities, 1992), 82.

[6] See Markovits and Gorski, *The German Left*.

[7] Karsten McGovern, "Kommunale Umweltpolitik in den neuen Bundesländern: Innovationsbedarf und Umsetzungsprobleme," in Susanne Benzler, Udo Bullmann, and

"real existing socialism" had produced neither a technological leader nor an industrial powerhouse, but a world-class polluter.

Damage to the environment was uniform and extreme. Only 3 percent of rivers and streams and 1 percent of lakes and ponds contained potable water. In some 1,000 local communities, the quality of tap water was so poor that the regime trucked in bottled water on a regular basis for infants and small children. The main culprits were obsolete production methods in industry, inadequate waste treatment procedures and infrastructure in industry and municipalities, and overuse of insecticides, herbicides, and chemical and organic fertilizers (including liquid manure) in the agricultural sector. Air quality was among the worst in Europe, largely as the result of the regime's reliance on domestic sources of lignite (brown, or soft, coal) to satisfy the country's energy needs. Dust and sulfur dioxide concentrations were between 8 and 11.5 times the levels measured in West Germany.[8] To top things off, the GDR suffered extensive soil contamination generated by industrial wastes, lignite strip mining, and numerous Soviet and GDR military installations.

The state of the GDR's environment posed two problems for the Bonn government. First, it created significant disincentives to new investment; firms, whether West German or foreign, could hardly be expected to commit large sums of capital to the eastern Länder amid conditions of great uncertainty about private liabilities for past environmental damage and about the impact of a degraded environment on production. Second, there was the basic issue of public health and safety. Although reliable data were still difficult to come by, average East German citizens, particularly those living in the southern, more industrialized parts of the country, were clearly worse off than their West German siblings: average life expectancies for both men and women were lower, rates of chronic bronchitis and asthmatic diseases, particularly among children, were substantially higher, and unsafe blood concentrations of heavy metals were prevalent in the population. These facts, coupled with widespread reports of extensive damage to wildlife and nature preserves in the GDR, generated an acute awareness of environmental issues among the general population.[9]

Dieter Eißel, eds., *Deutschland-Ost vor Ort: Anfänge der lokalen Politik in den neuen Bundesländern* (Opladen: Leske + Budrich, 1995), 168. On the GDR environmental movement, see, among others, Dennis, *German Democratic Republic*, 179–83.

[8] Figures are taken from the following sources: Bundesministerium für Umwelt, Naturschutz, und Reaktorsicherheit, *Basic Guidelines for Ecological Recovery and Development in the New Länder* (Bonn, 1991); Sinn and Sinn, *Kaltstart*, 129.

[9] Bundesministerium für Umwelt, Naturschutz, und Reaktorsicherheit, *Basic Guidelines for Ecological Recovery and Development in the New Länder*, 14–15.

Equalizing the standards of living of east and west meant, among other things, tackling environmental degradation head on and rapidly, which would involve substantial outlays of public money and potential conflicts with the objective of regional economic development. In a manner consistent with its general approach to unification, Bonn opted for a rapid and complete application of existing West German and EC environmental standards to the region. According to an official in the Federal Ministry of the Environment (Bundesministerum für Umwelt, Naturschutz, und Reaktorsicherheit: BMU), a consensus reigned in Bonn that the government had to pursue "a unified environmental policy for a unified Germany," with West German standards serving as the benchmark.[10] Article 34 of the Unification Treaty contained a commitment by the federal government to co-finance ecological recovery and development programs in consultation with the new Länder. It also enumerated the areas in which federal law would not take effect immediately.

These various exceptions, which covered areas such as emission standards, water quality, and waste management, required formal EC approval and, according to German officials who participated in the negotiations, became the subject of protracted bargaining between Bonn and several member governments. Bonn officials were convinced that the immediate application of EC standards in these areas would have required shutting down most East German industry, with catastrophic economic and social consequences. Therefore, Germany pressed for transition periods of up to six years to allow the public and private sectors in the (ex-)GDR time to adjust. These demands were a top priority for the Germans in the incorporation negotiations.[11]

According to a source in the BMU, German officials, as yet unaware of just how widespread and severe the environmental damage in the GDR was, requested transition periods much shorter than those granted the Iberian members in the 1980s.[12] The Commission ultimately recommended to the Council a differentiated approach that was virtually indistinguishable from the German position:

First, a distinction has to be made between plants where pollution is too high for them to be adapted (which will have to be closed down) and those where anti-pollution equipment could be fitted to bring them close into line with Community levels. For the latter, it is clear that transitional, and in some cases

[10] Interview with BMU official, Bonn, July 21, 1992.
[11] Interview with BMWi official, Bonn, October 2, 1992.
[12] Interview with BMU official, Bonn, July 17, 1992. According to this official, "there was a general sense within the Commission and among member governments that Germany had set some very ambitious goals for itself."

long-term, exemptions from Community standards will be necessary. Second, the new investment sectors will have to meet Community requirements.[13]

The Commission sought to balance the needs of the Germans against the concerns of other EC members, who were loathe to see East German firms gain a competitive edge thanks to lax or ambiguous environmental regulations.[14]

As the ecological disaster in the GDR came into sharp focus over the course of 1990, EC member concerns diminished considerably, and German worries that their proposed transitional arrangements were too ambitious increased. The Commission, sensitive to Germany's position, signaled that a decision on the existing package of exceptions by no means precluded consideration of a request for more flexible treatment further down the road, and the environmental derogations, which ranged from December 31, 1993 for certain categories of water quality to January 1, 1996 for various emissions standards, were approved by the Council of Ministers.

Environmental policy after unification, 1990–95

Federal officials resigned themselves to the fact that tackling the environmental mess in the former GDR would entail a complete departure from the guiding principle of both German and EC environmental policy: namely, the polluter pays. Strict adherence to this maxim would have condemned the goal of economic reconstruction in the east to failure. The main polluter – the SED regime – no longer existed, whereas investors would be frightened off by legal liabilities resulting from environmental damage. Thus, federal legislation passed in 1990 expressly included a clause that allowed the Länder to approve petitions from property owners for liability exemptions relating to environmental damage caused prior to July 1, 1990; in the case of state-owned assets, the THA retained this right.

The mammoth clean-up of the eastern German region would have to be funded largely out of the federal budget and, to a lesser extent, Land and EC programs. In 1990, the BMU allocated DM5 billion to cover the first phase of an environmental clean-up program. It also launched

---

[13] Commission of the European Communities, "The European Community and German Unification," 15. According to a BMU official, the German delegation insisted from the beginning that new investment be subject not only to EC standards, but to German ones, which were in many instances more stringent. Interview with BMU official, Bonn, July 17, 1992.

[14] David Spence, "Enlargement without Accession: The EC's Response to German Unification," The Royal Institute of International Affairs, *RIIA Discussion Paper* 36, 1991, 37–38.

studies to develop a more accurate picture of the state of the environment in the GDR, to outline measures that had already been undertaken to improve the environment (such as the closing down of especially hazardous plants), and to draw up a list of policy priorities. This resulted in the so-called *Eckwerte* ("Fundamental Principles") program, issued in November 1990. Three months later, the BMU introduced the Ecological Reconstruction Action Program, which implemented many elements contained in the *Eckwerte* initiative and carried a price tag of approximately DM17 billion for 1991 alone.[15] Estimates of the total costs of environmental clean-up in the new Länder varied wildly; even two years after unification, educated guesses ranged from DM30 billion to DM600 billion.

A salient feature of this policy area was the absence of intense, sustained interest group politics in the former GDR directed at the federal government. Much of this can be attributed to the federal government's conscious packaging of environmental measures for the former GDR as a public health issue, as a *Standort* issue, and as a job creation scheme. The health rationale was self-evident; even by the end of 1990, measurable improvements in air quality were evident, as plant closures followed from government regulatory decisions and from the fatal effects of market competition. Bonn officials connected environmental recovery in the east to the region's economic competitiveness – mobile capital flowed to environmentally attractive production locations, and the former GDR, with substantial federal support, had, over the long run, the opportunity to equip itself with the most advanced environmental technology available. The employment claims rested on more questionable assumptions, although the government was clearly able to show that laid-off workers were being put to work by publicly funded programs to clear and clean contaminated industrial sites.[16]

The government's approach found a receptive audience in the new Länder. Industry initially supported the government's position on environmental standards; new firms, according to a BMU official, had no desire to adjust to a lax set of requirements only to have to convert to a stricter regime three to four years down the road, whereas existing firms

[15] Klaus Zimmermann, "Ecological Transformation in Eastern Germany," in Ghaussy and Schäfer, eds., *The Economics of German Unification*, 217–19.

[16] Typically, these programs were structured as *Arbeitsbeschaffungsmaßnahmen* (ABM), funded by the Bonn social ministry. A BMU official estimated that of the 400,000 employed in ABM programs in mid-1992, 120,000 were involved in environmental clean-up projects of one kind or another. The government estimated 50,000 employed in soil reclamation projects in 1993 alone. "Die Umweltsanierung im Osten kostet 1994 rund DM4,2 Milliarden DM," *Frankfurter Allgemeine Zeitung*, October 8, 1993, 15.

were optimistic about their prospects and believed they could meet the various deadlines and remain competitive.[17] National environmental groups, such as the Bund für Umwelt und Naturschutz Deutschland (BUND), quickly expanded their operations eastward. Surprisingly, they encountered an organizational vacuum in the former GDR; the absence of a strong pro-environmental lobby, a startling fact in light of the central role of the ecology movement in the GDR's peaceful revolution, can be traced back to that very same revolution. Rapid democratization after November 1989 drew many prominent East German environmentalists into electoral politics and into the bureaucracy, which hampered the formation of an indigenous ecology movement oriented toward regional (as opposed to national) issues.

That said, the GDR ecology movement had created a political legacy, raising the environmental consciousness of the East German public.[18] To offset the perceived political influence of firm-specific and industry interests, several new Land governments created budget lines, administered by the state environmental ministry, to assist in the formation and maintenance of environmental interest groups.[19] An official in the Brandenburg environment ministry characterized this practice as temporary but necessary "bridging assistance," designed to create a balance between environmental and industrial interest groups in the Land.[20]

As the scale of the environmental challenges posed by unification became clearer in 1991 and 1992,[21] conflicts over the needs of post-socialist reconstruction versus the regeneration and protection of the environment materialized frequently at the local level, pitting conservationists against the interests of firms and their employees, and occasionally at the level of the Land, as state ministries for economics and for the environment clashed (typically behind the scenes) over development priorities. At no point, however, did these disputes cumulate to produce a regional challenge to the wisdom of applying the EC/FRG environmental regime to the east. Eastern German industry was largely silent, perhaps as a result of internal divisions; new firms, subject to existing EC and German standards, had very different interests compared to

---

[17] Interview with BMU official, Bonn, July 21, 1992.
[18] Catherine Kelleher, "The New Germany: An Overview," in Stares, ed., *The New Germany and the New Europe*, 39.
[19] See for example Boll, "Interest Organization and Intermediation in the New Länder," 124–25.
[20] Interview with Brandenburg environment ministry official, Potsdam, October 28, 1992.
[21] As a case in point, the number of suspected environmental "hot spots" in the former GDR rose from 26,000 in October 1990 to 61,000 by the end of 1992. "Teurere Ost-Altlastensanierung, *Frankfurter Allgemeine Zeitung*, May 11, 1993, 17.

pre-1990 firms operating under the various derogations.[22] The focus of discussion in the region was not on environmental goals *per se*, but rather on the size of the federal financial commitment and on fiscal burden-sharing between the new Länder and the federal government.

The eastern Länder grew increasingly critical of what they viewed as inadequate federal funding for the clean-up and an unfair financial division of labor between the federal and state governments. Both state and local officials in the east called for a moratorium on public investment in environmental projects in the west, and for the transfer of the resulting savings to desperately needed projects in the east. The complaints of the new Länder about the financial effort of the federal government also translated into leverage over an EC issue – specifically, the deadlines established by the derogations negotiated between Bonn and Brussels in 1990. The Land governments in the east coordinated their lobbying efforts on this issue; by 1991, they were already signaling to BMU officials, to the EC Commission, and to the press that many of the water and air quality targets were unrealistic, and very unlikely to be met. Slow progress was the result of technical difficulties, such as the pace of large-scale sewerage construction projects, as well as the lack of adequate funding. Bonn officials remained optimistic, at least in public; according to a BMU official, this was precisely the wrong time to signal flexibility to public and private actors in the new Länder, so the official position was "to keep the lid on."[23]

The ministry commenced an intensive round of formal consultations with the new Länder and commissioned several independent studies to ascertain whether extensions of the myriad environmental derogations were justified. The German government was reluctant to ask for special treatment at this time unless the request could be backed by hard evidence, since such entreaties invariably weakened Bonn's position in the European Council on environmental matters, opening up the prospect of special treatment for other, less deserving members. In light of Bonn's desire to continue to play the *Musterknabe* in this policy area, a BMU official characterized any request for extensions as "politically unfortunate."[24] The BMU studies revealed that although the new Länder would be able to meet the majority of the deadlines, several derogations were overly ambitious. The clearest cases involved water quality; in late 1993, as derogations were about to expire, Bonn requested and received a two-year extension from Brussels.

Unification's impact on German EC/EU environmental policy was

---

[22] Interview with Thuringia environment ministry official, Erfurt, November 25, 1992.
[23] Interview with BMU official, Bonn, July 21, 1992.
[24] Interview with BMU official, Bonn, July 17, 1992.

generally confined to the derogations issue. Debates in Brussels passed largely unnoticed in the new Länder; as a Land official in Potsdam explained, "we have so little influence on the process."[25] Germany, along with Denmark and the Netherlands, continued to be a force for strengthening European-level competencies and policies in this area. Institutionally, Bonn supported the expansion of qualified majority voting in the Council on environmental matters embodied in the Maastricht Treaty.[26] BMU officials believe that this will strengthen Germany's position in the long run, since environmental laggards in the EU will be able to make much less effective use of the national veto to impede progress; in the words of one civil servant, "Germany now has the opportunity to build winning coalitions around its positions."[27] Germany also blocked attempts by some member states, led by the UK, to "renationalize" environmental policy in the name of subsidiarity, an initiative that gained momentum in the aftermath of the Danish rejection of the Treaty on European Union in 1992.[28]

Substantively, Bonn provided crucial support to the Commission's environmental agenda for the 1990s, which was set out in the Fifth Environmental Program, "Towards Sustainability," issued by the Commission in April 1992. Building on the four programs that preceded it, the Commission emphasized the goal of integrating an environmental dimension into other EC policy areas, such as transportation and agriculture. It also stressed the need to develop general approaches and specific programs to facilitate international environmental cooperation, with a particular focus on the Central and Eastern European region. Both of these objectives spoke to core concerns of the Bonn government, and were greeted with enthusiasm.

Where differences arose between Bonn and Brussels, they involved areas such as energy, climate, and waste disposal policies in which the objectives of the Commission were not sufficiently ambitious for the German side.[29] Evidence also continued to surface in the post-unification period that the Commission looked to Germany both to lead the charge against less enthusiastic members on various policy issues, and to

[25] Interview with Brandenburg environment ministry official, Potsdam, October 28, 1992.

[26] See Alberta Sbragia, "EC Environmental Policy: Atypical Ambitions and Typical Problems?," in Alan Cafruny and Glenda Rosenthal, eds., *The State of the European Community* (Boulder: Lynne Rienner Publishers, 1993), vol. II, 343–44.

[27] Interview with BMU official, Bonn, July 17, 1992.

[28] Liefferink, Lowe, and Mol, "The Environment and the European Community," 8–9.

[29] Bundesministerium für Umwelt, Naturschutz, und Reaktorsicherheit, *Stellungnahme der Bundesregierung zum Programm der Europäischen Gemeinschaft für Umweltpolitik und Maßnahmen im Hinblick auf eine dauerhafte und umweltgerechte Entwicklung* (Bonn, 1992).

provide an example to the rest of the EC of how firm environmental standards and industrial competitiveness could be combined.

Germany maintained its pre-unification support for the need to harmonize "upward" in the EC/EU. On issues ranging from the preservation of the ozone layer to the regulation of refuse dumps to Community-wide standards for recycling and packaging to the illegal export of garbage (so-called "rubbish tourism" or *Mülltourismus*), German progressivism was at the source of oftentimes bitter debates in the Council over priorities, standards, and target dates. During Germany's six-month Council presidency in the second half of 1994, Bonn made environmental and energy policy reform – specifically, the introduction of an "energy tax" to reduce carbon dioxide emissions – a top priority, one that foundered ultimately on British intransigence.

In some instances where Bonn was unable to prevail with its stringent line, such as the setting of minimum standards for refuse dumps and the recycling and packaging directive, it insisted on the right to retain its more exacting national regimes, even at the cost of Commission legal challenges.[30] In other areas, like the energy tax, however, the government ultimately declined to go it alone, citing the limited benefits such a move would bring and the negative consequences for industrial competitiveness in Germany.[31] The federal government set its sights instead on collective action in Brussels and voluntary targets for reduced carbon dioxide emissions by German industry.[32] The sources of Germany's greater reluctance to engage in national policy "solos" resides in the changed domestic politics of the environment after 1990.

Although the BMU pushed an ambitious federal legislative program after 1990, seeking reform of national laws on waste disposal, a new law on soil protection and conservation (*Bodenschutz*), and an increase in auto emission taxes, to name just three initiatives, it encountered unusually strong opposition from national industry representatives and from within Bonn ministerial circles. Their long-standing concerns about the costs imposed by the country's environmental regulations on

[30] For example, in late 1995 the Commissioner for Internal Market Affairs stated that a German bottle-deposit scheme placed non-German producers of libations at a disadvantage, and that the resulting distortions to intra-Community trade could not be justified on the basis of environmental goals. The Bonn government rejected the Commission's criticism and its threat of legal action.

[31] The federal economics minister, Günter Rexrodt (FDP), announced in mid-1995 that Germany would introduce its own energy tax if the EU failed to act, but he was forced to back down in the face of powerful industry opposition and a lack of support from his coalition partners.

[32] Even here, Germany set a voluntary target – 25 percent reduction in greenhouse gas emissions by 2005 – that was a little over three times the target agreed upon by the EU membership as a whole.

industry resonated with greater effect in the context of the renewed debate about the German *Standort*.

Industry representatives insisted that Bonn continue its pursuit of European-wide harmonization of environmental regulations, in view of the importance of achieving a level playing-field for all firms in the internal market, but leavened this demand with warnings about the potentially disastrous consequences of getting too far out in front of the pack, particularly on issues like the energy tax and the refuse tax (*Abfallabgabe*). In other words, national solos not only generated few tangible improvements in the quality of the environment, but placed intolerable burdens on German firms trying to compete in an increasingly harsh international environment.[33]

The press, the Social Democrats, the Greens, and environmental interest groups spoke of an unofficial policy moratorium, more or less imposed on the BMU by the Chancellery and the ministries dealing with the economy in response to increasingly vocal industry demands.[34] Detractors pointed to the significant budget cuts incurred by the environment ministry beginning in 1992, as well as the apparent inability of the ministry to see many of its legislative proposals through to law. Opposition accusations that the government had crippled environmental policy featured prominently in the 1998 federal election campaign.

The charge of a complete policy moratorium is exaggerated.[35] Nevertheless, the impact of unification on German environmental policy, although subtle, is undeniable. The effects are largely contextual. For example, a more determined opposition to the BMU's environmental agenda hails not from eastern Germany, but from peak associations of business voicing concerns of western firms that predate unification. The BMU and its supporters have been forced to contend with standard industry objections to environmental regulations that are magnified in intensity by reference to the precarious fiscal and economic situation engendered by unification, not to mention the demands of eastern German public authorities for transfers of environmental policy re-

---

[33] In June 1992, the chemical giant Hoescht released figures purporting to show that the costs of meeting existing environmental standards had reached 30 percent of total production costs in some product categories, leading the company to discontinue some lines because they were no longer price competitive. "Umweltschutz wird für Hoechst immer teuerer," *Frankfurter Allgemeine Zeitung*, June 6, 1992, 15.

[34] Many industry concerns about the environment and *Standort Deutschland* were reproduced in an internal BMWi paper entitled "Qualität des Standortes Deutschland und Ansatzpunkte zur Verbesserung," January 27, 1992.

[35] For example, after unification the German parliament approved the so-called "economic cycle law" (*Kreislaufwirtschaftsgesetz*), which is designed to reduce the amount of waste that firms generate in their production processes.

sources from east to west. In this context, the pressure for a "breather" (*Atempause*) on environmental legislation has grown stronger, if not more persuasive in their eyes.

The perception in policymaking circles that environmental objectives can no longer be taken for granted is very real. On several occasions, the minister for the environment Klaus Töpfer, who held the post until 1994, spoke out about the threat to the quality of the German *Standort* posed by the introduction of an actual moratorium on environmental standards. The BMU reacted favorably to industry complaints, supported by the BMWi, that existing environmental procedures were so complicated as to represent an obstacle to new investment projects; the BMU introduced legislation in 1995 to speed up the environmental approval process for both public and private investment projects.

Thus, unification has produced subtle but tangible changes in this policy area, which are for the most part confined to the domestic level. In short, there has been no clear domestic "breakthrough" in this policy area, in which a new-found caution in national policy produces a corresponding shift in Brussels. In fact, Bonn continued to aspire to the role of *Musterknabe*, and succeeded in driving many EC/EU environmental debates, even if policy successes were infrequent. Yet although German environmental goals exhibit strong elements of continuity after 1990, there is one unmistakable change in the realm of strategy: Bonn is less likely to resort to unilateralism when its efforts to establish stringent supranational regulatory regimes are stymied.

Energy policy

West German energy policy sought to reconcile the ambitious and oftentimes contradictory goals of efficiency, conservation, security of supply, and environmental compatibility. The federal government's approach involved considerable intervention but little in the way of direct ownership or *dirigisme*. The EC was hardly a factor up through the 1970s; it was only after the OPEC shocks that the Community began to develop common policies in energy, and these remained for the most part indicative.[36]

At the heart of West German energy policy was coal. During the 1950s, the government fueled the *Wirtschaftswunder* by securing a steady

[36] Parnell speaks of the absence of a "supranational foundation for coherent national energy policies" in Germany during the 1960s. Martin Parnell, *The German Tradition of Organized Capitalism: Self-Government in the Coal Industry* (Oxford: Clarendon Press, 1994), 110–11. On the early failures of the common energy policy, see Stephen Padgett, "The Single European Energy Market: The Politics of Realization," *Journal of Common Market Studies* 30(March 1992), 56.

supply of cheap energy for the country's export industries; via a combination of subtle intervention and an open reliance on market forces, Bonn encouraged, or at least did nothing to hinder, the economy-wide switch from high-cost domestic hard coal, which was plagued by unfavorable geological conditions and the attendant high inputs of capital and labor, to cheaper imported alternatives like oil and foreign coal.[37] At the end of the 1950s, the weak competitive position of German coal touched off the first of many crises in the main centers of mining activity – the Ruhr Valley of North Rhine-Westphalia and the Saarland.

Bonn's energy policy gradually took on the objective of managing the contraction of the hard coal mining industry. It was clear to both major parties that the social and political consequences of a complete collapse of coal production were simply unthinkable.

Without protection, the uneconomic position of German coal would mean instant collapse of the industry, with the basic iron and steel industry emigrating and massive unemployment concentrated in particular *Montan*-districts The failure of business confidence and a dramatic, rapid rise in unemployment could have created a level of social unrest which would have threatened the political stability, indeed, the survival of the Federal Republic.[38]

In the aftermath of the 1973 OPEC crisis, coal policy assumed an additional rationale: national energy security. Coal, alongside nuclear power and natural gas, would enable the FRG to wean itself from an overreliance on petroleum, which had proved to be a geopolitically unreliable source of energy.

Between 1960 and 1980, the government put in place an elaborate and expensive lattice-work of support programs for coal, which included at one point or another the following: import controls on foreign coal; incentive and compensation schemes for pit closures; taxes on heating and fuel oil; early retirement incentives for older miners; retraining and social assistance schemes for unemployed miners; attraction-of-industry programs for the coal areas; and a state-financed rationalization cartel, Ruhrkohle AG.

The policy centerpiece comprised two price support programs. The first measure was designed to provide electric utilities with near full compensation for the added costs of using German hard coal instead of fuel oil or imported coal. Financed since 1974 by the so-called "coal penny" (*Kohlepfennig*), a levy of approximately 5 percent on consumer

---

[37] See Werner Abelshauser, *Der Ruhrkohlenbergbau seit 1945* (Munich: Verlag C. H. Beck, 1984), and Peter Schaaf, *Ruhrbergbau und Sozialdemokratie* (Marburg: Verlag Arbeiterbewegung und Gesellschaftswissenschaft GmbH, 1978).

[38] Parnell, *The German Tradition of Organized Capitalism*, 123.

electricity bills (industrial *and* private), this program sought to guarantee the coal industry a baseline production volume. In 1977, the government, coal producers, the miners' union (IG Bergbau und Energie: IGBE), and the utilities concluded a formal agreement, set to cover a ten-year period, to electrify 33 million tons of domestic hard coal annually. In 1981, the agreement was extended to 1995 as a result of the "Century Treaty" (*Jahrhundertvertrag*), and the annual production volumes supported by the levy were revised upward, to reach a target of 47.5 million tons in 1995.

The second measure, inaugurated in 1967, was designed to subsidize German coking coal used in steel plants (*Kokskohlenbeihilfe*). In the "Foundry Contract" (*Hüttenvertrag*) of 1969, Ruhrkohle AG committed itself for the duration of the contract (twenty years) to deliver coking coal to German steel producers at a price equivalent to the world market price. The federal government and the two coal Länder, North Rhine-Westphalia and the Saarland, pledged to subsidize this arrangement.

The financial costs of Bonn's energy policy ballooned in the 1980s as the price differential between domestic coal and imported alternatives widened. Between 1974 and 1977, the total cost of maintaining coal was approximately DM8.7 billion; the cost for a comparable three-year period beginning in 1983 nearly doubled to DM16 billion.[39] In 1983, the new center-right coalition government, confronting a major slump in steel production that had caused demand for coal to decline precipitously, launched the first of several "coal rounds" (*Kohlerunde*) with the coal Länder, producers, and the union representatives from IGBE. In 1987, the parties reached agreement after protracted and acrimonious negotiations that coal-mining capacity would be cut back by a little over 25 percent by 1995, to an annual production level of 65 million tons. To soften the blow, Bonn pledged to fund early retirement and generous unemployment schemes, and to increase the amount of subsidized coking coal produced by domestic coal mines.

By the end of the 1980s, the national energy consensus had frayed irretrievably. The place of nuclear power in Germany's energy mix was thrown into doubt after 1986 by the terrible accident at Chernobyl; drawing support from a stunned and anxious population, the Green Party and important sections of the SPD argued for a complete withdrawal (*Ausstieg*) from nuclear energy by the year 2000. The painful and increasingly expensive contraction of the coal industry opened up major differences not only between the Social Democratic opposition – champions of the maximalist demands of the coal industry – and the

---

[39] Parnell, *The German Tradition of Organized Capitalism*, 201 and 141.

governing coalition, but also within the latter. Free Democrats and CDU/CSU members from non-coal Länder were much more willing to consider substantial cutbacks in subsidies than their CDU colleagues from North Rhine-Westphalia and the Saarland.

The fractious politics of German energy policy came under pressure in the late 1980s from Brussels, too. After ratification of the SEA, the Commission's Directorate-General for Energy (DG-XVII) began to champion a barrier-free market in energy, leading to "an increase in energy trade between Member States, rationalization of the energy sectors, enhanced security of supply, and reduced energy costs."[40] Commission efforts to inject more competition into the Community energy sector revolved around breaking up national and regional monopolies in gas and electricity and dismantling subsidy programs for coal.[41] Both carried major implications for the German energy sector and government policy.

In 1988, the Commission outlined a three-stage transition to an internal energy market (IEM).[42] The first stage was launched in 1989, with the issuing of (1) a draft directive on the transparency of gas and electricity prices, which was designed to promote competition in these energy sectors; (2) a draft regulation requiring public notification of investment projects in the electricity, petroleum, and natural gas sectors, which was intended to facilitate the European-wide coordination of energy investment; (3) a draft directive on the transit of gas, which aimed to establish common transit rights ("common carriage") across national boundaries;[43] and (4) a similar draft directive on the transit of electricity.

The second phase was intended to force structural changes in the

---

[40] Padgett, "The Single European Energy Market," 57. The direct impetus was provided by France, which thanks to its maturing nuclear power sector had a surplus of electricity but was unable to sell it to interested consumers in Portugal, the Netherlands, and Germany because of national barriers. The resulting friction between France and Germany in the late 1980s led to France challenging the legality of Germany's support for its domestic coal industry, which many credit with intensifying Commission pressure on Bonn to change its coal policies. See Padgett, "The Single European Energy Market," 68; and Francis McGowan, "The European Electricity Industry and EC Regulatory Reform," in Jack Hayward, ed., *Industrial Enterprise and European Integration: From National to International Champions in Western Europe* (Oxford: Oxford University Press, 1995), 125–57 at 145.

[41] Klaus Matthies, "Hindernisse auf dem Weg zum Energie-Binnenmarkt," *Wirtschaftsdienst* (March 1993), 143.

[42] Commission of the European Communities, "The Internal Energy Market," *COM* (88)238.

[43] This was seen as a necessary precursor to "third-party access" (TPA). TPA means "free access for third parties (industrial energy users or distribution companies) to the principal transmission networks, breaking the exclusive rights of supply which utilities presently exercise in most Member States, and enabling industrial users and distribu-

member states' energy sectors that would encourage competition. These included "unbundling," which would require vertically integrated utilities to separate formally their production, transmission, and distribution operations to ensure greater transparency, as well as a TPA regime enabling large industrial consumers of power the ability to negotiate contracts with energy suppliers anywhere in the EC. The third phase was to extend the TPA regime to smaller users.

Although the Bonn government supported the general goal of energy market liberalization, since it dovetailed with national concerns about the German *Standort* and industrial competitiveness, it expressed grave doubts about what it saw as the overly centralized, regulatory, and bureaucratic means by which the Commission proposed to arrive at a single market for energy. The core elements of the IEM program were vigorously opposed by the power industry in Germany, whose long-standing monopoly positions were threatened by the long-term Commission objectives of common carriage and TPA. The government, needing the continued cooperation of the utilities on the coal electrification issue, declined to press the issue.

The other thrust of European energy policy during the late 1980s – coal subsidization – carried far greater implications for German energy policy in the short term and, as it would turn out, after unification. The Commission, eyeing the 1992 single market deadline, began to pressure the German government to rein in coal expenditures. In 1988, the Commission challenged the *Jahrhundertvertrag*'s compatibility with Article 85 of the Rome Treaty, which prohibits cartel arrangements, an action intended to prompt the government to set concrete timetables for industry rationalization and the reduction of subsidies.[44] In response, the federal government took the first steps toward a major reappraisal of its coal programs, and furthermore agreed to reduce the amount of coal slated for subsidized electrification and to undertake a progressive lowering of the *Kohlepfennig* between 1990 and 1993.

Energy policy and the unification settlement, 1989–90

Unification raised several questions about the future of the East German energy sector, the most pressing of which involved brown coal. Lignite

---

tion companies to 'shop around' for the most favorable prices." Padgett, "The Single European Energy Market," 58.

[44] In 1989, a ton of German coal cost DM170 more than a comparable amount of imported coal; coal subsidies in that year, which averaged out to DM66,000 per employee, surpassed the total wage bill in the industry. Parnell, *The German Tradition of Organized Capitalism*, 144.

accounted for over 70 percent of total primary energy consumption in the GDR. Three hundred million tons were mined annually at two major production sites, one at Lausitz and the other at Halle Leipzig, by a labor force of 135,000. Although lignite had the potential to be a cost-effective source of energy,[45] existing production techniques and staffing levels left the industry a long way from this point. Moreover, the SED's quest for energy autarky led it to use brown coal for purposes that had been abandoned long ago in the west, such as home heating with briquettes. Not only was this inefficient, but it bequeathed a disastrous environmental legacy: inordinately high levels of sulfur dioxide emissions and dust, and the physical devastation left behind by vast strip-mining operations.

In the unification settlement, large parts of West German energy and mining law were transferred seamlessly to eastern Germany, although the treaty expressly ruled out a safety net for lignite mining along West German lines.[46] The *Staatsvertrag* stipulated a rapid phase-out of the generous energy subsidies paid to industry and households in the GDR. Based on an agreement struck between the THA, the western German power companies, and the GDR reform government in August 1990, the building blocks of an energy supply system based on private owner-ship and the principle of regional monopolies were put in place.[47] Likewise, energy proved to be an uncontentious topic in negotiations between the German government and Brussels. The Commission noted many of the problems raised by the GDR's excessive reliance on brown coal, but shared the German government's view that a slimmed-down industry would help satisfy the region's energy needs. It also reminded German officials that the restructuring of the mining and electricity industries would have to take place in accordance with Community competition rules.

Energy policy after unification, 1990–95

Despite the favorable long-term prognosis for eastern German brown coal, the period after formal unification ushered in a dramatic and painful contraction of the industry. Between 1989 and 1991, annual production fell by 43 percent to 170 million tons, and employment

[45] The main brown coal fields in western Germany, located in the Rhineland region, had historically been very profitable. Nigel Lucas, *Western European Energy Policies* (New York: Oxford University Press, 1985), 214.

[46] Helmut Gröner, "Energy Policy in Eastern Germany," in Ghaussy and Schäfer, eds., *The Economics of German Unification*, 134–54 at 142.

[47] Hans-Hagen Härtel, Reinald Krüger, *et al.*, *Die Entwicklung des Wettbewerbs in den neuen Bundesländern* (Baden-Baden: Nomos Verlagsgesellschaft, 1995), 223–48.

shrank by an equivalent percentage to 75,000 over the same period. A McKinsey study issued in 1992 predicted that by the year 2000, annual production would be down to 90 million tons and total employment would stabilize at 14,600.[48]

For political representatives from the region as well as the brown coal Länder – Saxony-Anhalt, Saxony, and Brandenburg – these developments were cause for grave concern, particularly since the contraction of the industry was proceeding unchecked in the absence of the kind of expensive support historically provided to western German hard coal. The eastern German response, led by the Land governments, took several forms. First, the Länder targeted their brown coal regions for state and federal regional economic assistance, with the goal of attracting new industry to these areas and thereby diversifying the regional economy. Second, the Land governments developed energy programs that, in one manner or another, sought to provide a long-range perspective for brown coal.[49] Typically, this involved planning and, in some cases, financing the construction of lignite-fired power plants to stabilize coal production at nearby fields.[50]

Finally, Land officials as well as parliamentary representatives drew attention to federal policies and proposals that threatened the future of brown coal. Chief among these was Bonn's policy for hard coal, which was attacked on fairness grounds. The proposed national or EU energy tax on carbon dioxide emissions was also roundly criticized for potentially eliminating the cost advantages of brown coal over the long run. The new Länder voiced concerns about the EC's IEM program, noting that their brown coal power plants could not hope to compete against subsidized, nuclear-generated power from France.[51]

The altered context of national energy policy was by no means lost on the federal government. In a major statement on energy goals delivered to parliament at the end of 1991, the coalition government identified four sources of change in the existing parameters for energy policy: unification; global warming; European integration; and the upheaval in

---

[48] Ralf Neubauer, "Fluch des schwarzen Goldes," *Die Zeit*, May 1, 1992, 29.

[49] Continued mining was important not only for economic and social reasons, but for an environmental purpose as well. The land reclamation projects designed to heal the wounds left by decades of strip-mining required massive quantities of fill and topsoil, which could only be generated by further strip-mining.

[50] This particular strategy on occasion got the eastern Länder into hot water with competition authorities in Brussels. For example, in July 1997 the Commission initiated a legal challenge against Brandenburg, which it accused of having provided illegal subsidies to the town of Cottbus to construct a brown coal power plant in lieu of a much cheaper gas-fired alternative.

[51] Interview with Saxony economics ministry official, Dresden, November 23, 1992.

Table 4.1. *Change in energy consumption by fuel type, 1988–90 (percentages)*

Fuel type	1988 (West Germany)	1990 (United Germany)
Oil	41.9	35.4
Hard coal	19.2	15.6
Brown coal	8.1	21.6
Natural gas	16.2	15.6
Nuclear power	12.0	9.8
Other	2.6	2.0
Total	100.0	100.0

Source: Bundesministerium für Wirtschaft, *Energie Daten '94: Nationale und internationale Entwicklung* (Bonn, 1994), 28–30.

the former Eastern bloc countries.[52] By simultaneously altering the nation's energy mix (see table 4.1), straining the federal budget, and catalyzing the long-simmering debate over the future of *Standort Deutschland*, unification contributed new impulses to the larger domestic energy policy debate.

The government underscored the importance of liberalizing domestic energy markets, both to increase competition and, it was hoped, place downward pressure on energy prices, particularly for industrial users. Confronted with an abundance of cheap(er) energy alternatives on international markets and increasingly concerned about the implications of rising electricity costs and intractable budget deficits at home, the coalition government openly questioned the cost-effectiveness of "business-as-usual" in relation to hard coal. Since Germany's energy policy could not be developed in isolation from global, European, and national considerations, the government maintained that "in a united Germany, hard and brown coal will continue to make contributions to energy security, but at lower levels than is presently the case."[53] Ministers called on the SPD to enter into a dialogue designed to reforge a consensus over coal and nuclear policies.

Just prior to the release of the government's energy report, yet another coal round had concluded after long negotiations between government

[52] See Deutscher Bundestag, *Unterrichtung durch die Bundesregierung: Das energiepolitische Gesamtkonzept der Bundesregierung: Energiepolitik für das vereinte Deutschland*, 12. Wahlperiode, Drucksache 12/1799, December 11, 1991.

[53] Deutscher Bundestag, *Unterrichtung durch die Bundesregierung: Das energiepolitische Gesamtkonzept der Bundesregierung*, 5. Coal union and industry representatives, joined by SPD officials, rejected these arguments, pointing to continued instability in the Persian Gulf and the fact that brown coal, because of its high water content and therefore high transportation costs, was not a cost-effective substitute for users of hard coal in western Germany.

officials and representatives from the coal industry, which were accompanied by mass demonstrations in the Ruhr and angry rhetoric on all sides.[54] The European Commission played an important role in the discussions, by insisting on a concrete plan for the rationalization of the industry and a clear decision by the government to cut hard coal subsidies over the next decade. Government officials placed great store on the need for consensus with Brussels on the matter of coal policy, citing the imminent completion of the internal market. According to a BMWi official, the Commission pressure proved "not unhelpful" in concentrating the minds of industry and union representatives.[55]

The 1991 *Kohlerunde* produced a package of capacity cuts and mine closures, pledges of continued subsidization of a base level of coal production (50 million tons/year), retention of the traditional instruments for financing coal support programs, and social programs to cope with the projected loss of 40,000 jobs in the mining areas. The results were interpreted as a significant climb-down for the government's chief negotiator with the industry, federal economics minister Jürgen Möllemann. He had sought a capacity reduction to 34 million tons as a means of generating budgetary savings but ultimately gave in to "incredibly strong" political pressure from the western coal lobby.[56]

As the search for a national energy consensus got under way in 1992, hard coal policy jumped back onto the agenda, in spite of the fact that the ink was barely dry on the agreement reached the previous year. The decision by the government to set aside the hard-won results of the 1991 *Kohlerunde* was based in large part on market developments – specifically, a dramatic fall in domestic demand, the consequence of the burgeoning crisis in the steel industry (see chapter 5), and an ever-widening price gap between domestic and imported coal, which carried unwelcome implications for the federal budget deficit.

Mounting political pressures also contributed to the government's decision to reopen the coal round. As the economic situation in the

---

[54] SPD members of parliament repeatedly predicted – opponents say threatened – massive social unrest in the Ruhr mining regions if the government did not ease its position on capacity and subsidy reductions, whereas coalition government members indicated the growing impatience in eastern Germany and the non-coal producing Länder in the west with an exorbitant policy of protectionism that no longer corresponded to the changed fiscal, political, and economic circumstances of the 1990s.

[55] Interview with BMWi official, Bonn, September 25, 1992.

[56] Interview with BMWi official, Bonn, September 25, 1992. At the time of the *Kohlerunde*, annual subsidies to the hard coal industry had reached some DM10 billion, the result of a DM190/ton difference in price between domestic and imported coal. This subsidy figure translated into annual payments of DM76,000 per miner to the industry. Deutscher Bundestag, "Haushalt 1991: Bundesministerium für Wirtschaft," 12. Wahlperiode, 61. Sitzung, 28 November 1991, 5188.

eastern Länder worsened in 1992, Land officials and political representatives stepped up their calls for equal treatment for the east's brown
coal fields – that is, either equal subsidization levels in the east or equal
application of market principles in the west.[57] These actors also reiter-
ated their objections to an energy tax, and staked out a firm position on
the *Kohlepfennig*: eastern electricity users should retain their existing
exemption from the consumer levy for hard coal, which was due to
expire in 1996. Bonn was sensitive to these concerns; preserving a
slimmed-down and subsidy-free brown coal industry had become an
important component of the coalition's structural policy of maintaining
the industrial cores in the east.[58]

The chorus of complaints from business also intensified after 1991. In
additional to general industry worries about energy costs and coal
subsidies, specific challenges to the *Kohlepfennig* and the coking coal
subsidies began to emanate from the power utilities and the steel
concerns. Calls for an end to these subsidy regimes reached a crescendo
in mid-1993, as the price of domestic coal climbed to four times the
level of imported coal and as the EC's energy market liberalization
plans, which promised to expose industry and power utilities to even
greater competitive pressures, grew in salience.

The main impetus for a review of the 1991 *Kohlerunde* decision came
from Brussels. The Commission's prevailing subsidy code for coal was
due to expire at the end of 1993, and in August 1992 it circulated new
draft regulations designed to make state aid to coal more transparent
and less distortive to competition. Transparency meant placing all aid to
coal on budget, and moving away from production floors toward
subsidy ceilings. The goal of competition necessitated gradual but deep
cuts in both direct and indirect assistance over the course of the next
decade. According to the Commission, mines with operating costs
above the EC average after 1997 would be eligible only for assistance to
facilitate a complete shut-down of capacity and to cushion the resulting
social dislocation.

Although the Commission proposals dovetailed with Bonn's larger
fiscal goals, they provoked deep unrest in ministerial circles and in the
western coalfields. The goal of transparency took aim at the heart of the

[57] The chair of the FDP in Thuringia, Kniepert, quipped, "It would be cheaper to send
the Ruhr miners together with their families to the Canary Islands than to let them
continue working." As quoted in "Fundsache," *Frankfurter Allgemeine Zeitung*, February
18, 1993, 3.
[58] In 1993, Bonn and the three brown coal Länder in the former GDR agreed to provide
the industry with DM1.5 billion annually to assist in restructuring and environmental
clean-up operations. Federal and state representatives negotiated a five-year extension
of this agreement, entailing somewhat smaller financial outlays, in 1997.

German coal support regime, and the proposed criteria for subsidy payments, in particular the orientation to average EC production costs, threatened the very survival of the sector, at least according to industry sources. The average production cost per ton in the EC in 1992 was approximately DM220 – DM60 lower than the German average.[59] The IGBE and coal producers demanded that Bonn signal to its EC partners a willingness to use its veto in the Council to protect the domestic industry, and seek EC approval of the agreement embodied in the 1991 coal round. Minister Möllemann rejected the Commission's approach in a formal letter to Brussels, and gave public and private assurances to the hard coal industry that the government would not support any decision in Brussels that undercut the 1991 *Kohlerunde* agreement.

The government, however, was caught in an inescapable bind. On the one hand, it could not afford politically to impose a death sentence on domestic hard coal. On the other hand, it could hardly ignore the Commission or prevailing sentiment in the Council, since the *Kohlerunde* agreement still required Commission approval. Moreover, both the *Jahrhundertvertrag* and the *Hüttenvertrag* were due to expire in 1995 and 1997, respectively, and Bonn needed Community approval of whatever subsidy regimes – new, old, or modified – were to take their place.

Bonn faced a difficult situation in Brussels. The Commission was firmly committed to the basic objectives embodied in the draft regulations, even if the document did not represent its final word. In the Council, the Federal Republic confronted the very real possibility of isolation. In 1992, production assistance to hard coal in Germany dwarfed that of its competitors; on a per ton basis, German subsidization of the industry was twice the Spanish and three times the French levels.[60] Britain, having witnessed the rise of a competitive domestic industry during the 1980s and reduced production assistance to zero in 1992, supported the Commission's aims. Other coal-producing countries, such as Belgium and France, had already decided to prepare for the closure of the last of their mines in the near future, and thus were uninterested in the question of production subsidies. In fact, both Britain and France saw energy export opportunities in Germany if hard coal assistance were reduced, the former in coal and the latter in electricity generated by nuclear plants. Only the Spanish were expected to side with the Germans.[61]

[59] "Die EG ringt um ein Kohlekonzept," *Frankfurter Allgemeine Zeitung*, November 13, 1992, 17.

[60] Commission figures, as cited in Mike Parker, *The Politics of Coal's Decline* (London: The Royal Institute of International Affairs, 1994), 33.

[61] Matthies, "Hindernisse auf dem Weg zum Energie-Binnenmarkt," 146.

Bonn sought to blunt the Commission's proposal with arguments about energy security both in Germany and the Community as a whole – an ironic twist, in light of the government's heroic efforts during recent domestic energy debates to weaken the security rationale. Although Bonn's justification for its coal support framework found no support in the reworked version of the Commission's state aid guidelines approved in December 1993, the end result was a compromise between the EC and Germany. The Commission continued to regard state aid to coal as transitional, but it allowed greater scope for production subsidies, providing that these were attached to a formal modernization, rationalization, and restructuring plan designed to secure real reductions in production costs by 2002.[62] Bonn agreed to the Commission stipulation that full transparency in state aid to coal be achieved by the end of 1996, and pledged to promote industry rationalization and a reduction of subsidies.

By far the thorniest issue raised by the expiration of the *Jahrhundertvertrag* was the future of the financing regime for coal electrification. A straightforward continuation of the *Kohlepfennig* was rejected by a broad coalition of interests, including the power utilities, IGBE, the SPD, and even elements within the governing coalition. Several alternatives were proposed, most of which involved the imposition of a new energy tax. Supporters of a coal tax, based primarily in the government parties and in the IGBE, touted its capacity to reduce electricity costs to industry and to restore the political viability of coal programs by spreading the financial costs over a greater proportion of the population. For the SPD, the alternative of an energy tax would provide a vehicle for the pursuit of environmental goals, contributing to energy conservation and a reduction in carbon dioxide emissions. The SPD's position was rejected by industry, the FDP, and significant elements within the CDU/CSU, who were concerned about the impact of a carbon dioxide energy tax on general industry competitiveness and on the future of brown coal in the eastern region.[63] In late 1991, the government, citing the risks to the national economy and the trifling impact on the global warming problem, ruled out a German energy tax in the absence of EU-wide legislation.

The redrafting of Germany's coal policy came in increments, beginning with the government's announcement in October 1993 that it would raise the *Kohlepfennig* by one percentage point, to 8.5 percent, for

---

[62] Matthies, "Hindernisse auf dem Weg zum Energie-Binnenmarkt," 43.
[63] Proposals circulating in Brussels sought to tax energy use based on relative amounts of carbon dioxide emissions, which would have favored economies that relied more heavily on nuclear power (e.g. France) as opposed to petroleum and coal (e.g. Germany).

1994 and 1995 in order to close the program's chronic operating deficit. At the same time, it announced that with the expiration of the *Jahrhundertvertrag* at the end of 1995, coal financing would proceed according to fixed annual subsidy amounts, not guaranteed production levels. This was justified on both fiscal and efficiency grounds, as well as the need to meet the Community's new transparency guidelines.

As energy discussions with the SPD bogged down and ultimately collapsed over the issue of nuclear power, the government, in April 1994, introduced energy legislation laying out its conception of coal support policy after 1995. The proposal provided for DM7.5 billion in subsidies for the electrification of coal in 1996, and DM7.0 billion annually for the period 1997 to 2000.[64] Together with the coking coal subsidies and other flanking measures, annual assistance for the industry would remain at approximately DM10 billion. The period after 2000 was left to a future piece of legislation. Financing for years 1995 and 1996 would flow from an 8.5 percent *Kohlepfennig*, with the new Länder incorporated into the tax structure beginning in 1996 at the rate of 4.25 percent.[65] The government also announced that owing to budgetary constraints, it would be reducing its contribution to the coking coal subsidies henceforth, with the two coal-producing Länder, North Rhine-Westphalia and the Saarland, expected to pick up the slack.

The government's plans to rely on the *Kohlepfennig* were thrown into disarray in December 1994, when the Federal Constitutional Court declared the consumer levy unconstitutional. Although the government was allowed to continue operating the levy until its expiration at the end of 1995, it now faced the daunting task of devising an alternate financing mechanism to meet its legal obligations to the coal industry. The court's decision reopened the debate about the affordability of Germany's coal support program, since financing would now have to come from either the imposition of a new tax on energy or from savings within the existing budget.

---

[64] The government apparently calculated the DM7 billion figure from the fact that at the prevailing cost relationship between imported and domestic coal, this amount would finance the production of 35 million tons of coal – precisely the amount designated for electrification in the 1991 *Kohlerunde*. The fact that the government's decision represented potentially no great change with respect to the 1991 decision was roundly criticized by experts as overly timid on the issue of subsidy reductions. See Dieter Schmitt, "Energiepolitik nach dem Scheitern der Konsensgespräche," *Wirtschaftsdienst* (January 1994), 12–18 at 14.

[65] The government originally proposed a rate of 6.4 percent for eastern Germany, but was forced to lower it based on objections from coalition members of parliament, working in committee. These government backbenchers pointed out that the higher figure would have rendered electricity more costly in eastern Germany than in the west.

The debate was resolved in February 1995, when Chancellor Kohl ruled out an energy tax for the time being. In March, the government decided to fund coal subsidies from the budget at their present level up through the year 2000, and thereafter to seek reductions in the volume of aid.[66] In early March 1997, the government announced its intention to cut coal subsidies by 40 percent between 2000 and 2005, which sparked bitter opposition from the SPD and violent industrial action in the western coal fields and in Bonn. In a compromise reached with the unions in mid-March, the government agreed to pump almost DM1 billion into the industry up through 2000 in exchange for compliance with its original program of subsidy cuts thereafter.

Policy toward hard coal developed within a much larger issue space during this period: the structure and overall competitiveness of German and European energy markets. In parallel yet largely complementary developments, the government launched an initiative to liberalize its domestic energy market while reshaping and ultimately supporting Commission efforts to push through the IEM program. As we shall see, unification influenced the domestic context within which these policy debates were carried out.

The government's energy statement of November 1991 contained a pledge to introduce legislation designed to deregulate the nation's energy production and distribution sector. The goal of liberalization, which took concrete form over the ensuing months, entailed the introduction of the principle of common carriage, a version of TPA, and an end to "concessionary contracts" (*Konzessionsverträge*), in which energy distributors gained the long-term, exclusive right to use infrastructure networks in exchange for a usage fee paid to the municipal authorities that owned these networks. The parallels between this initiative and European energy policy were clear; indeed, the government noted explicitly that the EC, in pursuit of its internal market objectives, was narrowing the field of maneuver for national energy policy, which required close concertation between the two levels.[67]

Reactions to the government's energy market objectives revealed a good deal of continuity and some change in the terms of debate over energy politics in the united Germany. Manufacturing industry greeted the government's proposals with enthusiasm, pointing to the high cost of electricity in Germany and the strains this placed on competitiveness. These arguments resonated with increasing strength during 1992 in the

---

[66] This decision, ironically, undermined the BMF's 1996 budget deficit targets, and with it any possibility of meeting a key convergence criterion for EMU.

[67] Deutscher Bundestag, *Unterrichtung durch die Bundesregierung: Das energiepolitische Gesamtkonzept der Bundesregierung*, 38.

context of the unfolding *Standort* debate. Predictably, however, Bonn's legislative agenda drew a sharp, negative response from interest associations representing the utilities and municipal authorities, which stood to lose under market reform. The hard coal industry and IGBE opposed the proposal because of the threat to coal; utilities, under greater competitive pressures, would be even less willing to continue expensive arrangements to electrify German hard coal. The new Länder voiced opposition, arguing that an influx of cheap electricity would threaten the survival of brown coal and their fledgling power industry. The coalition itself, however, was by no means united on the objective. Spearheaded by the FDP economics minister, the proposal received the support of his party as well as the liberal wings of the CDU and CSU. Serious concerns were voiced by the finance and interior ministries, who were concerned about the financial impact on and legal challenge to local authorities posed by the *Konzessionsverträge* proposals.[68] Objections were even raised inside the BMWi, pointing to the dangers of liberalizing domestic energy markets ahead of tangible progress in Brussels.

The gulf between energy producers and users over liberalization of the national energy market reproduced itself over the IEM initiative. In parliamentary hearings and press statements, representatives of the power industry, municipal authorities, and hard coal warned against the threats posed to Germany's traditionally secure and reliable energy supply if the Commission proposals were to become law, whereas energy-intensive industries such as chemicals, backed by peak associations of business, underscored the need for liberalization if German firms were to compete successfully in the European internal market.

Bonn carried over its skepticism of a top-down approach by Brussels to energy into the post-unification period. It acknowledged that energy, as a tradable good, fell within the purview of the Commission's internal market and competition policy. However, government officials continued to reject Commission proposals for a sectoral (as opposed to market) policy, one that attempted to coordinate energy investment and planning activities. In fact, the German government's opposition was key to the rejection of an energy article in the Maastricht Treaty. Bonn also greeted the Commission's 1994 Green Paper on energy with deep mistrust, for many of the same reasons.[69] With this document, the Commission sought to develop momentum behind its goal of a separate

---

[68] According to one estimate, local authorities in Germany receive approximately DM5 billion from their concession treaties with the utilities, which go toward the financing of public services. Judy Dempsey, "Forward from 1995," *Financial Times*, June 20, 1994, IV.

[69] Commission of the European Communities, "Green Paper: For a European Union Energy Policy," *COM* (94) 659.

energy article in the treaty framework. Bonn officials maintained that there was no need for additional sectoral components in the treaty framework; energy policy was and is part and parcel of economic policy, and thus all the necessary instruments and legal infrastructure already exist at the European level. The Germans were keen to prevent the creation of a basis for a sectoral industrial policy in the treaty framework, and ambiguities on this point in the Green Paper led them to adopt a generally unsupportive stance.[70]

Bonn's resistance to an excessively bureaucratic and centralized European regulatory framework for energy also continued to characterize its approach to the Commission's IEM program. Although Germany joined fellow EC members in approving the 1989 Commission directives on price transparency and the transit of gas and electricity in 1990 and 1991, it rejected the regulation on energy investment as overly *dirigiste*. The government began to shed its gradualist approach to market liberalization in Brussels at about the same time that it launched its domestic initiative. By the time Germany took over the Council presidency in July 1994, it openly supported broad elements of the Commission's proposed second phase of the IEM, including unbundling and negotiated TPA geared for large industrial consumers of energy.[71]

The transformation between 1990 and 1994 was complete; at the end of the period, Germany had exchanged places with France, becoming the leading supporter of the Commission's IEM proposal and, by implication, a leading critic of the major alternative, the so-called single buyer system advocated by France which would have limited negotiated power exchanges to utilities.[72] After several abortive attempts at forging consensus with the French, in June 1996 the Germans settled reluctantly for a compromise entailing a three-stage opening of one-third of the internal electricity market over an eight-year period. With German prodding, work began immediately in the Council of Ministers on a

[70] In the words of a BMWi official, "DG-XVII operates under a big handicap in Brussels – since they have no own competences within the treaty framework, every time it wants to do something in the energy field, it has to search for legal justification . . . They seem to be suffering from a sense that they are not the constitutional equals of their colleagues in other Directorates General." Interview with BMWi official, Bonn, April 27, 1995.

[71] The criteria set out in the Commission's draft directive – 25 million cubic meters of gas or 100 gigawatt hours of electricity per year – effectively limited its reach to the largest users, such as those in the aluminum, steel, glass, and chemicals industries.

[72] Under this system, direct negotiations between purchasers and sellers of power would be precluded; instead, designated national monopolies would act as intermediaries for their users seeking to purchase power from suppliers elsewhere in the EU. Critics of the proposal charged France with trying to protect the position of its monopoly energy supplier, Electricité de France.

similar initiative for gas, which was eventually adopted after long and arduous negotiations in May 1998.

Progress in Brussels translated into parallel action at the domestic level; according to an official responsible for energy affairs in the BMWi, the IEM initiative at the European level provided a welcome impetus for the long-running objective of his *Referat* to reform the domestic energy market.[73] In April 1998, a new federal law liberalizing Germany's energy sector took effect.

Conclusions

In the areas of the environment and energy, unification led to discernible shifts in policy at the domestic level. Influence here was indirect and contextual. Specifically, mounting concerns about the health of the German *Standort* contributed to increased wariness about environmental regulation in government circles (except as applied to the eastern territories), and greater determination in pushing through deregulation of the domestic energy market and a reassessment of coal support programs.

Evidence of corresponding shifts in German policy approaches at the supranational level is at best subtle and nuanced. Most striking is the absence of a clear domestic "breakthrough" in environmental matters. Instead of applying the brakes in the Council of Ministers, the German government remained committed to its pre-1990 environmental agenda. The reasons behind the observed continuity reside in the interaction of policy-specific ideational systems, specifically German identity as the EU "golden boy," and the structure of the policy process in Bonn and Brussels.[74] At the same time, domestic politics matters: the German government has demonstrated a greater reluctance to engage in solo initiatives when its efforts to upgrade the EU's common interest fail. The implications for European environmental policy are potentially sobering: for the foreseeable future, Germany will not lead by example; Bonn can no longer afford to be holier than the rest of its EU neighbors. That said, with the costs of "exit" now far higher, the incentives for Germany to bring along its partners on environmental matters using "voice" are that much stronger.[75]

Germany's approach to European energy policy also retained its basic

---

[73] Interview with BMWi official, Bonn, April 27, 1995.

[74] I touch on this point only briefly here; chapter 7 presents a more thorough development of these arguments.

[75] Albert Hirschman, *Exit, Voice, and Loyalty* (Cambridge, MA: Harvard University Press, 1970).

pre-1990 contours. In fact, Bonn was blessed by unification, inasmuch as the rekindling of the *Standortdebatte* transformed the domestic energy debate, weakening the supporters of hard coal and strengthening the position of deregulation advocates both in government and in (western) industry. The rationale for liberalizing energy markets at home necessitated parallel action at the European level if German industry was not to suffer competitively. Consequently, the German government was able to throw its full weight behind an IEM program they had always supported in principle – apart from the Commission's *dirigisme*, which Bonn was able to thwart – but had been unable to sell domestically.

5 Change in competition policy

The immensity of the economic challenges posed by unification inevitably raised difficult questions of state aid, industrial policy, and the relationship between state and market. These questions led immediately to pitched domestic conflicts and, after 1992, to a widening gap between German rhetoric and German action on competition matters in Brussels. The effect was schizophrenic; Bonn's formal position on state aid remained true to its pre-unification heritage, but German behavior betrayed a new interventionist logic at work.

Pre-unification competition policy

Based on Articles 84–94 of the Treaty of Rome, the Community's competition regime confers considerable operational autonomy on the Commission to "investigate, codify, exempt, and fine" on questions relating to cartels, monopolies, and state aid to industry; it has evolved into a veritable "economic constitution, guaranteeing the maintenance of a liberal market order."[1] Competition matters often have been sharply contested in the Council, pitting more interventionist members like France and Italy against supporters of liberal orthodoxy, principally Germany and the UK.

On the question of state aid, West Germany was an enthusiastic supporter of a stringent application of the rules derived from Articles 92–94 of the Rome Treaty, which prohibit state subsidies that distort intra-Community trade. In practice, officials regarded state aid as a necessary evil, distinguishing between assistance to cushion the social upheaval caused by the structural decline of an industry and aid intended merely to prop up inefficient producers. West Germany was not averse to the former type of aid, consistent as it was with the basic

---

[1] Stephen Wilks and Lee McGowan, "Disarming the Commission: The Debate over a European Cartel Office," *Journal of Common Market Studies* 32 (June 1995), 259–73 at 261. Competition matters relating to regional economic assistance are discussed in chapter 6.

tenets of the social market economy, but regarded the latter with deep skepticism. In Brussels, Bonn found a supportive regulatory environment,[2] and sought to keep the level of state aid across the Community as low as possible, believing that German firms would thrive in a relatively subsidy-free environment. At the same time, it worked to ensure that German firms and regions retained access to state aid, whether provided by Brussels or Bonn, as long as the Community tolerated sectoral and regional aid.

Competition policy and the unification settlement, 1989–90

In the area with the most profound implications for competition policy – privatization – domestic institutional transfer swam against the prevailing west-to-east currents. The Treuhandanstalt (THA) was created on March 1, 1990 by the reform communist government to act as custodian of the public sector, which included virtually all of industry (some 8,000 firms, many of them organized as *Kombinate*) and vast agricultural and real estate holdings.[3] Its limited brief to privatize originated in widespread resolve among East German elites to prevent a fire sale of public assets to West German investors, who were making good use of the now permeable border to explore new business opportunities in the east. The commanding heights of the post-socialist economy were to remain in state hands for the foreseeable future.

The Unification Treaty brought the THA and its 12,000 firms employing approximately 4 million people into the Federal Republic largely as it was – an institution made in the GDR – although provisions were made for its transformation into a parapublic agency under the direct oversight of the Federal Ministry of Finance, as well as for other minor organizational modifications. The unproblematic nature of this reverse institutional transfer stemmed from the fact that officials in both Bonn and Berlin viewed privatization itself as an unproblematic task.

2　According to a German participant in Community affairs during the 1950s and 1960s, "The German Minister for Economic Affairs, Professor Erhard ... stated in 1962 that he himself could have written the competition provisions of the EEC Treaty." Hans von der Groeben, *The European Community, the Formative Years: The Struggle to Establish the Common Market and the Political Union (1958–66)* (Luxembourg: Office for Official Publications of the European Communities, 1987), 48f.

3　See "Beschluß zur Gründung der Anstalt zur treuhänderischen Verwaltung des Volkseigentums (Treuhandanstalt) vom 1. März 1990," *Gesetzblatt der Deutschen Demokratischen Republik*, part I, no. 14 (March 8, 1990), 107. See also Wolfram Fischer and Harm Schröter, "Die Entstehung der Treuhandanstalt," in Wolfram Fischer, Herbert Hax, and Hans Karl Schneider, *Treuhandanstalt: Das unmögliche wagen* (Berlin: Akademie Verlag, 1993), 25–6.

Not only did they expect it to take a few short years to complete, but they anticipated a substantial windfall from the sale of public assets. Estimates of the THA's future profits at this time ranged as high as DM600 billion.[4]

The THA quickly took on a pivotal role in the transformation of the eastern German economy, with responsibilities for negotiating the sale of its assets according to commercial criteria, evaluating which firms were candidates for restructuring prior to privatization, and closing unviable enterprises. As such, the THA's policy brief raised several thorny questions about EC competition policy.

The months leading up to formal unification saw little EC monitoring of, to say nothing of direct influence on, the THA and its privatization activities. Nevertheless, broader concerns about the implications of unification for EC competition law surfaced in negotiations between Bonn and Brussels. Commission officials were fully aware that in the short run, federal and state authorities would be providing considerable sums to GDR enterprises, actions which if left unregulated could easily generate market distortions and set undesirable precedents that could weaken the EC's regulatory regime. Their focus of attention was Article 92 of the Rome Treaty, with Articles 85–86, governing mergers and monopolies, drawing much less attention.

Initially, the West German government sought a blanket exemption from existing EC competition guidelines, at least as these related to state aid. The Germans looked to Article 92(2c) of the Rome Treaty, which allows state aids for "certain areas of the Federal Republic affected by the division of Germany, insofar as they are necessary to compensate for economic disadvantages brought about by division."[5] The Commission rejected Bonn's legal reasoning, maintaining that the article in question applied solely to postwar measures necessitated by the physical division of Germany, such as the regional assistance programs for West Berlin and the areas bordering on the GDR and Czechoslovakia. As the division of Germany came to an end, so too must the rationale for this particular treaty article.[6]

[4] Sinn and Sinn, *Kaltstart*, 70. In the end, the THA and its successor organizations will rack up a *deficit* of approximately DM270 billion.

[5] Thomas Läufer, *Europäische Gemeinschaft Europäische Union: Die Vertragstexte von Maastricht* (Bonn: Presse- und Informationsamt der Bundesregierung, 1992), 68.

[6] At Maastricht, the Commission favored striking Article 92 (2c) from the treaty text. Germany's foreign minister, Hans-Dietrich Genscher, insisted on its retention, pointing out that the wording covered the situation in the new Länder. According to a senior BMWi official interviewed in 1992, Bonn continued to refer to Article 92 (2c) as the legal basis for each state aid case reviewed by the Commission, which for its part refused to recognize the justification each time. The official explained that this impasse had posed no particular difficulties for Bonn, since the Commission had yet to reject a single

The Commission coupled its unbending treaty interpretation with a general insistence that with a few exceptions, Article 92 apply to the full range of assistance measures that had been and would be carried out by the THA and other public authorities. To do otherwise would represent a departure from standard EC practice during previous accessions, and constitute a damaging precedent in what had always been a politically charged issue area. However, the Commission promised to be flexible when evaluating individual aid cases, in light of

the desolate state of the GDR economy . . ., the absence of an economic structure adequate for a market economy, the requirement to rebuild, modernize and gear up industry and services, and the need to improve the environment significantly . . .[7]

The Germans, long-time advocates of a stringent EC competition policy, accepted these arrangements.

Competition policy after unification: continuity in theory

In an ironic twist, the implementation of the SEA – a neoliberal project – actually worked to the advantage of member governments and parts of the Commission favoring a more interventionist role for Europe's would-be polity. Led by DG-III in the Commission and supported by the French government, this coalition maintained that there was much the EC could do to foster internationally competitive industries if it were outfitted with appropriate legal competencies.[8]

Thus, industrial policy found its way back on to the EC agenda in the 1990s. The debate reached an early and decisive climax at the Maastricht summit, when the members agreed on treaty language that opened the door to the pursuit of so-called horizontal industrial policies, i.e. ones addressing the competitiveness of sectors, not individual firms. The Commission quickly followed up on the Maastricht decision with concrete proposals, known as "Action Programs," for the airline, automobile, electronics, and biotechnology industries.

Bonn reluctantly agreed to Article 130 as the price for a successful summit, but insisted on friendlier treaty language than that proposed by

---

aid case. "As soon as we have a significant case go against us," he added, "we will insist upon the clause's applicability." The significant case finally surfaced in 1996; see below. Interview with BMWi official, Bonn, December 11, 1992.

[7] Commission of the European Communities, "The European Community and German Unification," 74.

[8] See Commission of the European Communities, "European Industrial Policy for the 1990s," *Bulletin of the European Communities*, Supplement 3/1991 (Luxembourg: Office for Official Publications of the European Communities).

France and the Commission, including the stipulation that binding decisions about industrial policy required unanimity in the Council of Ministers.[9] Both politicians and bureaucrats acknowledged that Maastricht had opened the door to an expansion of Community competencies in the field of industrial policy; this would require strict vigilance on the part of Germany.

The government's actions matched its rhetoric on this issue. For example, Bonn resisted proposals circulating within the Commission in early 1992 to use the European Social Fund to co-finance workforce retraining programs to enable Community automobile manufacturers to fend off the Japanese import challenge. More generally, Bonn sought to starve the Commission's nascent industrial policy initiatives of budgetary resources,[10] and reacted with caution to the Commission's proposal in 1994 to use merger control policy to foster strategic alliances between firms. Save for a few firms and industry associations that stood to benefit from the Commission's initiatives, German business echoed the government's skepticism.[11]

Regarding Community policy on state aid, Germany initially maintained its pre-unification line as the Commission came under growing pressure from France, Spain, and other member governments to soften its approach with an eye to serving the competitive needs of European industry.[12] Commission pledges to scrutinize the subsidy practices of the wealthier member governments with greater intensity met with Bonn's approval, and in private German officials welcomed the prospect of supranational support for their own efforts to contain subsidy

[9] Article 130 empowers the EU to undertake measures to facilitate adjustment of industry to structural changes. In the German version of the treaty text, the operative noun is "easing" (*Erleichterung*), whereas the French version employs "acceleration." Each version carries equal legal weight. A senior BMWi official commented in 1992 that after Maastricht, the Commission attempted to get the Germans to change their text to bring it in line with the French version. The request was rejected firmly with the argument that the Chancellor had negotiated on the basis of precise treaty language, and he could not be expected to go back on his understanding of what he approved. The official stated that the textual difference provided Germany with a useful means of postponing developments in this policy area. Interview with BMWi official, Bonn, July 22, 1992. See also Henning Klodt, "Europäische Industriepolitik nach Maastricht," *Die Weltwirtschaft* (September 1992), 263–73.

[10] A senior BMWi official noted that during negotiations over the Delors II budget package in 1992, the Commission put forward no budget proposals under Article 130, knowing full well that these would have been "categorically rejected" by Germany. Interview with BMWi official, Bonn, July 22, 1992.

[11] See for example Deutscher Industrie- und Handelstag, "Antworten des DIHT auf die Fragen der CDU/CSU-Bundestagsfraktion zum Thema 'Standort Deutschland'," internal document, February 1992, 41; Bundesverband der Deutschen Industrie, "Antworten des BDI auf den Fragenkatalog zur Standortdiskussion der CDU/CSU-Bundestagsfraktion," internal document, April 1992, 79–85.

[12] Wilks and McGowan, "Disarming the Commission," 263–64.

practices in the western Länder. According to a BMWi official interviewed in 1992, "We have to be tougher than the Commission. Otherwise this job becomes impossible." He added that striking a softer line
than the competition police would put Germany in the position of
constantly appearing in Brussels asking for favors: "If one wants to
achieve anything in Brussels, one has to adopt stringent standards for
one's own conduct."[13] His words would take on an ironic quality only a
few years later.

Competition policy after unification: change in practice

Beneath the appearance of continuity, however, there lurked a growing
interventionism in the restructuring of the eastern German economy,
revolving primarily though not exclusively around the THA. The political pressures to respond forcefully to the emerging economic catastrophe in the new territories would eventually push the Bonn
government off its well-established position on state aid.

The domestic politics of privatization, 1990–94

By the end of 1990, the GDR blueprint for the THA, which called for
the reorganization of the agency into four stock corporations, was
quietly shelved in favor of a more unitary structure based on a division
of labor between the THA central office in Berlin and fifteen branch
offices.[14] Centralization promised greater administrative efficiency and
less exposure to political influence by trade unions and eastern Land
governments. As a parapublic agency with a legal mandate and the
capacity to raise its own capital within broad limits set by parliament,
the THA enjoyed considerable autonomy.[15]

During this period, Bonn was confronted with demands from eastern
German political representatives to transfer the THA's functions to the
new Länder.[16] State officials in the east regarded the THA with trepida-

[13] Interview with BMWi official, Bonn, November 12, 1992.
[14] Management and privatization of THA companies with fewer than 1,500 employees
were to be the responsibility of the branch offices (Niederlassungen), while the THA
central office assumed control of the larger firms and the formulation of general
privatization policy.
[15] According to THA president Birgit Breuel, the institutional arrangement was designed
to allow the federal government to use the agency as a scapegoat; "This was the idea of
our job – to have distance between the politicians and the Treuhand enterprises." Judy
Dempsey, "Treuhand Head Administers a Painful Cure," *Financial Times*, October 4,
1993.
[16] Roland Czada, "Die Treuhandanstalt im politischen System der Bundesrepublik," *Aus
Politik und Zeitgeschichte* 43–44 (October 28, 1994), 31–42 at 32; see also Frank

tion, seeing in it a powerful agency with the potential both to help and to harm their regional economies, but over which they had little control, their constitutional responsibilities for regional economic planning notwithstanding. With the THA's active support, the federal government turned aside calls for a territorial reorganization of the THA. The eastern Länder had to content themselves with representation on the THA's management board (*Verwaltungsrat*) and with informal contacts at various levels of the agency bureaucracy.

Up until the end of 1990, the THA enjoyed a reasonably broad field of maneuver. Thereafter, the THA moved rapidly out of the shadows into the political crossfire as the expected boom in sales failed to materialize and unemployment arising from firm closures began to increase dramatically. In the eyes of its many critics, the agency was not a solution to the east's problems, but a primary cause. Spontaneous protests by employees of THA firms fearful of imminent lay-offs broke out in early 1991. The SPD, supported by the unions and the eastern Land governments, demanded that the agency be reassigned to the BMWi, placed under closer parliamentary scrutiny, and allowed to pursue an active structural and regional policy in formal consultation with the eastern Land governments.[17] The agency drew criticism even from those who supported the policy of rapid privatization according to commercial criteria. In a six-point program published in January 1992, the Bundesverband der Deutschen Industrie (BDI) criticized the THA for inefficiency, opaque decision rules, and a lack of professionalism.[18] Western business associations in particular decried what they saw as the unrestrained subsidy practices of the THA, and warned of distortions to market competition that would drive many of their member firms out of business.

Many difficulties encountered by the THA were simply beyond its control. The settlement on property rights arising out of the unification treaties ("restitution before compensation"), as well as the rapid unmasking of the sorry state of East German industry, frightened off many potential buyers, complicated negotiations with those investors willing to bid for THA assets, and prompted the closure of many flagship GDR enterprises. The collapse of Soviet and Eastern European export

Nägele, "Strukturpolitik wider Willen? Die regionalpolitischen Dimensionen der Treuhandpolitik," *Aus Politik und Zeitgeschichte* 43–44 (October 28, 1994), 43–52.

[17] Noticeably absent from the coalition opposing THA policies were eastern-based employer associations, which were extremely weak. See Wolfgang Seibel, "Strategische Fehler oder erfolgreiches Scheitern? Zur Entwicklung der Treuhandanstalt 1990–1993," *Politische Vierteljahresschrift* 35 (1994), 33.

[18] Bundesverband der Deutschen Industrie, "BDI-Vorschlag für eine Weiterentwicklung des Treuhand-Konzepts," January 7, 1992.

markets also drove many firms to the wall, making it difficult for the agency to evaluate their long-term economic prospects. As a recessionary environment took hold after 1992, potential buyers drove harder bargains with the THA, expecting the agency to cover operating losses for the first several years after privatization.

Other difficulties, however, were entirely home grown. Incompetence, graft, and corruption permeated not a few privatization cases, and on top of all this, the THA suffered from what can only be described as a chronic public relations problem. To many eastern German citizens, the agency had taken on characteristics reminiscent of the discredited SED-regime: an all-powerful, centralized bureaucracy lacking transparency and public accountability. Even symbolic matters worked to the disadvantage of the agency. In March 1991, its Berlin headquarters moved into the massive facilities on the Leipzigerstraße, originally constructed in the 1930s to house the Third Reich's air ministry under Goering and more recently occupied by the GDR's industrial planning apparatus. At the regional level, many branch offices set up shop in vacated GDR military installations or, even worse, in offices formerly occupied by the hated Stasi.[19]

Surrounded by controversy, THA officials and the government carried out an internal debate over the direction of privatization policy. Should the THA emphasize rapid privatization of its firms (*Privatisierung*), or should it give priority to restructuring (*Sanierung*), quite possibly over a lengthy period, as a prelude to eventual privatization? To what extent should the agency develop an industrial policy to serve as an overarching framework for its more concrete privatization activities? In the end, the government and agency reaffirmed the policy of rapid privatization as "the best form of restructuring"[20] and as a means of containing the fiscal costs of privatization and its attendant political risks.

Rapid privatization in the midst of a mounting economic crisis practically required an element of social concertation. So in traditional German fashion, the THA leadership hosted and attended numerous conferences and mini-summits with representatives of the unions and the new Länder. These consultations led directly to two waves of formal agreements. The first was struck with the eastern Länder in March 1991, and provided for the creation of a "THA Economic Cabinet"

---

[19] Wolfgang Seibel, "Die organisatorische Entwicklung der Treuhandanstalt," in Wolfram Fischer, Herbert Hax, and Hans Karl Schneider, *Treuhandanstalt: Das unmögliche wagen* (Berlin: Akademie Verlag, 1993), 123.

[20] Wolfgang Seibel, "Das zentralistische Erbe," *Aus Politik und Zeitgeschichte* 43–44 (October 28, 1994), 6.

(*Treuhand-Wirtschaftskabinett*) attached to the political executive in each of the new Länder, which would bring together THA officials with state government officials on a regular basis to discuss the general progress of privatization in the Land as well as specific cases.[21] It also established an early warning system, according to which the THA pledged to inform the Land governments in advance of the pending liquidation of regionally significant enterprises, and to provide them with detailed information to assist in the preparation of flanking measures.

The second wave of agreements involved the unions. In April and then again in July, the THA, the Deutscher Gewerkschaftsbund (DGB), and the national white collar union federation (DAG) issued joint declarations, one establishing guidelines for social plans to cushion the effects of mass lay-offs caused by the THA, and the other outlining an agreement to fund and operate societies providing temporary employment and retraining for laid-off THA workers (so-called *ABS-Gesellschaften*). Neither declaration altered final THA authority over privatization cases.

Thus, the price of policy continuity – rapid privatization – was the political integration of the THA organization into two principal institutions of the (West) German polity: federalism and corporatism.[22] Yet the social embedding of the THA in no way ended the debate over privatization. Opponents of THA policies began to raise the specter of deindustrialization in eastern Germany. Absent a major change in the way the THA conducted business, they argued, the region would lose its manufacturing base, perhaps forever. This would result not only in permanent dependency on Bonn, but in social and economic hardship on a scale not seen since the Great Depression, with potentially ominous political implications. To the unions and elected Land officials, combating deindustrialization translated into the survival of particular firms or sectors and, within them, as many manufacturing jobs as possible.[23]

Critics of the THA proposed a halt to the THA's policy of rapid privatization, greater emphasis within the agency on active restructuring of firms (*Sanierung*) within regional and sectoral planning frameworks, and use of state holding companies to manage and restructure large employers lacking immediate privatization prospects. The ultimate goal

---

[21] An official in Mecklenburg-West Pomerania stated that the cabinet improved the capacity of the Land to monitor ongoing privatization cases and make its position known to the THA. As a result, "on big decisions nothing is decided against the Land." Interview with economics ministry official in Mecklenburg-West Pomerania, Schwerin, October 26, 1992.

[22] This is a point emphasized by Seibel in his numerous writings on the THA.

[23] As 1992 wore on, the unions asked for a moratorium on lay-offs while multi-year restructuring plans were implemented by the agency (*Entlassungsstopp*).

of these various proposals was to preserve the industrial cores (*industrielle Kerne*) of the eastern German economy.

Within government circles and the THA, aversion to the state holding model was particularly strong: (1) it would provide firms with a false sense of security, and relieve none of their adjustment imperatives, particularly those involving labor-shedding; (2) it would open the state to political blackmail; and (3) it would evoke "considerable head winds" from Brussels, particularly in cases involving sensitive sectors.[24] Similarly, THA officials were reluctant formally to orient privatization toward the preservation of regionally significant firms and/or industrial cores, despite the fact that they were fully aware of the consequences of liquidation. Placing this objective at the center of THA policy was unlikely to mollify critics and would merely expose the THA to an avalanche of demands from federal and state politicians to include "their firms" in the new policy.

The THA's initial response, announced toward the end of 1991, was to affirm the policy of rapid privatization, particularly for its larger enterprises, while creating a new organizational vehicle – the *Management-Kommanditgesellschaft* (MKG) – to carry out the restructuring of medium-sized firms with strong long-term prospects but for which there were no buyers in the short run. Firms were assigned to an MKG on the basis of their individual business potential; the THA expressly ruled out searching for constellations of firms that could generate sectoral or regional "synergies."[25]

This failed to silence the critics. By early 1992, Chancellor Kohl confronted increasing pressure from eastern members of his own party (CDU-Ost) in the Bundestag, who had organized themselves into a formal parliamentary caucus and were lobbying publicly and doggedly for the transfer of fifteen to twenty large firms from THA control to a state holding company, which would oversee their restructuring and eventual privatization via the stock market. The internal criticism struck a nerve; the leader of the CDU/CSU parliamentary caucus convened a working group to explore the matter, and newspaper reports indicated that the Chancellor had directed one of his advisors to assemble a list of likely candidates for rationalization under state auspices.[26]

---

[24] THA internal document, 13 December 1991; reprinted in Treuhandanstalt, *Dokumentation 1990–94*, vol. VII, 471–80 at 473.

[25] By 1993, sixty-nine firms – approximately 10 percent of the THA's holdings at the time – were grouped into five MKGs, each run by an experienced and well-paid western German manager. On the MKGs, see Seibel, "Strategische Fehler oder erfolgreiches Scheitern?", 24–29.

[26] H. Maier-Mannhart, "Werften als Präzedenzfall," *Süddeutsche Zeitung*, March 18, 1992, 4.

The continuing absence of a regional or sectoral dimension to the THA's activities posed real problems for the eastern Land governments, which faced the imminent collapse of geographically concentrated industries like steel, shipbuilding, chemicals, and coal. Beginning in 1992, large unprivatized firms often became the locus of public protests organized by unions, municipal authorities, and local political representatives. Various attempts at self help by the Länder, such as the creation of privately financed investment funds designed to facilitate the sale of small- and medium-sized THA firms, produced disappointing results.[27] Land-financed holding companies failed to catch on, because of wariness on the part of the THA, unease in Bonn and Brussels with the state aid implications, and the Länder's reluctance to underwrite the considerable financial risks.[28]

Ultimately, the search for a way to inject regional considerations into the privatization process led the eastern Länder back to the THA. The trendsetter was Saxony, which struck a formal deal with the THA in April 1992. Under the terms of the arrangement, Saxony agreed to identify "regionally significant" firms within its territory and bring them to the THA's attention. If the selected firms were deemed worthy of restructuring by the agency, the Land pledged to assist them with all its available policy instruments at the highest levels permitted under federal law. The THA for its part agreed to support restructuring of the firm over a twelve-month period. If the Land put forward a firm classified by the THA as unviable, the Land would be allowed to commission a restructuring concept from an outside source and submit it to the THA for consideration. Final decision as to the firm's eligibility for THA restructuring assistance remained with the agency, although the possibility of a Land "appeal" opened up the THA to political pressure in borderline cases.[29]

This arrangement was soon replicated in other eastern Länder; by

[27] In the fall of 1991, the Land of Saxony established the *Sachsenfonds*, which failed to attract sufficient capital owing to the reluctance of the banking sector to participate.

[28] The most celebrated case involved the Land of Thuringia. In June 1991, as a means of heading off possible liquidation by the THA, the Land government assumed full control of Jenoptik GmbH, a successor holding company to the famous East German manufacturer of optical equipment, precision instruments, and electronics, VEB Carl Zeiss Jena. The arrangement came under the scrutiny of the European Commission almost immediately, owing to concerns about the provision of state aid; by the middle of 1994, the restructuring costs incurred by Jenoptik had risen to DM1.2 billion. Management did not expect Jenoptik's holdings to yield a profit until after 1996, and disputes with the Land over the scale of job cuts were bitter and frequent.

[29] Pressure cut both ways, however. According to a Saxony official, this arrangement created an expanded field for THA blackmail. "It would be very easy for the THA to come to the Land and say, 'We have this firm, and the restructuring will cost DM500 million, which we are willing to provide. But you have to come up with 23 percent of

November 1, 1993, five participating Länder (all save Saxony-Anhalt) had identified 282 firms as regionally significant.[30] Via such mechanisms, the Land governments hoped to encourage better entrepreneurial management during the restructuring phase, and to elicit long-term financial commitments for many of the agency's problem cases – commitments that would extend beyond the THA's closure date set for the end of 1994.[31]

The coordination of THA and Land support typically entailed the creation of institutions at the Land level that brought together employer representatives, unions, elected officials, and local authorities. In Saxony the Land government created the Atlas team,[32] a special unit of independent management consultants attached to the economics ministry in Dresden. Two advisory committees were created to support Atlas, one bringing together employer and trade union representatives in the Land, and the other consisting of three members of the state parliament. The identification of regionally significant firms was a politically delicate task; as an official explained, "Every local authority official and member of parliament believes that his constituency contains one or more regionally significant firms."[33]

The diffusion of the Atlas model pulled the THA closer to acceptance of political responsibility for the survival of manufacturing industry in the former GDR. This subtle shift in approach was helped along in November 1992, when Chancellor Kohl, facing growing criticism of his economic policies from the government backbenches and declining popularity in the polls, announced that his government supported the

the figure in Land assistance, or we will back out.'" Interview with economics ministry official in Saxony, Dresden, November 23, 1992.

[30] Internal THA document, November 1, 1993; reprinted in Treuhandanstalt, *Dokumentation 1990–94*, vol. IX, 859–64. These exercises revealed the extent to which the Länder were unaware of the activities of the THA. For example, out of the fifty-three firms forwarded by the Land government of Brandenburg to the THA in October 1993, fourteen were already privatized and three were in the process of being liquidated. As such, the Land was completely in the dark about the status of almost one-third of its list! See THA correspondence, October 27, 1993; reprinted in Treuhandanstalt, *Dokumentation 1990–94*, vol. IX, 885–86.

[31] Interview with economics ministry official in Mecklenburg-West Pomerania, Schwerin, October 26, 1992.

[32] The acronym Atlas stood for Ausgewählte Treuhandunternehmen vom Land angemeldet zur Sanierung (Selected THA Firms Registered by the Land for Restructuring).

[33] Interview with economics ministry official in Saxony, Dresden, November 23, 1992. In a parliamentary debate held in mid-1992, the Minister of Economics for Brandenburg announced five priority areas targeted by the Land and the THA – and quickly noted that the list by no means devalued the importance of another six specific areas in the Land, and then concluded, "we have to be concerned about every industrial region in the Land." Landtag Brandenburg, 1. Wahlperiode, Planarprotokoll 1/49, June 24, 1992, 3567.

goal of preserving the industrial cores of the eastern German economy. His remarks received official expression in the Solidarity Pact of March 1993, which, among other things, singled out the MKGs and Atlas as appropriate vehicles for preserving the region's industrial cores.

Whether this constituted a sea-change in the THA's privatization brief is a matter of some controversy.[34] On the one hand, the government's public commitment to preserve industrial cores rendered it virtually impossible for the THA to actively seek the closure of many large employers in the near term. On the other hand, officials pointed out that the THA's accomplishments up through the first third of 1993 – 12,000 firms privatized, with promises of DM177 billion in investments and 1.45 million jobs – already had gone a long way toward preserving key industrial centers in the new Länder: automobiles in Eisenach; optics in Jena; shipbuilding in Mecklenburg-West Pomerania; microelectronics in Dresden; steel in Brandenburg.[35] Moreover, the Atlas and MKG models upheld commercial criteria; for example, each reaffirmed the goal of imminent privatization, ruled out a moratorium on THA lay-offs, and ensured that in the event of disagreement between the agency and a Land government over the prospects of a regionally significant firm, the Land would pick up the costs of restructuring over and above what it would cost to close the firm.[36]

The government's public embrace of eastern Germany's industrial cores altered few if any of the challenges facing the THA. By the end of 1992, almost 80 percent of the agency's holdings had been privatized and many of its branch offices had ceased operations, leaving the THA with what it identified in internal memoranda as the "big cases" that were destined to raise big political questions.[37] These included Eko Stahl AG in Eisenhüttenstadt, Brandenburg; Deutsche Waggonbau AG, Berlin; SKET Maschinen- und Anlagenbau AG, Magdeburg; brown

---

[34] Authors who support the notion of a sea-change include Jan Priewe, "Die Folgen der schnellen Privatisierung der Treuhandanstalt," *Aus Politik und Zeitgeschichte* 43–44 (October 28, 1994), 21–30 at 28; and C. H. Flockton, "The Federal German Economy in the Early 1990s," *German Politics* 2 (August 1993), 311–27 at 318. Wolfgang Seibel provides the most compelling argument that the Solidarity Pact represented more continuity than change in the THA's privatization line; see also Nägele, "Strukturpolitik wider Willen?," 48.

[35] "Konzept der Bundesregierung zur Sicherung und Erneuerung industrieller Kerne durch die Treuhandanstalt in den neuen Bundesländern," BMWi/BMF internal report, June 21, 1993; reprinted in Treuhandanstalt, *Dokumentation 1990–94*, vol. XI, 717–37 at 720–21.

[36] Treuhandaustalt, *Dokumentation 1990–94*, vol. XI, 731.

[37] See "Bericht für den Verwaltungsrat der Treuhandanstalt zur Entwicklung des Treuhandportofolios," September 17, 1993; reprinted in Treuhandanstalt, *Dokumentation 1990–94*, vol. VII, 436–48 at 443–44.

coal mining in Saxony and Saxony-Anhalt; and chemical manufacturing at sites in Bitterfeld-Wolfen, Böhlen, Buna, and Leuna.[38]

The federal government's affirmation of the Atlas model cleared the way, at least in theory, for an expansion of Land industrial holdings in the east, in that the THA officially had invited the Länder to pick up the costs of restructuring regionally significant firms in cases where the agency decided to pass. All the eastern Länder gave serious consideration to this option, and at least two, Thuringia and Saxony, set up holding companies designed to preserve industrial core areas. The others, however, eventually rejected such a radical policy innovation, largely because they were reluctant to take on the financial obligations in the absence of federal support for the state holding model.

In 1993, the THA began to prepare for its own liquidation. Ministerial officials in Bonn blocked a regionalization of the post-THA organizations, since they wished to avoid a further politicization of the privatization process. They were joined in opposition by the new Länder, which were leery of the bureaucratic burdens and incalculable financial risks of assuming the THA's management responsibilities for the unprivatized firms in their regions.[39]

After protracted negotiations with members of parliament and representatives from the new Länder, the government secured passage of legislation in 1994 that established four THA successor organizations, all under the supervision of the BMF; the key ones were the Bundesanstalt für vereinigungsbedingte Sonderaufgaben (BvS), which was responsible among other matters for monitoring the contracts of privatized firms, and the Beteiligungs-Management-Gesellschaft Berlin (BMGB), which was charged with the management, restructuring, and privatization of the THA's remaining firms.[40] The eastern Länder secured changes to the original federal proposals that guaranteed them representation on the management committees of the successor organi-

---

[38] "Konzept der Bundesregierung zur Sicherung und Erneuerung industrieller Kerne durch die Treuhandanstalt in den neuen Bundesländern," BMWi/BMF internal report, June 21, 1993; reprinted in Treuhandanstalt, *Dokumentation 1990–94*, vol. XI, 722–23.

[39] See Seibel, "Das zentralistische Erbe," 12–13. The European Commission, which stayed out of the domestic debates on the THA successors, would also have looked on the regionalization of the agency's functions with trepidation. Interview with Commission (DG-IV) official, Brussels, March 3, 1995.

[40] The others were the Liegenschaftsgesellschaft der Treuhandanstalt (TLG), which was to privatize the agency's remaining non-agricultural and non-forest real estate holdings, and the Bundesamt zur Regelung offener Vermögensfragen (BARoV), which was supposed to assume the BvS's unfulfilled tasks after 1996. In mid-1997, after extensive consultations with the SPD opposition and the eastern Länder, the government announced that the BvS would continue to carry out its ever diminishing responsibilities through the end of 1999.

zations, and in some cases the creation of regional advisory councils to assist the THA successors in carrying out their duties.[41] Bonn also conveyed to Brussels its view that the eastern region was still plagued by serious problems, and that some sort of transitional state aid regime would be required after 1994. At the end of 1994, approximately eighty unsold yet viable firms remained.

Privatization and the European Community, 1990–94

Over the course of 1991, the European Commission worked to bring the THA agency into the existing framework of EC competition rules. DG-IV created a task force early on to monitor the THA's activities and develop policy recommendations for the Commission. Officials continued to focus primarily on potential injuries to Articles 92–94 of the Rome Treaty (state aid).[42]

Initially, the German government balked at a formal role for the Commission in the privatization process. Pointing to Article 92(2c) and the unique situation confronting the now unified Germany, Bonn officials argued that the THA's activities did not constitute state aid, and thus they were of no concern to the Commission. Bonn was especially anxious to avoid the imposition of external constraints on privatization, since it expected eastern German firms to sell for good money, thereby rendering the THA a self-financing operation. Commission officials took a more skeptical view of things. According to one, "We felt that aid might be involved. The need to keep a close eye on THA activities was clear in our minds."[43] The Commission was afraid that unchecked leniency toward the THA could open the door to demands for similar treatment from other member governments.

By May 1991, the steadily worsening economic situation in the eastern region, combined with mounting domestic criticism of the THA, had caused German representatives to change their presentation in Brussels – the desire to prevent unwarranted intrusion into a profitable string of privatizations had been replaced by fear of unwelcome exacerbation of a catastrophe-in-the-making. During protracted and

---

[41] For an early agreement on these basic principles, see "Rahmenvereinbarung zur Konkretisierung der weiteren Zusammenarbeit von Bund und neuen Ländern in Erfüllung des Treuhandauftrags," June 14, 1994; reprinted in Treuhandanstalt, *Dokumentation 1990–94*, vol. XV, 350–57.

[42] The EC turnover thresholds for mergers and buyouts eliminated for all intents and purposes most eastern German firms from potential consideration. Härtel *et al.*, *Die Entwicklung des Wettbewerbs in den neuen Bundesländern*, 204–09.

[43] Interview with Commission (DG-IV) official, Brussels, December 1, 1992.

often tense exchanges with the Commission,[44] Bonn pointed to the developing economic crisis in the new Länder, and repeatedly underscored the unique and temporary challenges complicating the task of privatization. German officials described the basic mission of the THA in terms that distinguished it from state holdings elsewhere in the Community.

The THA conducts itself like a private firm of comparable size operating under comparable circumstances ... Its conduct ... is guided by commercial criteria that can be thoroughly compatible with state objectives in the area of structural or regional policy in a social market economy.[45]

In September 1991, the Commission issued a set of guidelines and procedures pertaining to the THA. Certain categories of assistance that normally would be considered questionable, such as the cancellation of pre-GEMSU debts (*Altschulden*) and state-financed environmental clean-up (*Altlasten*), were declared acceptable in light of the unique situation in the eastern territories. The Commission also pledged to look at pre-privatization financing by the THA more flexibly than standard regulations permitted, provided that privatization remained imminent. A DG-IV official, commenting in 1992, characterized these decisions as unprecedented, yet entirely reasonable.

The application of normal competition policy guidelines would require us to recommend a total shut-down of capacity [in the new Länder]. This is not a realistic option. We need to be lenient, perhaps more lenient than we normally are ... Eastern Germany is a poorest-of-the-poor region.[46]

The Commission required Bonn to submit a report on THA activities every six months, containing information about general privatization policy and internal guidelines, as well as aggregate data on the pace of privatization and THA financing. It also established detailed notification criteria for the THA. Privatization cases involving a single buyer, as well as those in which multiple offers were submitted and the THA accepted the highest bid, did not require notification. When the sale did not go to

---

[44] In May 1991, the Commission signaled to Bonn that it might lodge a formal complaint against the THA involving loan guarantees issued to a steel-producing firm in Brandenburg at below-market rates. The federal government made it clear to the Commission that it would regard any legal action with grave concern, since the THA was behaving "like a firm aware of its responsibilities and bound by the tenets of the social market economy." It vowed to take the case to the European Court of Justice if the Commission insisted on pursuing the matter. The Commission eventually dropped the matter. THA internal document, May 16, 1991, reprinted in Treuhandanstalt, *Dokumentation 1990–94*, vol. IX, 982–85.

[45] "Mitteilung der Bundesregierung an die Kommission der Europäischen Gemeinschaften," July 29, 1991, reprinted in Treuhandanstalt, *Dokumentation 1990–94*, vol. IX, 990–1009 at 1000.

[46] Interview with Commission (DG-IV) official, Brussels, December 1, 1992.

the highest bidder, notification was required if the firm exceeded specified size thresholds, which included employees (>1,500) and annual sales (>DM300 million), or if the firm, regardless of size, belonged to a designated sensitive sector.[47] As far as THA financing of its firms was concerned, the Commission demanded notification of all loans and credit guarantees issued to firms in sensitive sectors. All other financial assistance were subject to usual Commission notification guidelines.

The Commission pledged to rule on the state aid elements of notified cases within ten working days, a much faster turnaround time in comparison to its typical review procedure. With this decision, the Commission sought a transparent process to ensure that the THA adhered to "best offer" criteria and did not discriminate against foreign buyers.

On the whole, the German government was satisfied with the September 1991 decision; according to a THA official in Berlin, the decision evoked "no elation, but no horror either."[48] The official responsible for EC state aid in the BMWi stated,

For the Federal Republic of Germany, which traditionally has numbered among the proponents of a stringent control of state aids in the Community, the decision represents a reasonable solution to the inherent tension between the general goal of reducing state subsidies and the unalterable necessity of massive public support for the restructuring process in the new territories.[49]

A Commission official remarked in 1992 that Bonn "understood and accepted our need to fulfill our obligations under the terms of the Rome Treaty. Bonn has always shared our objectives."[50]

Close working relationships between the THA, Bonn, and Brussels soon developed on the basis of the September notification criteria. An official with the Treuhandanstalt stated confidently, "We believe we have a firm understanding of what the Commission categorically will not accept."[51] In 1992, the federal government turned over the THA's

---

[47] The list included steel, automobiles, shipbuilding, synthetic fibers, textiles, and certain categories of agribusiness – all sectors suffering from overcapacity and structural uncompetitiveness on international markets.

[48] Interview with THA official, Berlin, October 28, 1992.

[49] Peter Schütterle, "EG-Beihilfenkontrolle über die Treuhandanstalt: Die Entscheidung der Kommission vom 18.9.1991," *Europäische Zeitschrift für Wirtschaftsrecht* 2 (November 10, 1991), 662–65 at 665.

[50] Interview with Commission (DG-IV) official, Brussels, December 1, 1992.

[51] Interview with THA official, Berlin, October 28, 1992. A similar phenomenon quickly emerged at the Land level. According to a civil servant in the Thuringia economics ministry, the Land's ability to tailor sectoral and regional aid programs to meet Commission expectations meant that "we have no problems at all with Brussels." Interview with economics ministry official in Thuringia, Erfurt, November 24, 1992.

privatization handbook to the Commission, a gesture intended to promote full transparency with the competition authorities.[52] A BMWi official noted that it allowed the Commission to see to what lengths the THA went to minimize subsidy payments.[53]

Despite the good working relations, the THA was closely monitored in Brussels. There were frequent disagreements between DG-IV and the Bonn authorities over the definition of a "best offer." To the Commission, the highest offer was always the best offer. The THA often adopted a different definition, one that incorporated "a macroeconomic perspective," according to a finance ministry official,[54] such as which buyer was stronger and had a better reputation, and which bid guaranteed the greatest number of jobs for the longest duration. If a sale was made according to this conception of a "best offer," then the THA was required to justify the transaction to the Commission in a formal procedure requiring several written iterations.

Individual privatization cases also came in for close Commission scrutiny owing to the size and manner of public financing prior to privatization, the pricing policies of THA firms,[55] and the terms of sale. Despite the fact that privatization often entailed substantial amounts of public assistance paid out through the THA or the Land authorities, by the middle of 1993 only one case had failed to receive Commission approval. Generally speaking, the Commission determined that the unique situation in eastern Germany warranted a greater degree of flexibility toward state aid than elsewhere in the Community.

In 1992, as the THA began to take up the most difficult privatization cases, DG-IV conducted an internal review of the September 1991 notification criteria. Brussels officials were motivated by several concerns: (1) the THA's use of "negative" sale prices to rid itself of its least

---

[52] Interview with THA official, Berlin, October 28, 1992.
[53] Interview with BMWi official, Bonn, November 12, 1992. Initially, the THA board of directors was reluctant to turn over the handbook, since it feared the information would leak and come into the possession of potential buyers, thereby placing the THA at a disadvantage. In the end, the view at the agency's working level prevailed.
[54] Interview with BMF official, Bonn, October 2, 1992.
[55] In 1992, a Commission official in DG-IV remarked that his office had received numerous complaints about the pricing policies of non-privatized firms, many of them from western German concerns. This, he said, "is a matter of real concern for the Commission. The problem is especially acute in sectors suffering from overcapacity; it becomes difficult for the Commission to say to other members of the EC that they will have to passively stand by while their firms with relatively modern production processes shut down, when all the while eastern German firms with totally outdated technology charge dumping prices and are kept afloat by the THA." Interview with Commission (DG-IV) official, Brussels, December 1, 1992.

desirable (and typically largest) holdings;[56] (2) the use of "cluster" sales, in which the THA assembled mixes of desirable and less desirable firms in a single package to sweeten the deal for potential buyers; and (3) the greater risk of illegitimate state aid, as the THA opted to hold on to firms with remote privatization prospects and provide them with operating capital rather than to close them down. Under the existing notification criteria, however, DG-IV was not seeing many of these cases, and thus believed a review was in order.[57]

New notification criteria, which supplemented rather than replaced the old ones, were announced by the Commission in November 1992 and accepted by Bonn the following month. They represented a compromise between the desire of the Commission to enforce the competition rules and the desire of the German government to expedite an already tortured privatization program. The Commission established clear size and aid thresholds designed to increase the number of notifications sent to the Commission in each of the areas of concern listed above.

During the review of the 1991 notification criteria, the Commission, responding to unhappiness in the Council with the leniency showed the wealthy Germans as they coped with their problem region, began to signal intensifying concern over the secular trend in Germany's state aid practices in the eastern Länder. In a January interview with the German magazine *Capital*, the Commissioner for Competition, Sir Leon Brittan, noted that direct THA assistance to firms was on the increase, and pointed to the rising number of complaints filed by European firms about the artificially low prices charged by THA firms. Promising closer Commission scrutiny of THA activities, he added, "I fail to see market order and discipline in the new Länder."[58]

Officials working within the Commission questioned the elastic meaning of the term "industrial cores" in German domestic debates, and eyed the diffusion of the Atlas model warily. One DG-IV official,

---

[56] In order to contain deindustrialization in the eastern provinces, the THA increasingly resorted to negative sale prices, even when the cost of liquidation was lower. The Commission grew nervous about this practice because, as a BMWi official explained, "it held that in such cases, bankruptcy constitutes the best offer." The Commission, however, was not seeing these cases, since in the eyes of the THA, a solitary interested buyer receiving a negative sale price put forward the best offer, thereby obviating the need for Commission notification. Interview with BMWi official, Bonn, November 12, 1992.

[57] See letter from Commissioner Sir Leon Brittan to Foreign Minister Klaus Kinkel, December 8, 1992; reprinted in Treuhandanstalt, *Dokumentation 1990–94*, vol. IX, 1035–38.

[58] Reference to the Brittan interview taken from European Parliament, "Die Treuhandanstalt und die Gemeinschaft," April 1993; reprinted in Treuhandanstalt, *Dokumentation 1990–94*, vol. X, 17–34 at 24–25.

commenting at the end of 1992, expressed concern about the "Italianization" of eastern Germany, adding that a proliferation of regional IRIs was in the best interests of neither the Germans nor the EC.[59] The same official, interviewed two years later, noted with regret that the growth of Länder holding companies had become especially problematic, since they often became involved in the provision of "rescue and restructuring" assistance to privatized firms that subsequently encountered difficulties, a not uncommon occurrence in the new Länder. He went on to describe THA policy as having shifted from the targeting of firms worthy of restructuring (*Sanierungswürdig*) to the targeting of firms capable of restructuring (*Sanierungsfähig*). This left the agency more vulnerable to political pressures, and opened up a much greater potential for irregularities, since "virtually any firm is capable of restructuring, particularly if money is no object or if employment considerations are paramount."[60]

Bonn responded to these criticisms by assuring the Commission and its partners that the government remained as vigilant as ever on the question of state aid. In private, though, many German officials expressed doubts about the situation in the eastern Länder similar to those circulating inside the Commission.

In response to the THA self-liquidation at the end of 1994, the Commission decided in mid-December to issue a third round of notification criteria; these represented for all intents and purposes an extension of the existing set of regulations, but with some downward adjustment of the size and assistance thresholds to accommodate the changing complexion of the THA's holdings. The Commission attached an expiration date of December 31, 1995 to the new criteria, after which its normal notification procedures would apply to the remaining group of unprivatized firms.

Case studies

Shipbuilding and steel provide a window on to the changing relationship between Bonn and Brussels over EC/EU competition policy. Up through 1992, their policy lines dovetailed for the most part; indeed, the federal government usually was more than willing to let the Commission take the blame for difficult but necessary decisions. According to a senior member of the CDU, "It is very convenient to be able to point to

---

[59] The reference here is to Italy's national holding company, Istituto per la Recostruzione Industriale (IRI). Interview with Commission (DG-IV) official, Brussels, December 1, 1992.

[60] Interview with Commission (DG-IV) official, Brussels, March 3, 1995.

Brussels and say, in effect, the Europeans won't have this."[61] But as the economic situation grew more desperate in eastern Germany and the political pressures on Bonn multiplied, serious differences opened up between Bonn and Brussels, with telling consequences for Germany's larger competition policy aims.

Shipbuilding

GDR shipbuilding was concentrated in twenty-four shipyards and related industrial sites along the Baltic coast in what would eventually become part of Mecklenburg-West Pomerania (MWP) after 1990. At its peak, the sector was the sixth largest in the GDR, employing a workforce of 55,000. Close to 80 percent of its production went to customers in the USSR; every third fishing trawler in the Soviet fleet hailed from a single East German shipyard, the Volkswerft Stralsund.[62] By international standards, the sector was undercapitalized and overstaffed. The resulting vulnerability translated into a major regional problem for MWP – some 40 percent of the industrial workforce in this poor and largely rural Land was tied to shipbuilding.

West Germany, which showed little inclination to subsidize its own shipbuilding sector, had seen production capacity shrink by 50 percent between 1975 and 1990, with employment dropping from 78,000 to 50,000 over the same period.[63] In both 1989 and 1990, the government attempted to eliminate the federal shipbuilding subsidy program, settling in the end for sharp cutbacks in funding levels after encountering bitter opposition from coalition members representing major production sites in Lower Saxony, Bremen, Hamburg, and Schleswig-Holstein.

As one of several sensitive sectors, shipbuilding was the object of detailed and stringent EC regulations governing public subsidies.[64] In the 1980s, the European Commission began to pursue an OECD agreement to dismantle incrementally all forms of direct and indirect public subsidization of the industry. West Germany was on record as an ardent supporter of the Commission, and in fact consistently subsidized its firms well below the maximum allowed under EC guidelines.

East German shipbuilding surfaced as a topic of discussion between

---

[61] Interview with CDU member of the Bundestag, Bonn, December 10, 1992.

[62] Karin Gehrke, "An der Küste werden weiter Schiffe gebaut," in Die Wirtschaft, ed., *Kombinate: Was aus ihnen geworden ist* (Berlin, 1993); reprinted in Treuhandanstalt, *Dokumentation 1990–94*, vol. X, 105–18 at 106.

[63] Gehrke, "An der Küste werden weiter Schiffe gebaut."

[64] Since the mid-1970s, Europe's share of world shipbuilding capacity declined from 40 to 20 percent, and over the same period employment fell from 460,000 to under 120,000. Stefan Wgstyl, "Leaky Lifeboat of Subsidies," *Financial Times*, February 22, 1996, 11.

Bonn and Brussels in 1990. The Commission determined early on that the successful restructuring of the industry would require a higher level of operating aid than was permissible under the existing competition regime, and offered to draw up a set of derogations subject to Council approval by qualified majority. German officials realized that such a proposal would have to be backed by concrete figures on sectoral capacity and subsidy amounts, and by detailed data on individual enterprises – none of which was available in mid-1990.[65] The chances of the Council writing Bonn a blank check for a sensitive sector were effectively nil, unless the Germans agreed to pay dearly; as a BMWi official remarked, "There are no free lunches in the EC."[66] Since officials were confident that the restructuring of the industry could be accomplished quickly and within the existing state aid framework for shipbuilding, Bonn decided that the game was not worth the candle and declined the Commission's offer. Bonn viewed as prohibitive the risks of establishing an unwelcome precedent that could undermine Germany's position in the Council as a proponent of strict shipbuilding subsidy guidelines.

So, in December 1990, the Germans supported new EC state aid guidelines for the industry that contained no special provisions for the eastern German yards. The 7th Directive on Aid to Shipbuilding established a maximum ceiling of 13 percent for operating and restructuring subsidies (down from 28 percent in 1987 under the 6th Directive), and proscribed any restructuring and closure assistance that would result in net increases in national production capacity.[67] The Commission left the door open for Bonn to request derogations at a later date, as new information became available or the situation on the eastern German coast worsened.

Meanwhile, the THA took up the privatization of the twenty-four shipbuilding concerns, which had been grouped under the Deutscher Maschinen- und Schiffbau AG (DMS). At the request of the agency, the DMS submitted a formal proposal in mid-1991 that foresaw the restructuring of the various enterprises over a four-year period, followed by their sale *en masse* to a single buyer. This plan won popular support from the MWP Land government and the unions, both of which were anxious to preserve the coastal production sites intact.[68] The THA, leery of the incalculable costs of the DMS proposal, decided in the fall

---

[65] Interview with BMWi official, Bonn, June 4, 1992.

[66] Interview with BMWi official, Bonn, December 4, 1992.

[67] Investment assistance could not be used to create new production capacity or to increase the capacity of an existing shipyard unless it was tied to corresponding capacity reductions elsewhere in the national territory.

[68] The unions staged several highly visible industrial actions during this period to protest

of 1991 to press ahead with a rapid privatization of individual DMS assets, with particular focus on the three main yards: the Meeres-Technik-Werft (3,400 employees); the Neptun-Warnow-Werft (5,200 employees); and the Dieselmotorenwerk Rostock (1,100 employees).

This decision created divisions within the MWP Land government and sparked industrial action at the main shipyards and their supplier firms. The THA's rejection of the DMS plan prompted intervention from the Federal Minister of Transportation, Günther Krause (CDU), a politician whose political base and ambitions resided in MWP. Krause used the union protests as a platform for extolling the virtues of a state holding model for the industry. His proposed solution met with condemnation elsewhere in Bonn, however. A senior FDP official described his proposal as a direct challenge to the government's privatization policy, and sources close to the Chancellor described the model as a non-starter.[69]

The brouhaha complicated matters for the agency, which was negotiating a deal with Bremer Vulkan AG, a major western German shipbuilding conglomerate, to purchase the three core DMS enterprises at a final employment level of 5,300, a figure that had found acceptance within trade union circles.[70] State aid was a part of the offer, which necessitated European Commission approval. Although the THA was favorably predisposed, the offer elicited a great deal of skepticism in Bonn government circles, which saw another state holding in the making that could easily become a permanent drain on the public fisc and raise nettlesome questions in Brussels.

Amid the intensifying political and economic crisis in MWP, Bonn asked the Commission for a derogation from the 7th Shipbuilding Directive in order to facilitate the privatization of the eastern German shipyards. The government also requested that the THA be permitted to pay out state aid to DMS firms during the drafting of the derogation. Although the Commission concurred that special treatment was in order, it insisted on a detailed privatization concept from the government as a precondition, and warned Bonn that there had been too little in the way of capacity reduction, too much subsidization, and overly long time horizons for moving the firms to competitiveness. In March

---

the lack of movement by the THA, including occupying yards, blocking roads, and even interrupting a session of the state parliament.

[69] "FDP fordert Eingreifen Kohls," *Süddeutsche Zeitung*, March 3, 1992, 1; "Kohl mahnt Gomolka und Krause zur Zusammenarbeit," *Süddeutsche Zeitung*, March 5, 1992, 2.

[70] Of the 55,000 employed in the DDR's shipbuilding industry, 25,000 remained in March 1992. Estimates of the final size of the workforce, after privatization and rationalization, hovered around 10,000.

1992, the Commission informed Bonn that for the time being, no state aid could be paid to DMS firms.

Competition Commissioner Sir Leon Brittan refused publicly to rule out a state holding model, maintaining that the key issue was not the final form of ownership and management but the amount of state aid and the overall capacity of the sector after privatization. Nonetheless, the MWP economics minister indicated that his government had "received clear signals that neither the EC nor the federal government will approve this model."[71] A THA official remarked that "Bonn and Brussels were on the same wavelength" in expressing deep anxieties about the subsidy implications of a state holding model.[72]

The combination of federal and EC hostility to a state-holding solution led the THA in early March to abandon the package deal with Bremer Vulkan in favor of a modified version. Bremer Vulkan would take over Meeres-Technik-Werft and Dieselmotorenwerk Rostock, while a Norwegian firm, Kvaerner, would purchase Neptun-Warnow-Werft. THA president Birgit Breuel called it "one of the most difficult decisions taken by the Treuhandanstalt, because it had to be sensitive to political signals."[73]

Bonn supported the THA. Foreshadowing the reorientation of privatization policy toward the industrial cores of eastern Germany, Helmut Kohl remarked, "When I reflect on what we have done for the shipyards in the west and for coal, then we cannot allow an entire swath of territory to go to the dogs."[74] The Federal Minister of Economics defended the decision in parliament as having the best chance of approval in Brussels of all the available options, reminding the assembly that "the restructuring of the yards is possible only with Brussels' consent."[75] Both the unions and the SPD expressed dismay, and demanded that the original

[71] "Belegschaft halten Betriebe an der Ostsee besetzt, Krause attackiert CDU-geführte Regierung in Schwerin," *Süddeutsche Zeitung*, February 29–March 1, 1992, 1. Asked whether the EC was responsible for killing Krause's state holding, a Land official in the MWP economics ministry replied that once the Commission's thinking became known, "there was no more mention of Dr. Krause's proposal." This was a good outcome, he added. Interview with economics ministry official in Mecklenburg-West Pomerania, Schwerin, October 26, 1992.

[72] Interview with THA official, Berlin, October 28, 1992. A BMF official stated that the Commission let it be known that it would probably respond to a state holding solution for the yards with demands for much deeper capacity cuts, which would necessitate the closure of one or more of the smaller concerns held by the DMS. Interview with BMF official, Bonn, October 2, 1992.

[73] T. Enzweiler, "Machtwort aus Berlin," *Die Zeit*, March 13, 1992, 13. A THA source noted ruefully that Krause's intervention had cost the agency an additional DM1 billion, since the interested parties were now driving a harder bargain. "Die Großen rücken auf," *Der Spiegel*, March 23, 1992, 118.

[74] *Die Zeit*, March 13, 1992, 2.

[75] Deutscher Bundestag, *Plenarprotokolle*, 12. Wahlperiode, March 13, 1992, 6859.

Bremer Vulkan offer be reinstated if the government hoped to avert the deindustrialization of an entire region.

These developments provoked outrage from western German shipbuilders. Their advocates, including the industry association (Verband für Schiffbau und Meerestechnik), bitterly criticized the fact that in the absence of an EC regulation covering their eastern counterparts, Bonn had enacted a lower subsidy ceiling for the west than the maximum provided for under the 7th Directive, so as to create a spatial assistance gradient in favor of the east; as such, western German yards enjoyed the lowest subsidy rates in the EC, which threatened their competitiveness.[76] The western Länder's request for additional federal assistance for their shipyards was rebuffed by the federal economics minister.

Attention soon shifted back to Brussels, since the lack of an approved derogation to the existing Commission directive threatened to scuttle privatization talks with Bremer Vulkan and Kvaerner. In late May 1992, the Commission released a draft set of derogations for the eastern German industry. The Commission recommended that contracts concluded before July 1, 1990 be exempted from EC state aid guidelines until the end of 1993. During this period, the government would be allowed to subsidize the eastern German yards up to 36 percent of the value of the contracts, or four times the 1992 ceiling established under the 7th Directive. For all contracts concluded by the eastern German yards after July 1, 1990, existing EC guidelines would hold. The Commission linked the state aid derogation to a 40 percent reduction in capacity, leaving the sector with a final capacity of approximately 320,000 tons.

The Commission's recommendation met with protest from the MWP Land government officials, who believed the capacity cuts would push the industry below the point of economic viability, and in the process open up zero-sum conflicts among the various yards over capacity allocations.[77] Western German yards expressed deep reservations about the subsidy levels envisioned in the proposal. The Commission's capacity figures appeared to catch the federal government by surprise. Civil servants maintained that the capacity reductions pushed up against "the

---

[76] In 1991, the EC ceiling (and by extension the eastern German ceiling) was set at 13 percent, but western yards could receive a maximum of 9 percent; the figures for the first half of 1992 were 9 and 7.5 percent respectively.

[77] According to a civil servant in the Land economics ministry, the reaction to the Commission announcement demonstrated just how poorly Land politicians in eastern Germany understood EC integration. Many were guilty of "a misunderstanding of reality," thinking that they could ignore completely the 7th Directive on Shipbuilding. "They were shocked when the EC put its opinion forward, even though the EC did not act inappropriately." Interview with economics ministry official in Mecklenburg-West Pomerania, Schwerin, October 26, 1992.

border of the tolerable," and conceivably could force the closure of one of the smaller yards in MWP, which would be politically explosive.[78] Still, in their eyes the Commission had clearly taken politics into account in drafting its decision, particularly as regards the subsidy ceiling; as a BMWi official interviewed in late 1992 maintained, "If key industries go under in the east, we would have war over there; the Commission knows this, and doesn't want it."[79]

On June 18, 1992 the Council approved the Commission's recommendations largely intact. France, Italy, and Spain attempted to impose a capacity reduction of 57 percent,[80] but were dissuaded by the German delegation, which stressed the unique situation in eastern Germany and pledged that aid would neither benefit western German shipyards nor be used by the eastern yards to underbid their European competitors. Final Council approval of the package, over the objection of Denmark, occurred on July 20 in Lisbon. The Commission announced its intention to monitor the situation in MWP closely, to ensure that the capacity cuts were implemented and the subsidy guidelines observed.

BMWi minister Möllemann described the decision as a shot in the arm for the people of eastern Germany. Privately, a finance ministry official explained at the time, "Our minister was not at all upset with this outcome. Indeed, without Brussels, things could have turned out to be much more expensive." Under the prevailing fiscal climate in Germany, he added, "We have to use every brake possible [on public expenditure]."[81] The Bremer Vulkan and Kvaerner sales were finalized by October 1992, and many of the other DMS assets were successfully privatized.

Eastern German shipbuilding refused to slip into obscurity. In December 1995, responding to German press reports that Bremer Vulkan, in dire financial straits, had misappropriated subsidies intended for its eastern yards, the Commission formally asked the Bonn government for information on the matter. In mid-February, the Commission concluded that Bremer Vulkan had in fact diverted DM850 million in state aid earmarked for two eastern yards to its general coffers to combat a burgeoning liquidity crisis. The Commission instructed Bremer Vulkan to reimburse fully its public benefactors, and halted the payout of any further state aid to the firm until it had complied with the Commission's

---

[78] Interview with BMWi official, Bonn, July 27, 1992.
[79] Interview with BMWi official, Bonn, November 12, 1992.
[80] As a German industry official noted, "With unification Germany has become the largest national shipbuilder in the EC, and it is not surprising that its neighbors are worried about its potential influence." Interview with VSM official, Bonn, September 8, 1992.
[81] Interview with BMF official, Bonn, October 2, 1992.

order. As a Commission official stated, "It's not that we are being stubborn ... but we cannot have a different pair of spectacles for Germany."[82]

These revelations caused deep embarrassment in Bonn. It also generated a new regional crisis – with Bremer Vulkan teetering on the edge of bankruptcy, 23,000 jobs and key production sites in both western and eastern Germany hung in the balance. Unions, elected representatives, and the Land government in MWP responded swiftly with outraged demands for resolute action to save the two production sites. The Bonn government condemned the illegal actions of Bremer Vulkan and backed the position of the responsible THA successor, the BvS, which opposed the demands of the Land government and trade unions in MWP to renationalize the yards. A BvS spokesperson maintained that "we will find a private solution for every single production location."[83]

Bonn insisted that Brussels approve additional state aid, if necessary paid out through the BvS, to the two eastern German yards at risk. In February 1996, the Commission approved a request by the Land of MWP to issue up to DM600 million in loan guarantees to Bremer Vulkan for its struggling eastern shipyards to continue work on ships already in production, but attached strict conditions to prevent further irregularities. BMWi minister Rexrodt informed the Bundestag that he would seek Commission approval of DM500 million in fresh subsidies for Bremer Vulkan to support new contracts at the eastern yards. The minister's pledge came at a time when the federal government had already poured in DM6 billion to save the eastern yards,[84] and Commissioner Van Miert reacted coolly:

It will be difficult to replace the lost money with new money ... The EU Council of Ministers must approve such help unanimously. The fact [that] subsidies have been paid out already cannot be ignored. This will play a role in the discussions.[85]

In late March, the BvS announced that it would repurchase the eastern yards from Bremer Vulkan for a symbolic DM1 and reprivatize them under the auspices of a temporary holding company jointly financed by the THA-successor and the Land of MWP. The Commission, seeing the eastern yards as the victim of Bremer Vulkan's criminal practices, announced that it would seek special treatment for the yards in the

[82] "EU, Bonn to Continue Talks on Bremer Vulkan," *Reuters*, February 19, 1996.
[83] "BvS stellt Strafanzeige gegen alten Vulkan-Vorstand," *Frankfurter Allgemeine Zeitung*, February 27, 1996, 13.
[84] "Von der Vision vom Verbund mit dem Bremer Vulkan zur Illusion," *Frankfurter Allgemeine Zeitung*, February 23, 1996, 18.
[85] Svea Herbst-Bayliss, "Germany to Face Tough Battle on New Funds-EU," *Reuters*, March 7, 1996.

Council on the conditions that (a) Bonn provide a full account of the parent company's transgressions and a set of concrete proposals designed to prevent any misuse of public funds in the future; and (b) the federal government pledge to cut capacity at Bremen, the site of Bremer Vulkan, as the price of restructuring the eastern yards. The Council approved DM728 million in restructuring aid to the eastern German yards, along with subsidy payments to Spanish and Greek yards, in April 1997.

The messy aftermath of the shipyards' privatization exerted a subtle but strong constraint on Germany's approach to the reform of the shipbuilding aid regime, both at home and abroad. For example, Bonn supported in principle the Commission's efforts to secure stepwise reductions in the aid levels allowed under the 7th Shipbuilding Directive, but balked at setting firm, near-term deadlines for phasing out subsidies in light of the difficult situation in the eastern shipyards. This was in contrast to the Nordic countries and Britain, which consistently took a vocal, negative position on aid for shipbuilding. A BMWi official, commenting in 1992, stated, "We did not represent as hard a position as we did in past years."[86] Indeed, in May 1998, the Council of Ministers voted by qualified majority – over the objections of Germany, Portugal, and Sweden – to phase out operating subsidies to shipbuilders by the end of 2000, and to substitute regional aid for the defunct subsidy instrument.

And although Germany supported EU ratification of an OECD agreement in 1995 to begin phasing out shipbuilding subsidies after 1997, it was unable to prevent France from extracting a significant increase in aid to its shipbuilding industry as the price of approval. Much as Bonn disapproved of the concession, its defense of eastern German shipyards, combined with other pending state aid decisions, placed it in a compromised position. Thereafter, Germany showed little enthusiasm for the efforts of the Commission and other member governments (e.g. Finland and Sweden) to commit the EU to unilateral observation of the OECD agreement prior to ratification by key signatories like the United States.

Steel

In 1989, the GDR steel sector had a production capacity of 8.5 million tons, or approximately 18 percent of the West German figure. The sector was organized into three huge *Kombinate,* employing just under 67,000 workers, with 70 percent of production capacity concentrated in

---

[86] Interview with BMWi official, Bonn, July 27, 1992.

Brandenburg. Antiquated technology (the Siemens–Martins process), underinvestment, a lack of attention to integrated production facilities, and overemployment left the sector at a marked competitive disadvantage; productivity in GDR steel firms was 40 percent of the level achieved by West German concerns. Its export markets were almost exclusively in the former Eastern bloc.

For the West German steel industry, unification came at a time when its firms were reaping the benefits of the painful downsizing of the 1970s and early 1980s, which entailed significant reductions in production capacity and the loss of over 130,000 jobs.[87] Industry representatives were anything but complacent about their sector's medium-term prospects; EC competitors like the French and the British had closed the productivity gap in recent years, and the high costs of producing in the German *Standort* were beginning to take a toll on industry competitiveness.

As an EC-designated sensitive sector, steel was the subject of a comprehensive set of competition regulations administered by the European Commission. Historically, West Germany was an ardent proponent of reducing the amount of state aid paid out by member governments to their steel concerns. During the 1980s, Bonn provided various forms of assistance to steel companies, but at one-fifth to one-quarter the levels paid out by the French, British, and Italian governments.[88] At the same time, Bonn was always a reluctant participant in EC efforts to manage the sectoral adjustment crises of the 1970s and 1980s via protectionist measures, production cartels, and enforced capacity reductions.[89] The government encouraged private sector responses to the regionally concentrated steel crises in the Ruhr and the Saarland, and provided social flanking measures to cushion the social effects of firm closures and lay-offs.

During negotiations over the incorporation of the GDR, the Commission proposed that Bonn be permitted to grant aid to the steel industry providing it served the goal of improving competitiveness and did not increase overall production capacity. The EC's standing competition rules for the industry, which sanctioned aid for closure, research and development, and environmental protection only under certain conditions, and prohibited aid to cover operating losses and regional assistance, were applied to the territory of the former GDR, and a

---

[87] Josef Esser and Wolfgang Fach, "Crisis Management 'Made in Germany': The Steel Industry," in Peter Katzenstein, ed., *Industry and Politics in Germany* (Ithaca, Cornell University Press, 1989), 223.

[88] Esser and Fach, "Crisis Management 'Made in Germany'," 228.

[89] See Yves Mény and Vincent Wright, eds., *The Politics of Steel* (New York: Walter de Gruyter, 1987).

derogation of finite duration allowing certain types of regional and investment assistance was attached.[90]

The THA quickly dismantled the *Kombinate*, leaving fifteen major steel firms and an assortment of related enterprises to be privatized. An internal THA study in 1991 painted a generally optimistic picture of the industry's long-term prospects, assuming adequate capital investment and hard-headed rationalization measures were undertaken. The THA estimated that the number of jobs in the industry would fall by 75 percent over the next two years. As such, privatization promised to be especially difficult, since many of these firms employed several thousand workers and were located in areas where alternative manufacturing jobs were scarce.[91] Estimates of the total cost of privatizing the steel industry were pegged at DM8 billion.[92]

One of the THA's most difficult privatization cases was Eko Stahl (Eisenhüttenkombinat Ost). Located a stone's throw from the Polish border in Eisenhüttenstadt (Brandenburg), Eko Stahl was the GDR's flagship steel producer. The city, originally christened Stalinstadt, was built around the steel works in 1951, and few of its 52,000 inhabitants lacked ties with the enterprise, which in 1990 employed almost 20,000 workers. In short order, Eko became synonymous with deindustrialization.

The firm faced an uphill climb; in addition to the standard list of handicaps afflicting eastern German manufacturing concerns, Eko lacked an interim processing step – a warm continuous rolling-mill – to complement its six blast furnaces and cold continuous rolling-mill. In the eyes of Eko managers, the construction of a warm rolling-mill was the only route to long-term viability; unions, local leaders, and the Land government viewed it as a precondition for the retention of 3,000 to 3,500 jobs. In 1991, the firm, hard hit by the collapse of export markets in Eastern Europe and the Soviet Union, posted a DM100 million loss on earnings of DM1.14 billion.[93]

The THA adopted the Eko board's analysis, and turned away bids that did not include a new rolling-mill. By mid-1991, several major steel concerns had shown an interest in Eko; each saw in the firm the

[90] Commission of the European Communities, "The European Community and German Unification," 108.

[91] Treuhandanstalt, "Bericht über die Privatisierung der Stahlindustrie in den neuen Bundesländern," 1991; reprinted in Treuhandanstalt, *Dokumentation 1990–94*, vol. IV, 563–78 at 573.

[92] Haushaltsausschuß (Unterausschuß Treuhandanstalt), "Information über die Stahlindustrie in den neuen Bundesländern," March 12, 1992; reprinted in Treuhandanstalt, *Dokumentation 1990–94, Vol. 4*, 563–78 at 573.

[93] "Eisenhüttenstadt hofft auf Krupp und Möllemann," *Süddeutsche Zeitung*, January 31, 1992, 36.

potential to tap profitable markets in eastern Germany and, further down the road, in Eastern Europe. By November 1991, Krupp Stahl had emerged as the leading contender, offering to finance half of the necessary investment, with the THA, the Land, and the federal government covering the other half. Krupp pledged to retain 2,800 jobs at Eko.

In privatizing eastern German steel, the THA could not ignore Brussels, particularly when the subsidized creation of new capacity was in the offing as at Eko. Western German industry representatives warned Bonn against seeking EC approval for state aid that generated unviable, new capacity in eastern Germany, which could easily open the door to even more egregious subsidy practices elsewhere in the Community. As Ruprecht Vondran, a CDU member of parliament and president of the national steel association WS, stated on the floor of the Bundestag, "German policy must remain internationally credible."[94]

In 1992, the THA's negotiations with Krupp began to unravel. Thyssen, an unsuccessful competitor for the Eko bid, signaled that if the THA sale to Krupp contained what it viewed as an abnormally high level of subsidy, it would lodge a formal complaint with the Commission and, if necessary, the European Court of Justice. Clearly, the THA was concerned about the subsidy question too; around this time, the agency consulted a retired Commission official with experience in the steel sector, who concluded that the terms of its agreement with Krupp Stahl, reached at the end of February, stood little chance of securing Commission approval.[95]

In subsequent negotiations with the THA, Krupp balked at closing the deal; its reluctance sprang from unfavorable developments in the steel market and its own mounting liquidity problems. In October 1992, the European Commission expressed doubts about the terms negotiated between Krupp and the THA, since they entailed subsidies amounting to 65 percent of the net investment package, or 30 percentage points higher than the maximum allowed under normal guidelines applying in the region (see chapter 6, note 11). That same month, Krupp backed out of the negotiations, leaving the THA to search for another buyer. A new potential buyer surfaced quickly: the Italian concern Riva, which had already acquired two other eastern German steel firms.

As 1992 wore on, concerns about deindustrialization began to shape the government's rationale for privatizing eastern German steel. The SPD, CDU-Ost members of parliament, representatives of the metalworkers' union IG Metall, and the steel-producing Länder in the east called on the government to develop a comprehensive sectoral policy for

---

[94] Deutscher Bundestag, 12. Wahlperiode, 65. Sitzung, December 6, 1991, 5613.
[95] Interview with THA official, Berlin, October 28, 1992.

eastern German steel, but they were rebuffed by the Bonn coalition. Each privatization case would be dealt with individually by the THA. By the end of 1992, seven of the seventeen major steel producers held by the THA had been privatized, and three had been closed. Government ministers provided public guarantees that the Eko production location would be secured, in light of its regional significance.

As a result of recession and increased market access by Eastern European steel producers, steel prices dropped dramatically across the EC in 1992, plunging the sector into what would turn out to be its worst crisis in the postwar period. By early 1993, experts were predicting between 30 and 40 thousand lost jobs in Germany by year's end, three-quarters of these concentrated in the west. Politicians and industry officials based in the Ruhr area, pointing to growing labor unrest, called on Brussels and Bonn to continue the EC's prohibition on state aid to steel firms, and demanded that the inevitable job losses be cushioned by social plans. In mid-1993, the western steel Länder, the SPD, and IG Metall asked the EC to declare a "manifest crisis" under Article 58 of the European Coal and Steel Community Treaty, which would enable Brussels to organize a European-wide crisis cartel to allocate production quotas and assign capacity cuts among Europe's steel producers.

The government's response initially focused on maintaining subsidy discipline in Brussels and on encouraging private sector-led adjustment to the crisis. Any form of state aid to western German producers was ruled out *a priori*.[96] The German government showed no interest in organizing capacity cutbacks in the industry, arguing that such arrangements would invariably disadvantage the eastern German producers, many of which remained with the THA.

Initially, Brussels responded to the European-wide sectoral crisis by attempting to control the volume of Eastern European steel imports reaching member markets (see chapter 3), a move that Germany supported. In November 1992, the Commission announced it was drafting a plan to address the sector's problems, which entailed a 50 percent increase in the EC funds available to cushion job losses resulting from firm closures. The Commission, anxious to respond to the crisis but reluctant to relive the technical difficulties and political divisiveness of the EC-managed crisis cartel of the early 1980s, also began to explore the existing scope for voluntary capacity reductions, and set February

[96] When Klöckner Stahl, a Ruhr firm with a significant steel production site in Bremen, was forced to seek protection from its creditors at the end of 1992, the government expressed concern, but rejected demands from the city-state to guarantee the steel production site there. A BMWi spokesperson pointed out that the government's policy of preserving industrial cores applied only to eastern Germany.

1993 as the deadline for arriving at an acceptable, fair plan to reduce the sector's aggregate capacity by up to one-fifth.

In this context, the privatization of Eko Stahl AG became a matter of intense, Community-wide interest, since the German government was seeking approval of a DM2 billion assistance package for Riva that would result in an increase in overall production capacity. Strike action at Eko throughout 1993, much of it expressing frustration with the Commission's stance, underscored the political centrality of the case.

In April 1993, the Commission rejected the new restructuring plan put forward by the Eko management, arguing that the DM2 billion in state aid was too high and the proposed warm rolling-mill would only add to chronic excess capacity in Europe. The Commission's position received the support of key Council members, including the UK, the Netherlands, and Denmark. Bonn and the THA expressed dismay at the decision; the federal economics minister complained that the Commission had already approved large steel subsidies in Italy and Spain without substantial capacity cutbacks, and by that logic it was obligated to extend Eko similar treatment. At the same time, government ministers acknowledged privately the internal contradiction in their official position – flexibility toward Eko from their European partners combined with toughness on steel subsidization elsewhere in the EC. Western German steel producers argued that Bonn's ill-considered support for Eko had cost it the support of traditional allies like Britain, Denmark, and Luxembourg.[97]

As long as member governments were unable to resolve outstanding state aid cases in Germany, Italy, Spain, and Portugal, each of which required a unanimous vote in the Council, Europe's steel producers refused to agree to a voluntary program of production cuts. In December 1993, as part of a larger package of state aid cases, the Council approved a revised Eko plan, which contained a reduced subsidy figure (DM813 million), strict limits on production at Eko, and a commitment from Riva to close down one of its other eastern German mills to offset the new capacity at Eisenhüttenstadt. On aggregate, over ECU7 billion in approved German, Italian, and Spanish subsidies were linked to 5 million tons in capacity cuts. The THA and the eastern German lobby voiced enthusiastic support for the Council's decision, whereas the WS and western German producers decried Bonn's unwillingness to look after the interests of the German steel sector, which would be harmed by the scale of state aid approved for Italy and Spain.

On the eve of the Eko privatization in May 1994, disagreement

[97] "Vondran: Deutsche Stahlindustrie gefährdet," *Frankfurter Allgemeine Zeitung*, November 16, 1993, 17.

between Riva and IG Metall arose over the pace of workforce reductions post-privatization and the composition of the firm's supervisory board (*Aufsichtsrat*). Within two weeks, the sale to Riva had fallen through amidst a round of bitter recriminations. Meanwhile, the THA's bill for Eko kept rising; in the three-and-one-half years since unification, the agency had paid out DM2.6 billion to keep the firm afloat. The collapse of the Riva deal prompted solemn pledges by the THA and the federal government to guarantee Eko's future; according to an agency official, "We have to restructure and look to the long term because we have to turn some of these regions of eastern Germany into highly competitive industries. Otherwise there will be a desert. That is what Eko Stahl means."[98] Government officials ruled out a state-owned solution to Eko's problems, pointing out that Brussels would never approve of it anyway.

Meanwhile, the Council's December decision on steel aid reverberated negatively among Europe's steel producers, ultimately dooming Commission efforts to encourage voluntary cuts in production capacity. Commissioner Van Miert announced in May 1994 that the EU had scrapped its steel rescue plan. Efforts to rescue the rescue plan continued into the summer months, which involved, among other things, a Council decision to allow a looser interpretation of state aid rules to facilitate capacity cuts in Italy – a move that was opposed by the UK and Denmark, but not Germany. The Commission, hoping to restore its credibility with Britain, Denmark, and private steel producers, also announced in mid-1994 that it was launching probes into state aid to two German steelmakers, including Eko Stahl. In October, the Commission officially declared the EC rescue plan dead.

For Eko, the Riva debacle cast a shadow reaching all the way to Brussels. Immediately after the collapse of talks with the Italian firm, the Commission agreed to allow the THA to continue providing operating and restructuring assistance, but indicated that this could not go on indefinitely. The Commission also signaled that its approval of the DM813 million state aid package for Riva's purchase of Eko was rescinded, since the precondition for aid – the closure of a smaller Riva plant elsewhere in the new Länder – no longer held.

In July 1994, after two months of unsuccessful attempts to interest major German steel producers in taking over Eko, the THA announced that it had launched exploratory discussions with a Belgian firm, Cockerill Sambre SA. The negotiating parties were working against an October deadline set by the Commission, after which the payout of

[98] Judy Dempsey, "Hopes at Eko Stahl Dashed as Riva Pulls Out," *Financial Times*, May 16, 1994, 2.

assistance by the THA to Eko would have to cease. As talks moved toward closure in early October, Cockerill Sambre and the THA agreed on a package that included approximately DM200 million in state aid over and above the DM812 million contained in the failed Riva offer; Cockerill insisted on this in order to cover operating losses since December 1993 as well as its more ambitious investment proposal. The THA announced that it was considering having Eko purchase the smaller Riva plant in order to close it down, thereby preserving the capacity cuts desired by the Commission.

After numerous meetings with Commission officials, the German government announced its willingness to compromise on the question of state aid, and cleared a slimmed-down subsidy package with Cockerill (approximately DM100 million more than the Riva offer) that won the Commission's backing, on the condition that Germany cut a total of 361,000 tons of capacity in eastern Germany, or 41,000 more than the Riva package. British hints of a possible Council veto of the Eko package caused the German economics minister to send his UK counterpart a letter in which he threatened to veto state aid for a Belfast textile firm if the Eko aid package fell through on a British veto.[99] Ultimately, France held up final approval of the Eko package to win Council support for subsidies to its ailing shipyards, which were facing the prospect of an end to assistance at the end of the year. After placating the French and the British,[100] Bonn won Council approval of the Eko scheme on December 9, 1994. Cockerill Sambre assumed majority control of Eko on January 1, 1995.

Post-1994 privatization and the EU: mounting controversy

The increasingly softer German line on state aid was paralleled by an increasingly tougher Commission stance in Germany. In February 1996, the Commission announced that it was setting up a separate division to monitor aid practices in the eastern Länder, in light of the sheer number of state aid cases (upward of 2,000) and growing evidence of irregularities and even illegalities.[101] With specific references to

[99] "'Rexrodt droht in London für Eko'," *Frankfurter Allgemeine Zeitung*, November 7, 1994, 17.

[100] Bonn agreed to reduce the level of commercial loan guarantees contained in the Cockerill package.

[101] In May 1996, Commissioner Van Miert noted that Germany had the largest number of state aid cases before the Commission, with more than 1,000 originating in eastern Germany alone. Of the 527 state aid decisions taken by the Commission in 1994, 39.1 percent involved German firms. Frederik Dahl, "Van Miert Worried about State Aid Lies," *Reuters*, May 30, 1996; Amelia Torres, "EU Gets Tough on Aid to German Firms," *Reuters*, March 14, 1996.

Bremer Vulkan and the THA, Commissioner Van Miert stated that there was no longer reason to treat the region as a special case.[102] The German government responded to the Commission in May with a memorandum outlining why the region deserved continued special handling, particularly with regard to cases involving soon-to-be and recently privatized firms. The government stood by its claim that a continuation of special treatment was consistent with Article 92(2c), a position the Commission rejected.[103]

Brussels also demonstrated a greater willingness to question and even reject aid packages. DG-IV initiated legal inquiries into subsidies paid out in high-profile privatizations like the Leuna 2000 petrochemical refinery, owned by the French giant Elf Aquitaine, and Buna SOW Olefinverbund, a complex of chemical plants owned by Dow Chemical of the USA.

The most spectacular case involved Volkswagen. In mid-1996, the Commission required the multinational to forego DM240.7 million of a DM780 million regional aid package put together by the Land of Saxony, after determining that elements of VW's investment plans for car and engine plants at two locations in Saxony did not meet standing competition guidelines for the sector. When VW responded by suspending the planned investment projects indefinitely, the Commission threatened to reject the entire aid package and require VW to repay the Land and the federal government for assistance already received.

The Land of Saxony, arguing that over 20,000 jobs in a structurally weak region were now at risk, then filed a lawsuit with the European Court of Justice challenging the Commission's decision on the basis of Article 92 (2c), and at the same time granted VW DM631 million, or DM91 million more than the figure approved by the Commission. Defiant Land officials characterized the Commission as a "Euro-dictatorship" staffed by "oligarchs," and they received strong statements of support from other eastern Land prime ministers, prominent SPD politicians, and even the head of the BDI.[104]

---

[102] "Keine Sonderbehandlung für Ostbeihilfen," *Frankfurter Allgemeine Zeitung*, February 1, 1996, 11.

[103] A Commission official in DG-IV commented in 1992 that Bonn had sought a blanket derogation from the start, which would have enabled the Germans to maintain their liberal line while gaining a free hand in the eastern states, and thereby "avoid the schizophrenia." Interview with Commission (DG-IV) official, Brussels, December 1, 1992.

[104] Tom Heneghan, "Saxony Fights for VW Subsidy Despite EU Ban," *Reuters*, July 31, 1996. Not all eastern Länder desire a weaker Commission presence in competition matters. According to a Land official in Mecklenburg-West Pomerania, stringent competition regulations "serve us well," since they limit the ability of economically stronger Länder (like Saxony) to disadvantage economically weaker Länder (like

The Commission characterized the Land's actions as an unprecedented, flagrant violation of EU competition rules, and threatened a countersuit of its own against the federal government, the Land of Saxony, and VW. The Commission immediately froze all pending subsidy payments to VW, and Competition Commissioner Van Miert issued a pointed warning:

Germany has been European champion in state subsidies for a long time. Before the German government criticizes others, it should examine its own heart. We completely understand the difficult situation in eastern Germany, but they are also a part of the European single market now.[105]

Although Bonn supported Saxony's treaty rationale, it concurred with the Commission that the Land had breached EU regulations, and urged the Land to resolve the situation through dialogue, not confrontation. In extensive discussions with the Commission, Bonn argued on the basis of Article 92(2c), but signaled repeatedly a willingness to find a practical solution. The Commission insisted that existing competition rules governing regional and sectoral aid, *not* the disputed Article 92(2c), constituted the appropriate treaty basis for judging the case, and vowed to press on with a court challenge if the funds for VW were unfrozen or if Saxony made additional subsidy payments.[106] In a terse missive aimed at the German chancellor, Van Miert warned, "Saxony has called into question the basic concept of the EU . . . I see the fabled Project Europe under threat, the work of Monnet, Schumann, Adenauer, Delors, and Kohl."[107]

A few days later, Bonn filed a legal challenge to the Commission's original decision against VW and Saxony, in the hopes of resolving the larger dispute over Article 92's "Germany clause." A compromise solution to the VW crisis eventually took shape in November 1997, according to which the firm repaid Saxony the disputed DM91 million, with the German government providing guarantees to Brussels that it would monitor the transaction and ensure that the funds did not find their way back to the auto manufacturer. In return, VW received a favorable decision from the Commission on a DM100 million subsidy package for investment plans in the Land of Hessen.

MWP) through their subsidy programs. Interview with economics ministry official in MWP, Schwerin, October 26, 1992.

[105] Michael Shields, "EU Ups Pressure in Subsidies Row with German State," *Reuters*, August 17, 1996.

[106] The Commission noted that Article 92 (2c) had been used only twice since unification; both cases involved aid to firms in those regions – Berlin and the former zonal border areas – to which the Article had applied prior to unification.

[107] Ruth Walker, "A Test of EU Unity Ends in Suspended Subsidy for VW," *Reuters*, September 5, 1996.

The VW case is a sizable piece of a much larger mosaic. Reform proposals put forward by the Commission in 1997, which entailed more stringent EU controls over large subsidy cases coupled with delegation of responsibility for monitoring small-scale state aid practices to the national governments, met with opposition from the usual suspects in the Council of Ministers. Although the Commission eventually prevailed, Germany adopted a much more conflicted position than in the past. Bonn affirmed the value of a stringent regulatory framework, but expressed deep reservations about any enhancement of the Commission's competition powers that might impair the ability of German authorities to deal with economic problems in the former GDR. Bonn's new-found ambivalence can be traced directly to the exigencies of unification.

Conclusions

The THA's record represents an impressive act of political will. In just four short years, the agency privatized all but a handful of the 13,687 firms under its control. It secured investment commitments of almost DM200 billion, along with promises to retain or create 1.5 million jobs.[108] The Bonn government could point to numerous success stories in the former GDR, including state-of-the-art automobile plants in Thuringia and Saxony.

The price of rapid privatization was high, though. By the end of 1994, estimates of the THA's final debts had reached DM275 billion – a far, far cry from the tidy profit forecast in 1990. Key industrial core regions in the east had been preserved, but at considerable cost to the taxpayer; each of the 7,000 jobs saved in the shipbuilding industry in Mecklenburg-West Pomerania carried a price tag of DM700,000.[109] And after unification, Germany has become the largest aggregate subsidizer of industry in the EC/EU bar none. Its per capita assistance rates to the eastern Länder are the highest of any region in the Union.[110]

Unification did not lead to a formal shift in Bonn's position on state aid in Brussels. German officials insisted that their departures from social market orthodoxy were necessitated by unique but transitory conditions, and would have no long-term effects on competition policy either at the national or supranational level. Despite the official policy of

---

[108] Birgit Breul, "Treuhandanstalt: Bilanz und Perspektiven," *Aus Politik und Zeitgeschichte* 43–44 (October 28, 1994), 14–20 at 18.

[109] Judy Dempsey, "The End of the Sales," *Financial Times*, December 30, 1994, 12.

[110] Emma Tucker, "Commissioner Promises Crackdown on State Aid," *Financial Times*, January 23, 1997, 2; Emma Tucker, "Commissioner Urges Tighter State Aid Rules," *Financial Times*, April 17, 1997, 3.

continuity, however, German officials in practice adopted a visibly softer line in Brussels in order to secure favorable outcomes for the eastern region; one civil servant in Bonn characterized the change as "a break with the past ... a discontinuity."[111]

The end result has been serious damage to Germany's credibility; Commission officials regularly mention the Federal Republic in the same breath as Italy. In the process, the EU's state aid regime has weakened too. A Commission official, who in 1992 predicted that Germany would be "back in our camp" as soon as the situation eased in the east, offered this sober reappraisal a little over two years later:

The Germans believed that unification would generate a few skeletons in the closet where competition policy was concerned, but that they would remain in the closet ... Well, I'm here to tell you that the skeletons are spreading ... Bonn first has to restore discipline on its home front before it can turn to Europe and demand a rigorous approach from the Commission and its member governments.[112]

Central to Bonn's unofficial slide into a policy of "state interventionism with a bad conscience"[113] were the eastern Länder, which utilized their legislative prerogatives and institutionalized access to the THA to push Bonn into actions that diverged increasingly from its competition rhetoric. A similar Land-led dynamic of policy change emerges in two other regulative areas: the structural funds and the Common Agricultural Policy.

[111] Interview with BMWi official, Bonn, May 28, 1995.
[112] Interview with Commission (DG-IV) official, Brussels, March 3, 1995.
[113] Lehmbruch, "Die deutsche Vereinigung," 597.

6   Change in structural funds and the CAP

After 1990, German objectives and actions changed discernibly and officially in two EC/EU policy areas, the structural funds and the Common Agricultural Policy (CAP). New government positions in Brussels, which began with adjustments to federal policies, came about in response to the profoundly novel regional and agricultural challenges thrown up by unification and its aftermath. In each case, the eastern Land governments were at the forefront of pressure for changes in federal policy, and were able to utilize the access and information granted them under formal policymaking arrangements at the national and supranational levels to good effect.

Structural funds

Both the European Community and its member governments administer programs designed to achieve a spatially balanced pattern of economic development.[1] Typically, these programs designate assisted areas within which applicants are eligible for capital grants, soft loans, accelerated depreciation allowances, and tax concessions for business, as well as job training for workers and infrastructure grants to municipalities. There existed three main programs at the European level prior to Maastricht, which together constituted the EC structural funds: the European Regional Development Fund (ERDF), the European Social Fund (ESF), and the Guidance Section of the European Agricultural Guidance and Guarantee Fund (EAGGF).

In West Germany, federal regional policy targeted two types of problem region: underdeveloped rural areas, and areas vulnerable to or suffering from the decline of a dominant industry. Administratively, the program was conducted as a "joint task," or *Gemeinschaftsaufgabe* (GA), in which formal negotiations among Land and federal representatives

---

[1] See Harvey Armstrong, "The Role and Evaluation of European Community Regional Policy," in Barry Jones and Michael Keating, eds., *The European Union and the Regions* (Oxford: Clarendon Press, 1995), 23–64.

produced annual framework plans that set funding levels, designated assisted areas across the country, and established assistance rates.[2] The Länder were responsible for program implementation and administration. The designation of assisted areas followed from clearly defined decision rules and multiple statistical indicators. Certain regions were eligible *a priori* for assistance – that is, they were not required to qualify via the indicators. Included in this special category, but assisted out of their own separate programs, were the zonal border areas (*Zonenrandgebiete*), a twenty-five-mile-wide strip along the borders with Czechoslovakia and the GDR, and West Berlin. These regions, disadvantaged by the postwar division of Germany, enjoyed the highest assistance rates.

Prior to 1979, Germany, like other member states, received its EC structural fund allocations in the form of a fixed national quota negotiated in the Council of Ministers. Between 1975 and 1979, Germany garnered 8.4 percent of European Regional Development Fund allocations, and posted the second lowest per capita share of regional fund expenditure for its assisted areas: ECU8.6 per capita, as compared to the Community average of 27.2.[3] These modest sums colored the position adopted by the Germans in Brussels. Germany blocked a Commission initiative in the early 1970s to establish a much larger regional fund, and thereafter remained wary of proposals to increase spending on the structural funds.[4] That said, Bonn consistently endorsed efforts to improve the effectiveness of grants and to concentrate resources on the neediest regions in the Community.

Reform of the structural funds commenced in 1979, and gained momentum throughout the 1980s as concern about the regional impact of a barrier-free internal market grew.[5] The structural funds budget expanded, approaching one-quarter of total EC annual outlays, and programs were oriented to Community-wide objectives and criteria set largely by the Commission, which also gained the capacity to interact directly with regional and subregional actors, on occasion bypassing the national governments. To improve the targeting of assistance, the Commission in 1988 identified five priorities:

---

[2] A comprehensive overview of the GA can be found in Dieter Ewringmann *et al.*, *Die Gemeinschaftsaufgabe "Verbesserung der regionalen Wirtschaftsstruktur" unter veränderten Rahmenbedingungen* (Berlin: Ducker and Humbolt, 1986), and Fritz Scharpf *et al.*, *Politikverflechtung* (Kronberg/Ts.: Scriptor Verlag GmbH, 1976).

[3] Jeffrey Anderson, "Skeptical Reflections on a 'Europe of Regions': Britain, Germany, and the European Regional Development Fund," *Journal of Public Policy* 10 (October–December 1990), 417–47 at 426.

[4] See Bulmer and Paterson, *The Federal Republic of Germany and the European Community*, 202–22.

[5] See Marks, "Structural Policy in the European Community."

Objective 1: Promoting the development and structural adjust-
              ment of lagging regions, defined as those in which per
              capita GDP is 75 percent or less of the Community
              average. These regions were to receive up to 80
              percent of structural fund allocations.
Objective 2: Converting regions seriously affected by industrial
              decline.[6]
Objective 3: Combating long-term unemployment.
Objective 4: Facilitating the occupational integration of young
              people.
Objective 5a: Promoting the adaptation of agricultural production.
Objective 5b: Promoting the development of rural areas.[7]

The Commission was empowered to draw up its own list of assisted
areas, which did not overlap perfectly with those identified in national
regional programs. For the period 1989–93, the Objective 1 regions
encompassed 21 percent of the EC population, and were situated on the
western and southern periphery of the Community.[8] Objective 2 and
Objective 5b regions contained 16 and 5 percent of the EC's population
respectively.

Until unification, the Federal Republic continued to receive modest
amounts from the structural funds. Between 1979 and 1989, Germany's
share of ERDF commitments fell from 6.2 percent to 3.9 percent.[9] As
the wealthiest Community member, it had no Objective 1 regions, and a
scattering of Objective 2 and 5b regions in all but one of the eleven
Länder. Moreover, in the 1980s, Germany became the target of
sustained efforts by the Commission's DG-IV to limit the area coverage
of federal and state regional programs as well as their assistance rates.
The pressures of EC competition policy produced results; in 1988,
Bonn agreed to reduce the percentage of the population covered by

---

[6] These regions are designated according to three criteria: (1) average unemployment
rates above the Community average over the last three years; (2) a percentage of the
regional workforce employed in manufacturing above the Community average since
1975; and (3) a decline in the number of manufacturing jobs, compared with a
benchmark of 1975. Commission of the European Communities, *Der EFRE 1989*
(Luxembourg: Office for Official Publications of the European Communities, 1991), 7.

[7] In 1995, in the wake of the accession of Austria, Finland, and Sweden, the Union
created a new category of assisted area: Objective 6 regions, which targeted thinly
populated regions in the Arctic Circle.

[8] Commission of the European Communities, *The Regions in the 1990s* (Luxembourg:
Office for Official Publications of the European Communities, 1991), 14.

[9] Commission of the European Communities, *XXIIIrd General Report on the Activities of
the European Communities 1989* (Luxembourg: Office for Official Publications of the
European Communities, 1990), 216.

federal and state assisted areas from 45 percent to 39 percent; a further reduction to a figure below 30 percent was scheduled for 1991.

Bonn officials bridled at the Commission's interventions, arguing that DG-IV's actions interfered with their constitutional obligation under Article 72 of the Basic Law to secure an equality of living standards within Germany. They also criticized the EC competition authorities for subverting the fragile compromises reached in the GA between rural and industrial Länder. Nevertheless, federal officials used the Commission as a welcome scapegoat in their attempts to push expenditure cuts and reductions in area coverage through the GA in response to tightening federal budget constraints in the 1980s.[10]

Structural funds and the unification settlement, 1989–90

Bonn incorporated the eastern Länder into the GA with minor procedural modifications. The federal government sought to check distributional conflicts among the Länder by keeping many potentially divisive issues off the agenda. For example, Bonn declared the ex-GDR in its entirety an assisted area *sui generis* for a period of five years, and provided the region with additional federal funds over and above those already earmarked for the western Länder. Both actions were intended to avert a zero-sum battle between east and west over assisted areas and budget allocations.

The federal government, however, was unable to evade difficult distributional choices. Federal and state representatives agreed to confer the highest assistance rates in the country on the eastern Länder.[11] Furthermore, assistance criteria were relaxed for certain categories of

---

[10] See Jeffrey Anderson, *The Territorial Imperative: Pluralism, Corporatism, and Economic Crisis* (New York: Cambridge University Press, 1992), ch. 5.

[11] In the east, the upper limit for GA grants to support new investment was set at 23 percent of the total costs of the project; the corresponding figures for expansion of existing premises and for restructuring were 20 percent and 15 percent respectively. These could be combined with an automatic 12 percent investment grant (*Investitions-zulage*) to generate maximum assistance rates of 35 percent, 32 percent, and 27 percent of total costs, depending on the type of project. Comparable GA limits in the western Länder were set at 18 percent (new investment), 15 percent (expansion), and 10 percent (restructuring), and the options for combining these with other forms of aid were severely restricted, rendering these assistance ceilings as maxima for all intents and purposes. These ceilings required Commission approval; according to one source in DG-IV, German officials apparently believed that the 35 percent figure for eastern Germany was sufficiently high to generate an efficacious subsidy gap between east and west, and proposed this to the Commission. "If the negotiations had taken place a year later, in a changed economic context, the German demand would have been higher," he surmised. Interview with Commission (DG-IV) official, Brussels, December 1, 1992.

projects in the new Länder to improve take-up and to acknowledge the markedly different investment circumstances prevailing in the region.

At the European level, the structural funds proved to be one of the more contentious items to surface in discussions between Bonn and Brussels. Community members expressed grave reservations about the continuation of regional assistance programs for West Berlin and the zonal border areas, arguing that their claims to special status based on Article 92(2c) had crumbled along with the wall. With unification increasingly likely, Chancellor Kohl made an offer at the Dublin summit in April 1990 to waive structural fund assistance for the ex-GDR in exchange for EC permission to restructure the region on the basis of domestic initiatives consistent with Community law. In this manner, Bonn hoped to calm southern EC members, who saw the new Länder as potential competitors for assistance, and to minimize supranational influence on the regional economic dimension of unification. The Commission never gave serious consideration to this offer. In August 1990, it allocated ECU3 billion in regional assistance to the five new Länder over the period 1991–93, and listed the region as an assisted area *sui generis* in view of the absence of reliable economic data.[12] The Commission announced that it would withhold final approval of the assistance package until Bonn committed to a timetable for phasing out aid to West Berlin and the zonal border areas, and carried out a reduction in GA assisted-area coverage from 39 to 27 percent of the western German population by the end of 1993.

EC pressure dovetailed with new domestic conflicts to render continued federal support for Berlin and the zonal border areas untenable. Bonn officials were well aware that the absence of intense distributional conflicts between east and west was due in large part to the willingness of political leaders in the old Länder to acknowledge the unique, daunting situation in the former GDR.[13] Federal officials calculated that this goodwill would evaporate if Bonn were to ask the Commission to permit a continuation of the Berlin and zonal border area programs, since the Commission would almost certainly require massive cuts in assisted area coverage within the old Länder (upward of 40 percent, by

---

[12] According to a DG-XVI official interviewed in 1992, since there was no way to schedule the new Länder accurately in 1990–91, a decision was made to allocate an amount equal to the average per capita receipts of the Community's Objective 1, 2, and 5b regions. The Commission arrived at the total of ECU3 billion, or approximately DM6 billion. Interview with Commission (DG-XVI) official, Brussels, December 2, 1992.

[13] "We accepted these changes [to the GA] with clenched teeth," said an official from North Rhine-Westphalia. Interview with State Chancellery official in North Rhine-Westphalia, Düsseldorf, June 10, 1992.

some estimates) as compensation. In May 1990, the federal and state governments agreed to a phase-out of the zonal border area and Berlin programs. Bowing to intense pressure from supporters of these regions, Bonn set a time horizon of seven years. At the Commission's insistence, the government moved the phase-out deadline forward to the end of 1994.

Structural funds after unification, 1990–95

German regional policy confronted growing pressures to adjust even after formal unification in October 1990. Elected governments in the eastern Länder consistently characterized their GA allotments as inadequate, and demanded more cash to galvanize the restructuring of their regional economies. Furthermore, they asked Bonn to loosen GA eligibility restrictions on infrastructure investment, specifically to allow their local authorities to finance a broader array of projects (e.g. sewerage schemes and trunk road construction).[14] The latter demand came in response to a qualitatively different set of spatial problems in the east; four decades of socialist rule had left the country's basic infrastructure and environment in a state of total disrepair.

Annual GA expenditure limits rose from just under DM1.2 billion in 1990 to a peak of DM15.3 billion in 1994, and dropped down to a still considerable DM7.5 billion in 1997 (see figure 6.1).[15] The bulk of the federal spending increases were reserved for the new Länder; between 1991 and 1994, the east's share of total federal GA expenditure limits rose from 73 percent to 95 percent; by 1997, the region's share had fallen back to just under 89.2 percent. The BMWi refused steadfastly to amend GA provisions pertaining to infrastructure, arguing that the massive budget transfers to the east under the aegis of environmental and transportation policies would close this deficit in a few years. In January 1991, Bonn pushed through the required reduction in GA assisted area coverage in the western Länder, and received Commission approval of GA assistance for eastern and western Germany until the end of 1993.

The new Länder, still lacking administrative capacity, had to rely on Bonn to a degree unknown in the west. The eastern Länder viewed the GA not simply as a means of diversifying their manufacturing bases, but

[14] Historically, infrastructure projects were eligible only if they bore a direct relationship to capital investment; these included the building of access roads and the preparation of development sites.
[15] Federal expenditure is actually half the aggregate figures given, since the Länder are required to match federal GA funds with their own contributions.

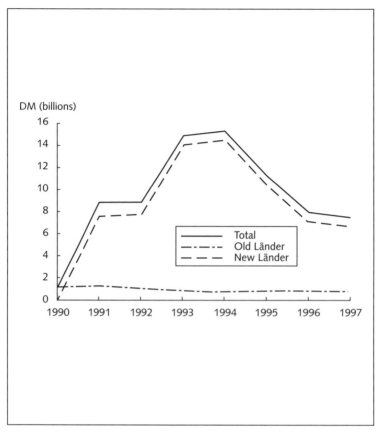

Figure 6.1.   GA expenditure limits, 1990–97
(*Source:* GA Annual Framework Plans, 1990–97).

as a way to solidify their pre-unification industrial cores, and moved quickly to establish formal relations with the THA (see chapter 5). With encouragement from the federal economics ministry, the new Länder began to establish spatial priorities in 1992 to guide the allocation of regional assistance. Creating systems of spatial triage was no easy task for these Land governments, since there were obvious political risks associated with relegating certain subregions to lower priority categories, especially in light of the fact that subregional and local actors in the former GDR, although initially slow to mobilize, soon formed local development coalitions to attract industry and jobs and to put pressure on public authorities at the state and federal levels.

The period 1991–93 represented the first phase of eastern German inclusion in the EC structural funds. A Community Support Framework (CSF) for the eastern region was drafted in record time and issued in March 1991, and a separate monitoring committee, bringing together EC, federal, state, and local officials, was formed to implement it. Community resources were allocated among the new Länder and East Berlin on the basis of population size. Experts from DG-XVI, the directorate-general responsible for regional affairs, held training seminars in the east to introduce Land personnel to the fine art of running the various programs funded by the EC.

Beneath these formal linkages between the supranational, national, and regional levels, however, the Commission maintained at best a rudimentary presence in the east during this initial period. In fact, the Commission declined to construct the kind of supranational-subnational partnerships heralded by the reforms of the late 1980s, largely because the eastern Länder were not equipped administratively to handle such arrangements.

The Commission was absent in other ways too. In negotiations with Brussels over the terms of acceptance for the 3 billion ECU, the BMWi insisted that the structural funds be subject to national (GA) and not Community assistance criteria. The ministry's objective was first and foremost to maintain the direct link between project assistance and the economic goals of building and diversifying the regional economy. Officials believed that the GA criteria preserved this link, whereas the EC criteria permitted assistance for basic infrastructure that lacked any immediate connection to capital investment or the creation of manufacturing jobs. Second, by subordinating EC funds to the national policy regime, Bonn officials hoped to create a unitary administrative process, which was viewed as absolutely essential in light of the infant bureaucracy in the new Länder.

The new Länder chafed under this regulation; many expressed a desire to co-finance sewerage schemes and trunk roads, in this case with EC money, and they tried to use the Brussels criteria as a lever to pry open the more restrictive GA guidelines. They received little support from the Commission, which basically supported Bonn's line. DG-XVI officials acknowledged that basic infrastructure projects were eligible in Objective 1 regions across the Community, and that this kind of assistance played an important role in the development of Spain, Portugal, and Greece. They maintained, however, that the needs and requirements of eastern Germany were simply not on the same scale as those in the poorer Community members.[16]

---

[16] Interview with Commission (DG-XVI) official, Brussels, December 2, 1992.

The results of EC regional aid for the period 1991–93 were impressive. The structural funds contributed to the financing of over 5,500 projects with a combined projected investment volume of just under DM30 billion; Commission estimates placed the number of created and/or preserved jobs at approximately 190,000.[17]

The ex-GDR's place in the structural funds was far from settled, however. In the Treaty on European Union and attached protocols, the signatories pledged to create a new cohesion fund, and to increase expenditure levels for the three original funds over the course of the Community's next five-year budget plan. The Commission's Delors II budget proposal, released in early 1992, gave fiscal expression to these commitments. Delors II proposed to double structural assistance (defined as structural plus cohesion funds) for Spain, Portugal, Greece, and Ireland over the period 1994–97. The Commission recommended that eastern Germany be classified as an Objective 1 region *sui generis*, and suggested a two-thirds increase in its structural fund allotment.[18]

These proposals elicited contradictory responses within Germany. The eastern Länder complained bitterly that their region had been underfunded in relation to the scale of its misery back in 1991, and that the gap would widen under Delors II. Bonn, joined by other wealthy member governments, voiced strong dissatisfaction as well, but focused instead on what it viewed as an unacceptable increase in the EC budget ceiling, from 1.2 to 1.37 percent of Community GDP, to pay for Maastricht's cohesion policy.

Soon after the publication of the Commission's original package, the new Länder launched a campaign for Objective 1 status and a substantial increase in funding. Regional advocates sought to build an objective case, employing comparative data on unemployment rates, infrastructure, and per capita GDP. The eastern Land governments pointed to data collected by the BMWi that placed the region at 36.8 percent of average Community per capita GDP – the lowest in the EC, and well below the Objective 1 eligibility threshold of 75 percent.

Eastern representatives put forward two especially controversial demands. First, they asked the Commission to incorporate current

---

[17] Kommission der Europäischen Gemeinschaften (Generaldirektion Regionalpolitik), "Deutschland: Gemeinschaftliches Förderkonzept für die Entwicklung und die strukturelle Anpassung der Regionen mit Entwicklungsrückstand (Ziel 1), 1994–99," 1994, 20.

[18] The Commission's figure for the new Länder was in line with its proposed increases for the Objective 1 regions. About two-thirds of the increase for the "poor four" (Spain, Portugal, Greece, Ireland) was to come via the three main structural funds, with the other third contributed by the new cohesion fund. No part of Germany was (or is) eligible for cohesion fund assistance.

statistics on eastern German per capita GDP into the EC data base used to determine Objective 1 status. This seemingly innocuous proposal contained political dynamite. According to unpublished data collected by the Bonn economics ministry, the inclusion of the ex-GDR data would have lowered average per capita GDP in the Community by a little over three percentage points in 1991, which in turn would have left a handful of existing Objective 1 regions above the program's threshold. This demand evoked consternation not only in Brussels but also in Bonn, since to lend it support would have required German officials to backtrack on their pledge not to advance eastern German interests at the expense of poorer Community members.

The new Länder pressed for a statistical (as opposed to a political) classification in order to make it more difficult for the Commission and the federal government to ignore their second demand – a two-step increase in funding: (1) parity with other Objective 1 regions, measured in terms of ECU per capita;[19] and then (2) a proportional increase in line with other Objective 1 regions. The eastern lobby argued for a two- to threefold increase in its structural fund allotment, placing it on a par with Objective 1 regions in the Mediterranean periphery, such as Greece or Portugal.

For the new Länder, the task in Brussels was to bring the Commission over to their side while dispelling worries in other Objective 1 regions. In a series of mini-summits with Delors and representatives from DG-XVI during 1992, the leaders of the new Länder pressed their case. Early on, the Commission came round to the notion that the new Länder deserved Objective 1 status, but balked at their demands for a data-derived classification and a larger funding allotment. East Berlin's future designation also proved to be an especially thorny issue. The eastern Germans argued that the entire ex-GDR, including the former capital, should be treated as an integrated whole by the Community, whereas the Commission was reluctant to grant eligibility to part of a city, and thereby depart from standard classification criteria.

Representatives from other Objective 1 regions reacted defensively to the demands of the eastern Länder, principally by stressing a glaring omission in their case: the size and wealth of the German national economy bestowed upon the eastern region a considerably higher devel- opment potential in the long run than those of the Greek or Portuguese

---

[19] The 1991–93 structural fund package for the eastern Länder worked out to ECU65 per capita, as compared to the EC average for Objective 1 regions of ECU127 per capita, or Portugal's take (ECU165 per capita) or Ireland's (ECU252 per capita). Europäisches Parlament, "Arbeitsdokument: Die Sozio-Ökonomische Lage in den 5 neuen Bundesländern und die Maßnahmen der Kommission," April 1993; reprinted in Treuhandanstalt, *Dokumentation 1990–94*, vol. IX, 1058–82 at 1069.

economies. In response, the eastern Länder cultivated direct contacts with these representatives via the regional consulate network in Brussels. Their strategy was basically to apprise foreign officials of the desperate situation in many parts of the new Germany, and to assure them that their demands were for fair treatment and nothing more.

The new Länder also had to contend with possible opposition from the old Länder, which feared that, in exchange for a favorable settlement of the eastern German question, the Commission might demand further cuts in their share of GA and EC assistance. Eastern representatives were in no position to provide any guarantees, but, toward the latter part of 1992, were able to convince their western compatriots that their demands were being made in good faith and on the basis of objective data.

The package of demands pushed by the eastern Länder placed federal officials on the horns of a complex dilemma. First, Objective 1 designation, especially if granted on the basis of hard data, would put the German government in the position of challenging the structural fund entitlements of the poorer members. As for the funding equation, Bonn had no desire to sanction what it viewed as an irresponsible expansion of the EC budget at a time when German public support for a more perfect European union was disintegrating, along with its willingness to foot the bill. The principal cleavage ran between the Foreign Ministry and the BMWi's Europe Division (*E-Abteilung*) on the one hand, which favored data inclusion and maximum funding levels, and the BMWi's Economic Policy Division (*Abteilung I*) on the other.[20]

Support for the eastern Länder also threatened to undermine one of Bonn's overarching objectives *vis-à-vis* the structural funds. According to a BMWi official,

the structural funds cannot be expanded indefinitely ... We cannot double the funds every five years. Instead, more attention has to be paid to the efficacy of policy and to the movement of assisted regions out of assisted area status as their economies improve.[21]

However, the government could ill afford to ignore the demands of the eastern Länder. Thus, Bonn appeared in Brussels not only in its traditional garb as Community paymaster, but also in a new costume –

---

[20] Officials in the Economic Policy Division feared that the Commission would insist on domestic symmetry, i.e. the inclusion of eastern Germany in the national (GA) data base, resulting in the wholesale ejection of western assisted areas from federal regional policy. According to a BMWi official, a unitary data base in Brussels would have pushed the western Länder to the brink of opposition to further special treatment for the new Länder. Interview with BMWi official, Bonn, July 22, 1992.

[21] Interview with BMWi official, Bonn, March 16, 1992.

that of supplicant. This placed German officials in an unaccustomed and indeed uncomfortable position.[22]

Circumstances at this time threatened to play into the Commission's hands. Jacques Delors missed few opportunities to remind Bonn and the rest of the EC that if Germany wanted more money for its eastern region, it would have to agree to an increase in the Community's budgetary ceiling. The federal government resisted what it saw as Commission blackmail by recommending internal shifts in Delors II spending priorities to free up the necessary resources for the eastern Länder. With these proposals, Bonn also hoped to allay the fears of poorer member governments, who saw their slices of cohesion pie shrinking if Bonn pushed for equal treatment of the eastern provinces at no extra cost.

One horn of Bonn's dilemma broke off with the Danish rejection of the Maastricht Treaty in June 1992, which threw the Commission and its ambitious vision for Europe on the defensive and killed the center-piece of the original Delors II package – the 1.37 percent increase in the budgetary ceiling. Thereafter, Bonn was free to support the demands of the eastern Länder without fear of automatically endangering its EC budgetary priorities. Indeed, within two months, a senior BMWi official (Europe Division) publicly demanded a funding level comparable to that received by other Objective 1 regions, including Portugal and Greece.[23] Figures circulating within the Commission showed not only that the eastern Länder constituted the poorest region in the entire Community, but that Germany now had the largest regional disparity between rich (Hamburg) and poor (new Länder) of any member.[24]

At the Lisbon summit in June 1992, the heads of government agreed that the five new Länder and East Berlin would be classified as an Objective 1 region beginning in 1994. The decision looked to extend eastern Germany's special status, since the Commission, backed by the poorer EC members, argued strenuously against the inclusion of the eastern German data on technical grounds, and Bonn declined to press the issue for fear of touching off a redistribution crisis within the Community. According to sources within the Chancellery, the German

---

[22] A senior Foreign Ministry official, commenting in late 1992, stated with considerable exasperation, "It is as if we were standing before the Wailing Wall ... We sound like the Spaniards." Interview with Foreign Ministry official, Bonn, December 20, 1992.

[23] A BMWi official described this demand as a poker game: the government was aware that the new Länder were not entitled to the same level of assistance as Portugal, but was aiming for something around Spain's level of assistance. Interview with BMWi official, Bonn, July 22, 1992.

[24] Commission of the European Communities, *Competitiveness and Cohesion: Trends in the Regions* (Luxembourg: Office for Official Publications of the European Communities, 1994), 35.

government declined to air its long-standing concerns about the efficiency and efficacy of the new cohesion fund for fear of creating an unsympathetic audience in the Council for the demands of the new Länder.[25]

At the Edinburgh summit in December, the Community resolved most of the thorny budgetary issues raised by Delors II (see chapter 2). Within the larger settlement, the budgetary parameters for the structural funds were also discussed. Bargaining snagged on a last minute reversal in Bonn's negotiating position. Adopting the line supported by the Foreign Ministry and the Europe Division of the economics ministry, the German delegation pushed for the inclusion of eastern Germany in the Commission's data base. Officials maintained that increased assistance for the east was entirely consistent with the fund's long-standing goal of targeting the neediest regions in the EC, a fact that called for an objective decision-making approach. In private, they expressed hopes that inclusion of the data would bolster Germany's claims to the maximum possible allotment for the new Objective 1 region. Both the Commission and Council accepted Bonn's request in principle, but insisted that any region receiving Objective 1 status prior to the inclusion of the data be so designated for the period 1994–99.[26] The final agreement doubled the assistance levels reserved for the poorer member governments.[27] Overall cohesion expenditure (structural funds plus cohesion fund) would rise by ECU165.6 billion (in 1992 prices) between 1994 and 1999. Eastern Germany was to receive an amount somewhere in the range of DM20 to 28 billion.

During the next several months, Bonn adhered to the logic of its new position, and demanded a funding allotment for the eastern Länder on a par with Portugal or Greece. This approach created much ill will within the Council, particularly among the Southern members. In July 1993, after intense negotiations, the Commission announced that the eastern Länder would receive approximately DM28 billion over the 1994–99 period – a doubling (and then some) of the 1991–93 allotment that brought the region up to the EC average in this category of regional assistance.[28] Reports out of Brussels indicate that the Commission was

[25] Interview with Federal Chancellery official, Bonn, November 20, 1992.

[26] Examples include the Italian region of Abruzzi and the UK's Highlands and Islands area. R. Waniek, "EG-Regionalpolitik für die Jahre 1994 bis 1999," *Wirtschaftsdienst* (January 1994), 44.

[27] Commission of the European Communities, *Community Structural Funds, 1994–1999: Revised Regulations and Comments* (Luxembourg: Office for Official Publications of the European Communities, 1993), 16.

[28] A BMF official stated that Germany had asked for more, in the range of DM34–38 billion, but "we did not get it." Interview with BMF official, Bonn, May 17, 1994.

inclined to support a substantial increase in part because of concerns about rising anti-EC sentiment in Germany, but did not feel that the German region was in any way comparable to underdeveloped regions in Europe's southern periphery.

For 1994–96, a slightly smaller set of German Objective 2 regions received ECU733 million (in 1994 prices), or 10.5 percent of the EU total for this class of problem region. Bonn was able to ensure that West Berlin continue to receive Objective 2 status, an achievement that officials thought would lessen the assistance gap between the two halves of the city and cushion the overall effects of phasing out special assistance programs for the western part. Germany's Objective 5b regions received ECU1.2 billion for the period 1994–99.

The price tag for the new Objective 1 region in eastern Germany included an overall expansion of EU assisted area coverage.

In terms of population covered, the proportion for the Community as a whole for all regional Objectives, has risen from 43% in 1989 to 1993 to 52% in 1994–96/99. Except for Greece, Ireland, and Portugal, where all the population was already covered, coverage has increased in all Member States ... but half of this increase relates to the addition of the new Länder. Spain and the UK have experienced the smallest rise – 1–2% points – while in the other countries, apart from Luxembourg, the increases range from 7 percentage points (Belgium) to 20 (Germany).[29]

Objective 2 coverage remained at 16.8 percent of Community population – 1.8 percentage points over the Commission's original target of 15 percent; coverage was maintained at existing levels for the second three-year period (1997–99), despite original Commission intentions to overhaul the map.[30]

The urgency with which the government pushed the eastern region's case left it little room to take up the concerns of German academicians and business representatives, who expressed pointed criticism of waste and inefficiency plaguing the structural funds.[31] Nevertheless, under the combined banners of subsidiarity and efficiency, Bonn, joined by Paris and London, also pushed through several administrative and substantive reforms. For example, the federal government secured a greater role for the member states in the designation of Objective 2 and 5b regions,[32]

[29] Commission of the European Communities, *Competitiveness and Cohesion*, 128.
[30] George Parker, "Industrial Regions Receive Aid Boost," *Financial Times*, December 19, 1995, 7.
[31] See for example Deutscher Industrie- und Handelstag, "Reform oder Fortschreibung der EG-Regionalpolitik?," Bonn, August 1992.
[32] Officials responsible for domestic regional policy were especially interested in this proposal, since they feared that the Commission was moving in the direction of setting all assisted areas, whether in EU or national policies. Arguing on the basis of subsidiarity, one noted, "We know the regional problems best, and have better insights

and a simplification of the CSF implementation process, as well as a greater emphasis on cross-border regional initiatives with Eastern European neighbors. In insisting on these and other changes, the Bonn government gave voice to the complaints of both federal and state policymakers about an increasingly burdensome and unresponsive European decision-making process.

A bone of contention between Bonn and Brussels surfaced during subsequent negotiations over the CSF and related operational programs for the eastern German Objective 1 region. The dispute centered on ERDF funds, which represented the lion's share of EU assistance for the region. The BMWi, backed by the economics ministries of the eastern Länder, sought a continuation of the 1991–93 arrangement, under which these funds were routed through the GA and disbursed according to its criteria. However, the prospect of Objective 1 assistance, which elsewhere in the Union was used to fund basic infrastructure and environmental projects, generated strong claims from previously excluded ministries at the federal and state levels. They hoped to open up the aid criteria beyond the confines of the GA, so as to address the full range of development problems confronting the former GDR. BMWi officials interpreted this initiative not as a mission by other ministries to improve policy efficacy in the new Länder, but as an attempt to snare increasingly scarce budgetary resources.

Spearheaded by the transportation and environment ministries in Bonn and the Länder, this bureaucratic campaign won the Commission's support.[33] Publicly, DG-XVI officials cast their position in terms of subsidiarity – the regions themselves should determine their own priorities. Privately, they expressed unhappiness with the GA criteria, pointing out that the channeling of EU resources into pre-existing domestic programs invariably hampered coordination between the funds, limited the Commission's ability to monitor policy impact, and robbed the EU of credit in the eyes of recipients and the general public. The Commission also recognized an opportunity to export its Southern development model to the region, and thereby expand its contacts and

into what is achievable in the regions. And, finally, we are in the end politically responsible. If something goes awry in the Ruhr, we – not Brussels – are democratically accountable to those affected." Interview with BMWi official, Bonn, April 9, 1992.

[33] A DG-XVI official interviewed in March 1995 stated that discussions within Germany and between Bonn and Brussels began to heat up after August 1994, when Commissioner Bruce Milan wrote to the heads of the eastern Länder as well as to the federal economics minister, Günther Rexrodt, to convey his surprise that the proposed CSF for the Objective 1 region intended to channel all ERDF moneys through the GA. The letter recalled Delors' numerous visits to the region, during which the Länder consistently lodged complaints about the narrow GA criteria. Interview with Commission (DG-XVI) official, Brussels, March 2, 1995.

influence there.[34] At the Commission's urging, Saxony and Berlin signaled their intent to bypass the GA with a significant portion of their EU allotments. The Commission's opening demand was that 50 percent of ERDF funds be reserved for special programs relating to the environment, research and development, small- and medium-sized firms, and urban development.

After protracted, often bitter negotiations between and among EU, federal, and state representatives, proponents of looser aid criteria were able in the end to insert a clause in the CSF that essentially leaves it up to each Land, in consultation with Bonn *and* Brussels, to determine the amount of structural funds that flow outside the GA after 1995. Although it appears that the bulk of the relevant ERDF aid will continue to be subject to GA criteria, some Länder, notably Saxony and Berlin, planned to allocate substantial sums to non-GA pursuits, particularly in the area of environmental infrastructure.[35] At the same time, representatives from the new Länder showed little interest in intensifying partnership with the Commission. Their actions revealed a distinct preference for the policy discretion offered by the Objective 1 development model, but did not embrace a weightier role for the Commission as part of the bargain. In short, the new Länder took the principle of subsidiarity very seriously, which led them to act against not only the interests of parts of the Bonn bureaucracy, but also the Commission.

Thus, the designation of the former GDR as an Objective 1 region resulted in the importation of an EU regional development model against the express wishes of a key Bonn ministry. In the process, previously excluded federal and state agencies gained access to the regional policymaking process. And finally, because of the actions and policies of the Commission, governments in the new Länder realized a long-standing demand – namely, to escape the confines of the federal regional policy regime.

Bonn's demands on behalf of the new Länder, combined with the fact

---

[34] According to a DG-XVI official, the Commission actively developed contacts with the excluded ministries in Bonn and the Länder, and the Länder ministries in particular wasted no time beating a path to DG-XVI to make known their unhappiness with the BMWi proposals. Interview with Commission (DG-XVI) official, Brussels, March 2, 1995. BMWi officials reacted to the Commission's actions with considerable dismay; in the words of one, "Here we have a situation where the EU Commission is trying to set priorities that contradict this house's standing policy." Noting the sheer scale of the resources to flow from Brussels to the new Objective 1 region in the east, he remarked that "this puts us in a new position as receiver (*Empfänger*)," and warned of "centrally directed influence" from Brussels. Interview with BMWi official, Bonn, May 18, 1994.

[35] Estimates are that 22 percent of the relevant funds will be used outside of GA parameters. Friedemann Tetsch, "Gemeinschaftsaufgabe 'Verbesserung der regionalen Wirtschaftsstruktur' am Scheideweg," *Stadt und Gemeinde* (8/1994), 3–8 at 7.

that the Commission's approval of the GA expired on December 31, 1993, left the federal government vulnerable to continued Commission pressure to reduce the scope and intensity of regional assistance measures in the old Länder. The Commission made it clear to Bonn that a renewal was contingent on additional cuts in the west.[36] The 1994 GA Framework Plan reduced assisted area coverage in the western Länder (including West Berlin)[37] from 27 to 22 percent of the population for a period of three years, from 1994 to 1996;[38] at the same time, participants extended the new Länder's status as an assisted area *sui generis* to the end of this period. These decisions received Commission approval in early 1994.

In conjunction with Land representatives, federal economics ministry officials commenced a major review of the GA in 1994. Their decision was prompted in large part by growing east–west tensions in the GA; although few old Länder disputed the needs of the new Länder, they were becoming restive over the dualism built into the GA – one set of procedures for the east, another for the west – and in particular the absence of a fixed time frame for "normalization" of assistance criteria in the former GDR.[39] The review was also necessitated by the Commission, which continued to press for additional cuts in regional assistance for the old Länder[40] and which, in the eyes of BMWi policymakers, had undermined the consensus underpinning the GA with its support for a loosening of aid restrictions on Objective 1 assistance for the new Länder. In short, the GA was squeezed from above and from the east, prompting federal officials to respond with a thoroughgoing reassess-

---

[36] A Commission official, referring to the regional problems in eastern and western Germany, remarked, "When you have two sick patients, only one of them can be doing worse." Another commented in blunter terms: "It is a scandal really that regional policy is still on offer in western Germany." Interviews with Commission officials (DG-IV and DG-XVI), Brussels, December 1 and December 2, 1992 respectively.

[37] Previously, West Berlin had not been counted as part of the western German territory. Inclusion of West Berlin, which contained 3.3 of the "west" German population, required cuts of 8.3 percent in the ten contiguous western Länder.

[38] Interviews with officials in Bonn and Brussels revealed that the Commission originally pressed for more drastic coverage reductions in western Germany, of the order of 10–12 percent of the population. By the end of this period, the GA framework plan established a slightly lower coverage figure for western Germany: 20.8 percent. Interview with BMWi official, Bonn, December 4, 1992.

[39] This would involve, among other things, a removal of the blanket designation of the region as an assisted area, and its replacement with a more differentiated system as obtained in the west, with assisted areas of various intensities as well as non-assisted areas.

[40] By early 1995, the Commission had backed off this position, and was sending signals to the BMWi that it would not be pressing for reductions in coverage beyond the existing 22 percent figure for western Germany after 1996. Interview with BMWi official, Bonn, May 28, 1995.

ment of the policy instrument. BMWi officials expressed doubts that the GA would survive intact into the next century.[41]

After a long and arduous process lasting the better part of a year, in March 1995 the GA emerged with its basic principles intact – a joint policymaking framework targeting business-related development of the problem regions – but also with a more streamlined, flexible, and transparent set of assistance criteria, increased latitude for Land initiative, and a greater role for the federal government in implementation, monitoring, and impact assessment. Federal and state officials agreed on mechanisms to reestablish a uniform set of assistance criteria for the entire country and to allow for the descheduling of economically stronger parts of the new Länder.[42]

Thus, BMWi officials succeeded in reestablishing a strong consensus among the sixteen Länder that the federal government should continue to occupy a significant place in the reformed regional policy framework. According to one, the feeling in the regions is that "the federal government must remain involved, to serve as a cushion between the Länder and Brussels. Otherwise, the Länder haven't got a chance against Brussels."[43] The reform of the GA enabled the BMWi to reassert a measure of control over the bulk of ERDF funds flowing to the Objective 1 region, and thereby cope more effectively with the bureaucratic challenges emanating from other Bonn ministries and above all the Commission.

The episode underscores the changing implications of subsidiarity in this policy area post-unification. In the past, the Commission's many direct relationships with the Länder did not overly concern Bonn, since the volume of structural funds flowing to German regions was too small to influence the principles and procedures (if not the intensity) of federal policy. With unification and the subsequent infusion of Objective 1 resources, the federal government confronted a dramatically changed situation, in which the risk of losing control over development priorities, procedures, and budgetary outlays had risen substantially. Direct links between Brussels and the (eastern) Länder henceforth had to be monitored much more closely in the relevant Bonn ministries.

Even after the reform of the GA, east–west tensions, often intensified

---

[41] Friedemann Tetsch, "Bund-Länder-Gemeinschaftsaufgabe: Verbesserung der regionalen Wirtschaftsstruktur," *Die Neue Verwaltung* (May–June 1993), 24–28 at 28.

[42] The new Länder had moved above the EU's per capita GDP average for the first time in 1993, leaving Greece behind as the poorest region in the EU. Between 1991 and 1993, per capita GDP in the eastern Länder rose from 34.1 percent to 49.1 percent of the western German average. Pockets of prosperity could be found in numerous areas, including Dresden, Leipzig, and the environs of Berlin.

[43] Interview with BMWi official, Bonn, December 4, 1992.

by steady Commission pressure, persisted. In 1995, Berlin waged a successful campaign, over the objections of the western Länder, to accord its western half the same assisted area status as (former) East Berlin. This action received Commission approval in June of the following year, but placed a spotlight once again on the question of western area coverage; in response, western Länder stepped up their demands for a descheduling of prosperous parts of the new Länder in the GA after 1996. Subsequent negotiations between the federal government and the Länder produced an agreement that up through 1999, western area coverage would remain at 22 percent of the population and the eastern Länder in their entirety would receive *a priori* assisted area status. After 1997, however, eight prosperous subregions in the former GDR (Berlin, Dresden, Leipzig, Erfurt, Weimar, Jena, Schwerin, and Halle) would move to a lower category of assistance, albeit one still higher than that offered in the west. The Commission approved the plan in late 1996, but insisted that western coverage remain at its current level of 20.8 percent.[44]

Caught between domestic and supranational constraints, Bonn's approach to the larger issue of structural funds policy grew more tentative. In early 1996, the Commission expressed its concern that the scope and intensity of regional programs operating at the European, national, and subnational levels were generating distortions to competition within the single market, and floated a proposal to create a new EU framework governing regional aid. Although many member governments supported the initiative, German officials expressed concern that any changes in the existing regime might complicate restructuring efforts under way in the new Länder. Upon receiving favorable responses from the Commission over the course of 1996 to its request that the new Länder retain their Objective 1 status after 1999, the federal government joined the Commission in calling for an overhaul of the EU's regional aid regime, one that would concentrate resources on the poorest regions in the Union.

The Commission's reform proposals, which took shape over the course of 1997 and were formally published in March of the following year, called for a ECU275 billion structural fund budget for the period 2000 to 2006, ECU45 billion of which would be set aside for new members expected to join during those years. This overall figure repre-

---

[44] Since West Berlin was now counted as part of the new Länder, the Commission wished to prevent Bonn from scheduling additional western German areas in its place. The Commission drove a hard bargain, pointing out that if assisted areas were designated according to EU and not German criteria, area coverage in the west would have to fall by about one-third.

sented a freezing in real terms of structural fund expenditures; German officials nevertheless criticized the proposed budget as overly generous. The Commission's substantive reform proposals included a reduction in the number of assistance categories from seven to three, which entailed, among other changes, folding Objective 5b into Objective 2, and a streamlining of program administration procedures. Its most controversial recommendations were to shrink the area coverage of EU-assisted areas from a little over 50 percent of the Union population to around 40 percent while bringing the assisted area maps of national regional policies into line with that employed by Brussels.[45]

With publication of the Commission's blueprint for the structural funds, bitter conflicts for Germany loomed on the horizon, especially back home. The Commission's goal of targeting only the poorest regions in the EU augured well for the new Länder, which were still languishing at the bottom of the EU regional growth table.[46] On the other hand, it spelled disaster for assisted areas in western Germany, particularly underdeveloped rural communities, which faced the very real prospect of a total cut-off of both national (GA) and EU (Objectives 2 and 5b) assistance. This in turn jeopardized the fragile east–west truce worked out by the Bonn government during the recently concluded GA policy review. BMWi minister Rexrodt expressed deep concerns about the implications of the Agenda 2000 proposals for the western half of the country, stating that "In general it is essential that the results of the reforms be politically acceptable within Germany."[47]

In Brussels, Bonn faced even thornier choices as it attempted to reconcile its conflicting roles as Community paymaster and structural funds beneficiary. The Commission repeatedly reminded the Kohl government of the practical budgetary implications of continued EU structural assistance for the new Länder. Germany could not expect to make much headway with its demand for a reduction in the structural funds expenditures – and by extension its aggregate EU budget contributions – so long as the eastern German region continued to receive Objective 1 assistance. As if to underscore the point, Bonn's campaign to discontinue cohesion fund assistance for the EU's poorer member

[45] Commission of the European Communities, *Agenda 2000*, vol. I, 14–21. Journalistic sources estimated that up to eleven regions would lose Objective 1 status under the reformed structural funds: Lisbon (Portugal); Valencia (Spain); Corsica and Valenciennois (France); Sardinia and Puglia (Italy); Hainaut (Belgium), Flevoland (Netherlands); and the Republic of Ireland.

[46] The Commission's proposals envisioned a continuation of eastern Germany's status as an Objective 1 region, with the exception of east Berlin, which would be upgraded to Objective 2 status.

[47] "Rexrodt verlangt schlankere und wirksamere EU-Strukturpolitik," *Frankfurter Allgemeine Zeitung*, February 20, 1998, 13.

countries fell victim to the politics of consensus-building in the Council of Ministers.

Moreover, concentrating benefits on the neediest EU regions would almost certainly exacerbate Germany's position as a net contributor to the EU budget – the eastern Länder were slated to receive a small increase in their allotment, but this would be more than compensated for by the ejection of western German regions from the EU assisted areas map. Minister Rexrodt indicated that Germany planned to raise the controversial issue of reforming the EU's assistance indicators to assign greater weight to the problem of rural underdevelopment, which would not only address real problems but also increase Germany's net return from the structural funds.[48]

Common Agricultural Policy (CAP)

The Common Agricultural Policy replaced national agricultural programs with a common framework of price supports, variable levies on imports, and programs to address structural weaknesses in Europe's agricultural sector. The CAP is often portrayed as the centerpiece of the grand Franco-German bargain that launched the EEC in the late 1950s. In exchange for the creation of an internal market open to German industrial and manufacturing might, Bonn agreed to the common management of agricultural policy, a sector in which the French were expected to excel. Although there is a grain of truth in this tale, it ignores the tangible benefits that Germany derived from both ends of the bargain.

West German agricultural policy was tailored to the relative structural homogeneity of the domestic farming sector.[49] The removal of the vast Junker estates in the east through division left the western occupation zones with a shrunken agricultural sector that was decidedly Catholic and dominated by small family farms. This led to a sectoral convergence of interest; for the first time in its history, German agriculture was represented by a single association: the Deutscher Bauernverband (DBV). The DBV cast its primary goal as the defense of farming not just as an economic vocation, but as a way of life, drawing on a long (and tarnished) tradition in German politics.[50]

---

[48] "Rexrodt verlangt schlankere und wirksamere EU-Strukturpolitik," 12.

[49] The following discussion of pre-unification Germany and the CAP is based on Gisela Hendriks, *Germany and European Integration: The Common Agricultural Policy: An Area of Conflict* (New York: St. Martin's Press, 1991).

[50] The German literature on the DBV is voluminous. For a recent analysis containing a comprehensive bibliography, see Rolf Heinze and Helmut Voelzkow, "Der Deutsche Bauernverband und das 'Gemeinwohl'," in Renate Mainz, ed., *Verbände zwischen*

The principal patrons of agriculture were the CDU and its Bavarian sister party, the CSU. These parties, which together headed coalition governments in twenty-seven of the forty years of West Germany's existence, placed one of their own in the Ministry of Food, Agriculture, and Forestry (Bundesministerium für Ernährung, Landwirtschaft, und Forsten, or BML) in each of those years. With electoral bases in the largely rural south (Baden-Württemberg and Bavaria), they strongly defended the interests of their small-scale farmers, and supported a generally protectionist policy. During the other thirteen years, when a social democratic-liberal coalition governed, the ministry was headed by a member of the Free Democratic Party (FDP), which had strong ties to the somewhat larger farms in northern Germany. North–south tensions were mirrored in Germany's principal domestic agricultural program, the *Gemeinschaftsaufgabe "Verbesserung der Agrarstruktur und des Küstenschutzes"* (GAK). The GAK was organized and operated along lines very similar to the joint regional policy framework described in the previous section, and its structural policy instruments served through the years to preserve and maintain the basic structural features of the country's farm sector.

German governments pursued a consistent CAP policy that centered around the maintenance of high prices for its farmers and a structural policy supportive of small-scale farming. The introduction of Europe's agri-monetary system after the collapse of Bretton Woods, based on so-called green exchange rates, offered Bonn the opportunity to shield German farmers from the agricultural price reductions otherwise demanded by the appreciation of the Deutsche Mark.[51] The source of many conflicts between Germany and its EC partners, above all France, green money was the cornerstone of Germany's "renationalization" of the CAP beginning in the 1970s; thanks to the "green Mark," prices for agricultural products in Germany during the 1970s were 10 percent or more above the average EC price level.[52] When CAP reform took center-stage in Brussels in the 1980s,[53] in the midst of wine lakes, butter mountains, and spiraling budgetary costs, Germany shunned any

---

Mitgliederinteressen und Gemeinwohl (Gütersloh: Verlag Bertelsmann Stiftung, 1992), 122–61.

[51] With the collapse of fixed exchange rates in 1972, the EC implemented a grid of green exchange rates to neutralize the impact of shifts in exchange rate parities on national agricultural prices, and employed the mechanism of monetary compensatory amounts (MCAs) – in effect, a system of export refunds and regulatory levies on imports – to preserve the target prices agreed by the Agriculture Council.

[52] Hendriks, *Germany and European Integration*, 60.

[53] On the CAP reform of the 1980s, see H. Wayne Moyer and Timothy Josling, *Agricultural Policy Reform: Politics and Process in the EC and the USA* (Ames, IA: Iowa State University Press, 1990), chs. 3–4.

proposed solutions that entailed price reductions; in 1985, Bonn's veto threat prevented the Council from acting on a Commission proposal to cut the price of cereals by a mere 1.8 percent.[54] Instead, Germany sought to address the problem of overproduction and runaway costs through set-asides and co-payment procedures when and if guaranteed production thresholds were exceeded.

CAP and the unification settlement, 1989–90

Agricultural property relations in the GDR were dominated by two forms of collective enterprise: agricultural production cooperatives (*Landwirtschaftliche Produktionsgenossenschaften*, LPG),[55] which accounted for approximately 50 percent of the farms, over 80 percent of employment and total acreage, and a little more than 70 percent of annual agricultural output; and state-owned farms (*Volkseigene Güter*, VEG), which accounted for 6.7 percent of the country's agricultural enterprises, 15 percent of the employed, 7.5 percent of the acreage, and approximately 17 percent of annual production.[56] On the eve of unification, the level of employment in the sector stood at approximately 850,000 (two-thirds of which were directly involved in production), or 10 percent of the GDR workforce – double the figure for West Germany. The average farm in the GDR encompassed 11,120 acres (4,500 hectares), a scale that dwarfed the typical western farm of just over 40 acres (16.8 hectares). Indeed, with unification Germany now possessed the largest farms in the entire Community.[57] Finally, GDR agriculture was highly specialized, with the vast majority of farms concentrating exclusively on either crop production or livestock. This led to both extreme economic inefficiencies and excessive environmental burdens on the land.

Taken together, these four characteristics meant that the federal government would have to contend with sharp conflicts in Bonn and in Brussels. Given the sheer magnitude of the transition to a smaller agricultural sector based on private ownership and markets, eastern farmers could be expected to demand structural assistance and favorable

---

[54] Hendriks, *Germany and European Integration*, 100–09.

[55] Members of LPGs retained formal ownership of the land, but usage rights were held by the cooperative.

[56] Privately owned and operated farms accounted for the remainders in these categories. All figures are from 1989. See Presse- und Informationsamt der Bundesregierung, *Unsere Landwirtschaft* (Bonn, 1992), 20.

[57] Grit Viertel, "Gemeinsame Agrarpolitik und neue Bundesländer," in Barbara Lippert *et al.*, *Die EG und die neuen Bundesländer* (Bonn: Europa Union Verlag, 1993), 211. Large farms in the eastern part of Germany were not an artifact of the SED regime; the region, after all, was at one time the seat of the Prussian landed aristocracy.

pricing policies to cushion and perhaps even delay adjustment. Moreover, the prospect of large, efficient producers in the five new Länder was bound to generate high anxiety among the smaller, family-owned farms in western Germany. Bonn faced the distinct possibility that regional conflicts would shift from a north–south to an east–west axis and, moreover, that these conflicts would spill over onto the Brussels agenda, which, largely but not exclusively at Bonn's insistence, had been tailored to accommodate small-scale farmers. Adjustments to both the CAP and to the GAK required Council approval, which placed Bonn once again in the position of supplicant in Brussels.

The technical process of incorporating the eastern German agricultural sector into national and supranational policy frameworks threw up few intractable obstacles, a surprising development in light of the many complex and politically sensitive issues involved. Bonn paved the way by insisting that the GDR adopt the main elements of the CAP – a system of price supports and external protection – by July 1, 1990, the official starting date of GEMSU. In late June, the GDR government established a legal framework for regulating property relations on the land during the transition to a market economy, which included a deadline of December 31, 1991 for the transformation of all remaining LPGs into jointly owned and managed cooperatives or private farms.

During intense negotiations with Bonn over the course of 1990, the Commission acknowledged the need "to adjust the existing measures of the Community's structural legislation in a way that fits the needs of present large cooperative holdings and of family farms equally well."[58] Bonn was allowed to compensate eastern German farmers financially for income losses incurred during the transition to the CAP regime until the end of 1993.[59] The government also succeeded in winning EC approval of special measures implemented through the GAK to speed the restructuring process in the eastern agricultural sector, as well as more flexible set-aside schemes to facilitate the downsizing of the sector. Finally, the EC approved transitional regimes for quality and health standards, marketing standards, and the like. Member governments, concerned about the possible health risks posed by substandard food

[58] Commission of the European Communities, "The European Community and German Unification," 83.
[59] Producer prices set by GDR livestock concerns were two to three times the level obtaining in the EC. Conversely, consumer prices were held artificially low through subsidies, which resulted in chronic waste and misallocation of resources; for example, 200,000 tons of bread baked for human consumption were converted to animal feed annually. Sabine Jarothe, "Konfliktfeld deutsch–deutsche Landwirtschaft," *Politische Studien* 43 (January–February 1992), 97–106 at 98.

products from eastern Germany or its Eastern trading partners, were granted the right to seek protection through the Commission.

CAP after unification, 1990–96

The state of eastern German agriculture after October 3, 1990 told a familiar tale: aging capital stock, outdated production techniques, over-manning, environmental degradation, high production costs, uncertain property relations, and fragile regional markets. Virtually overnight, demand for eastern German food products collapsed, as store shelves filled with western German and foreign goods which, though not invariably of higher quality, were more attractively packaged and bene-fited from the allure of novelty. The resulting liquidity crunch hit the LPGs hard, leading among other things to a massive sell-off of livestock at dumping prices, which in turn put pressure on prices in western Germany and even other parts of the Community.[60] In this context, many eastern farms opted to participate in set-aside programs operated by Bonn and Brussels, recognizing in these measures a ready source of cash. For the 1991 harvest, approximately 600,000 hectares of agricul-tural land were taken out of production under a one-year special program operated by Bonn; this represented 12.8 percent of the 1989 total in the new Länder. For the 1992 harvest, a combination of federal and EC programs led to just under 360,000 hectares in set-asides.[61]

Reactions on the land were emphatic and anxious, yet at the same time diffuse and uncoordinated. This can be traced directly to stresses and strains in interest representation within the sector after 1990. The DBV moved quickly to extend its reach eastward by offering member-ship to the regional associations of the Bauernverband der DDR, itself recently reconstituted out of the Verband der gegenseitigen Bauernhilfe (the former SED transmission belt organization), rather than by creating its own branch organizations *de novo*. The DBV's decision prompted the creation of competitor organizations in each of the Länder representing the interests of existing or soon-to-be family farmers, who resented the domination of the "official" regional associations by LPG interests. Although the resulting conflicts were largely resolved by the end of 1992 after long and arduous work by the DBV, they undermined the unity of

---

[60] The BML responded by negotiating a treaty with the USSR that entailed the delivery of massive amounts of ex-DDR surplus food, including 200,000 tons of beef and 140,000 tons of pork. Brussels approved the shipment of the heavily subsidized food, which defused the mounting crisis. Interview with BML official, Bonn, June 11, 1992.

[61] Bundesministerium für Ernährung, Landwirtschaft, und Forsten, *Agrarpolitik der Bundesregierung in den neuen Bundesländern* (Bonn: BML, 1992), 3.

the farmers' organization and virtually paralyzed interest representation in many eastern Länder.

Matters were complicated by the fact that many eastern German farmers perceived the western German agricultural lobby, including the DBV, as indifferent, if not outright hostile to their interests. Bavarian farmers in particular were singled out for criticism; they were accused of orchestrating a campaign through the CSU parliamentary caucus and the BML to bias post-unification agricultural policy exclusively in favor of the small family farm and against large-scale, cooperative enterprises.[62] A BML official remarked, "One has to realize that to the typical southern German farmer, the LPG represented the class enemy – a nightmare."[63] In many respects, the DBV was itself paralyzed after unification. At worst, the association appeared to eastern Germans "as the chief lobbyist of the . . . family farms."[64] At best, the DBV left itself open to the charge of indifference.[65]

Into this representational vacuum stepped the eastern Länder, which emerged as the principal voice of agriculture in the former GDR.[66] In numerous legislative debates on agriculture across the region, state officials voiced their concerns about the crisis, raising the specter of rural depopulation if current trends were not reversed.[67] Land officials in the east were especially agitated about federal and EC set-aside programs, which they believed were hastening the collapse of agriculture and aggravating the problem of rural unemployment. Efforts by Land governments to amend the national and EC set-aside programs or to

[62] In 1991 and 1992, western German newspaper accounts were filled with apocalyptic descriptions of "agri-factories" in the east, as contrasted with the idyllic, harmonious fit between farm and nature that obtained in the west. An SPD leader in Mecklenburg-West Pomerania stated categorically in 1992 that the LPGs had been destroyed at the end of 1991 because the BML, beholden to western farming interests, feared competition from large-scale farming concerns. Christoph Dieckmann, "Der Spuk im Schloß," *Die Zeit*, March 27, 1992, 10.

[63] Interview with BML official, Bonn, May 29, 1992.

[64] Interview with DBV official, Bonn, May 27, 1992.

[65] In a position paper on the CAP reform published in September 1991, the DBV mentioned the new Länder only once, and almost in passing. Deutscher Bauernverband, *Für Marktausgleich gegen Preissenkung: Der Deutsche Bauernverband zur Reform der EG-Agrarpolitik* (Bonn, 1991).

[66] Many Land officials interviewed in the fall of 1992 commented on the large amount of autonomy they enjoyed as a result of the fragmented condition of farmers' associations at the state level. That said, the Land ministries were unable to rely on regional associations for support or information; according to a Brandenburg official, "We have no partners." Interview with agriculture ministry official in Brandenburg, Potsdam, October 28, 1992.

[67] According to the federal government, agricultural employment in the new Länder dropped from 850,000 in September 1989 to approximately 300,000 at the end of 1991. Bundesministerium für Ernährung, Landwirtschaft, und Forsten, "Agrarwirtschaft in den neuen Bundesländern," January 1992, 1.

offset their effects through Land measures ultimately proved ineffective.[68]

Early on, the eastern Länder recognized the need for a coordinated response, and worked to fashion a general consensus on interests and aims among the new Länder. In some regards, their demands overlapped with the traditional position of western farming interests. For example, high price supports were a priority; so too was access to state aid designed to promote restructuring and competitiveness. On other matters, such as policies that would accommodate large-scale farms and property forms other than the small family farm model, the eastern agenda pushed out into new territory. The eastern Länder vehemently resisted a key element of institutional transfer in agriculture – the model of the small family farm. Their voices were instrumental in shaping the coalition agreement negotiated by the CDU, CSU, and FDP after the December 1990 federal elections, which expressly included a provision that all farms in Germany, regardless of size, would remain eligible for state assistance.

Based on this uneasy political consensus, which left many questions unresolved,[69] the BML set about adapting the national agricultural policy regime to accommodate the distinctive needs of eastern German agriculture. In July 1991 and again in December, new federal legislation clarified and expanded opportunities for LPG members to seek out cooperative forms of private ownership, and to soften provisions that would have levied crippling sanctions on those LPGs unable to meet the deadline for transition to some form of private ownership at the end of the year. Despite these and other initiatives, the bitter struggle between the LPG successors and individual farmers continued unabated in the eastern Länder.

The federal government also pushed ,through adjustments to the

[68] For example, officials in all but one of the eastern Länder, against the express wishes of their own farmers, asked both Bonn and Brussels to modify the set-aside programs; farmers, instead of automatically receiving a set-aside premium in exchange for taking some of their land out of production, would be required to obtain Land approval before applying for the aid. In Brandenburg, the Ministry of Agriculture requested a complete suspension of both federal and EC set-aside programs, at the same time as its farmers' organizations were demanding higher premiums to take land out of production! These entreaties were rejected at both the national and EC levels as inconsistent with the larger goals of the CAP. As for compensatory Land programs, Brandenburg attempted to create an alternative program to encourage farmers to reject set-asides in favor of environmentally oriented extensification. Labeled the "Brandenburg Way" (*Brandenburger Weg*), the initiative faltered. The exception was Saxony-Anhalt, blessed with high quality land, which made no effort to neutralize the set-aside programs since its farmers participated at very low rates.

[69] The property rights question was fudged, as was the extent to which farms of differing sizes and types were to enjoy equal or differentiated access to public funds.

GAK. In addition to modifying the eligibility terms of its various policy instruments, Bonn and the Länder agreed to create several new programs, effective from January 1, 1991, exclusively for eastern farms: (1) to promote the (re)creation and modernization of family farms; (2) to promote the restructuring of LPGs; (3) to promote energy conservation throughout the sector; and (4) to improve the marketing of agricultural products. In 1992, GAK measures benefiting the new Länder were expanded to include a program for so-called disadvantaged regions as well as start-up assistance for young farmers. Aid ceilings for both family farms and juridical persons (*juristische Personen*, i.e. non-family farms) were raised, and the definition of the latter was expanded.[70] By 1992, the GAK for all intents and purposes contained two distinct sets of policy instruments: one for the old Länder, and one for the new. In 1991–92, total GAK expenditures were DM7.3 billion, of which DM2.4 billion went to the new Länder.[71]

Effecting these changes in the GAK was not an easy task; the policy process was marked by frequent clashes between representatives of the old (especially Bavaria) and new Länder over size and aid ceilings.[72] Modifying the GAK also required EC approval; at the end of 1990, Bonn secured special derogations from EC regulations that enabled it to provide special forms of assistance to eastern farmers until the end of 1993.

Unification and the adjustment of domestic agricultural programs coincided with ongoing pressures for change in Germany's CAP policy. An important external impetus came from the Uruguay Round of the GATT – specifically, the US-backed initiative to reduce the level of farm support paid out by treaty signatories.[73] In the midst of the GATT negotiations, the European Commissioner for Agriculture, Ray MacSharry, published a set of reform proposals that broke with the CAP

---

[70] In a measure designed to underscore the priority accorded to private property, though, juridical persons in which public authorities (i.e. Länder or municipalities) owned shares totaling 25 percent or more were declared ineligible for assistance.

[71] The funding formula was/is 60 percent federal contributions, 40 percent Land contributions.

[72] In a Landtag debate on January 16, 1991, Brandenburg's agriculture minister referred to prior meetings among the new Länder to hammer out a common GAK position, and stated emphatically, "The eastern Länder categorically reject the Bavarian way, which envisions no aid for juridical persons [i.e. non-family farms]." Brandenburger Landtag, 8. Sitzung, "Aktuelle Stunde: Schnelle Hilfe für die Landwirtschaft und den ländlichen Raum," 295.

[73] See the general discussion of GATT in chapter 3. On the agricultural issues specific to GATT, see Robert Paarlberg, *Leadership Abroad Begins at Home* (Washington, DC: The Brookings Institution, 1995), 66–75; and John Keeler, "Agricultural Power in the European Community: Explaining the Fate of CAP and GATT Negotiations," *Comparative Politics* 28 (January 1996), 127–50.

orthodoxy of using the price mechanism as the principal means of insulating farmers from the vagaries of the market.[74] Central to the MacSharry reforms, published in 1991, was a substantial reduction in price supports for cereals. Farmers were to be compensated for resulting income losses by means of direct transfer payments, the receipt of which was conditional on their participation in compulsory set-aside schemes. According to the principle of "modulation," small farms were to receive full compensation for land set aside, whereas larger farms would be entitled only to partial compensation.

Combined with the Uruguay Round, the MacSharry initiative challenged Germany's traditional position on the CAP. Ignaz Kiechle (CSU), Germany's agriculture minister, stated publicly on numerous occasions his principled opposition to cereal price cuts, and questioned the conceptual foundation of the reform package: direct income transfers. Kiechle's statements drew angry responses from representatives of the BDI and other German industry associations, as well as the federal economics minister, who accused him of subverting their efforts to bring the GATT round to a successful conclusion. Kiechle advocated additional set-aside programs, quota schemes, and co-payment programs to address the problems of overproduction. His position differed imperceptibly from that advanced by the DBV and the transnational peak association in the agricultural sector, COPA.

In October 1991, after long and arduous negotiations between the three coalition partners, the Bonn government issued a cabinet decision laying out four guidelines for Germany's negotiating position *vis-à-vis* the CAP reform:

(1) The problem of surplus production should be addressed by means of an effective and balanced bundle of measures involving both price and production instruments. The aim is an enduring improvement in the efficiency of European agriculture.

(2) Cuts in price supports can be undertaken only in connection with lasting and reliable income compensation, for which only those firms that participate in measures to reduce production levels are eligible. Compensation should not impede the construction of larger competitive farms, which is essential to the structural development of agriculture; this means that income compensation arrangements may not discriminate against larger enterprises.

(3) An adequate measure of external protection must be guaranteed.

(4) State incentives to promote extensification and environmentally

---

[74] See, among others, Alan Swinbank, "CAP Reform, 1992," *Journal of Common Market Studies* 31 (September 1993), 359–72.

compatible production are to be strengthened; set-asides alone cannot control the problem of excess production in the long run.[75] The guidelines represented a compromise between the BML and the BMWi, but one that left plenty of leeway for the agriculture minister to bargain in Brussels.[76]

The government's general position won the support of eastern German farmers, who opposed price cuts of the magnitude sought by the Commission. Yet price cuts were the least of their concerns. The eastern Land governments launched an all-out campaign soon after regional experts had finished working out the implications of the MacSharry reforms for the region. Specifically, modulation, acreage premium formulas, and various eligibility criteria relating to product categories like grains and beef would have seriously disadvantaged large farms in the former GDR at a critical point in their transition to capitalist agricultural production.[77] As Brandenburg's agriculture minister stated to the Land parliament in June 1992:

When I and my ministry looked over the CAP reform proposals circulated by EC Commissioner MacSharry for the first time, a shiver ran down our spines. The original reform proposals were – if I might be permitted to express myself casually – tailored for Irish agriculture. Based on our impact assessment of the 1991 proposals, around 90 percent of Brandenburg's farms would have received no premiums or income payments.[78]

Brandishing expert studies that forecast dire consequences if the reforms were enacted as written, Land leaders first convinced the BML of the urgency of the situation. With Bonn's help, the new Länder commenced a supranational lobbying campaign directed at both Commissioner MacSharry and Commission president Jacques Delors. The eastern Länder initially demanded a complete exemption from the reforms; tabled in April 1992, this proposal, which Land officials understood perfectly well stood no chance of acceptance, was designed to make the set of demands eventually tabled by Bonn more palatable.

Kiechle approached the final negotiating round in Brussels firmly

---

[75] See *Antwort der Bundesregierung auf die Grosse Anfrage "GATT-Welthandelssystem,"* Deutscher Bundestag, 12. Wahlperiode, Drucksache 12/1745, December 5, 1991, 6.

[76] A DBV spokesperson said that the association was quite pleased with the cabinet decision, which it interpreted as giving price reductions a lower priority than production caps. Interview with DBV official, Bonn, July 8, 1992. This view was contested in the BMWi, which saw both as given equal weight; according to one official there, had it not been for pressure from the ministry, Kiechle would have made no mention whatsoever of price cuts. Interview with BMWi official, Bonn, May 14, 1992.

[77] For example, the original MacSharry reforms specified that "existing" farms were eligible for direct income payments, a formulation that would have excluded new farms, whether family-owned or juridical persons, that were cropping up continually in eastern Germany.

[78] Landtag Brandenburg, 1. Wahlperiode, Plenarprotokoll 1/49, June 24, 1992, 3521.

opposed to a price reduction of the magnitude proposed by the Commission, and was counting on the French to hold the line at a 20 percent reduction or less. However, in the weeks prior to the decisive Council meeting, France signaled a willingness to accept much larger reductions, a conversion based on tactical considerations related to the GATT negotiations. The French reversal, described as "retreat to the front" (*eine Flucht nach vorne*) by one Bonn official, was designed to take the steam out of the GATT export subsidy spat with the Americans by unilaterally bringing European grain prices closer to the prevailing world price, an outcome that would not necessarily harm the more efficient French grain farmers.[79]

Abandoned by the French, the Germans found themselves isolated in the Council, a position that officials described as unacceptable. This assessment was grounded in the specific issues facing the twelve agriculture ministers; Germany would be perceived as blocking any possible agreement on GATT, something to which its leaders were publicly committed. For Bonn, said one ministry official, "GATT and CAP have been from the beginning two sides of the same coin."[80] Remarking that the Council veto had become an option devoid of legitimacy, the same ministry official explained that Kiechle's only option was to change tack.[81] Resigned to the inevitable, Kiechle sought full compensation for farmers through the direct transfer mechanism, as well as additional flanking measures to cushion the shock and a comprehensive package of derogations for eastern German farmers. Bonn's assent represented not just a sharp break with its past position in the Council, but also a last-minute, public U-turn by its minister.

Thus, after long and often acrimonious negotiations, EC farm ministers agreed to a CAP reform that bore a strong familial resemblance to the original MacSharry proposals. The agreement called for an average 29 percent reduction in the price support for cereals over a four-year period. As compensation for the resulting income losses, farmers were to receive direct payments based on fixed acreage premiums. To remain eligible for the income compensation, farmers were required to set aside 15 percent of their land, for which they were to be compensated through set-aside premiums, again based on established formulas. The Council rejected the principle of modulation; all farms, and not just smaller enterprises, would be eligible for full compensation for lost income.

---

[79] Interview with BML official, Bonn, June 11, 1992.
[80] Interview with BML official, Bonn, June 11, 1992.
[81] Interview with BML official, Bonn, June 11, 1992. Apparently, the agriculture ministry and (by implication) the German government were willing to write off a GATT agreement if this was the will of the Council, but they were unwilling to carry the blame alone.

Moreover, small farms (those less than 20 hectares) were exempted from the set-aside requirement.[82] The member governments also approved the derogation package for eastern German farmers, as well as new policy instruments to encourage farmers to adopt more environmentally sound production techniques.

Although government officials denied any linkage between their demands on behalf of the new Länder and the broader reform package, it appears that there was indeed a connection. Bonn made a tactical decision to seek derogations of limited duration for its eastern German farmers, instead of pressing for EC-wide changes in the various offending regulations,[83] and won concessions from the Commission and Council members in exchange for support for the larger MacSharry reform initiative.

Reaction to the CAP reform was predictable. The DBV decried the price reductions, and predicted that the reforms would transform farmers from independent entrepreneurs to wards of the state. Officials in the new Länder greeted with relief the various derogations and adjustments achieved on their behalf, but expressed concern about the magnitude of the price cuts and the bureaucratic overhead created by the reforms, which would tax their infant administrative structures.

Kiechle described the reform package as a "turning point" (*Wende*) in Community agricultural policy, and proclaimed that the EC had now done its part to make a GATT agreement possible. His statements on the agreement struck a defensive tone; addressing Germany's farmers, he explained that the agreement was the least objectionable of the various options considered in the Council, and that to have adopted an all-or-nothing position would have placed in jeopardy the very real concessions he had won for German farmers in both east and west.[84] Interestingly, the government refrained from publicizing the various approved derogations for the new Länder, since it hoped to avoid generating pressures for comparable treatment from western German

---

[82] The BML estimated that this would exempt over 80 percent of farming enterprises in the Federal Republic. Bundesministerium für Ernährung, Landwirtschaft, und Forsten, "Bericht über die Tagung des Agrarrates vom 18. bis 21. Mai 1992 in Brüssel: Zusammenfassung," internal document, May 1992, 3.

[83] The one exception was the abandonment of modulation, which was brought about by EC members with significant numbers of farms above the full-compensation threshold (e.g. Germany and the UK). A Commission official interviewed in 1995 stated that the main impetus for abandoning modulation came from the UK. Interview with Commission (DG-VI) official, March 1, 1995.

[84] Bonn also received EC approval of a transitional measure, to last up through the end of 1995, to continue providing compensation to German farmers (including those in the east) for income losses resulting from the appreciation of the Deutsche Mark; dating from 1984, this program had originally been designed to expire at the end of 1991.

farmers. According to a BML official, "There has not yet developed a sufficient level of solidarity in the all-German farming sector to bear the weight of this information."[85]

With the CAP reform behind it, the German government gained some leeway in pushing for a resolution of the Uruguay Round, and worked to arrange a compromise between the French and American positions on reductions in the volume of subsidized agricultural exports as well as cuts in production subsidies. Domestic battle lines over the GATT remained clear-cut, with the BMWi and business associations lining up on the side of agreement, and farmers, led by the DBV, calling for solidarity with the French position, and even taking to the Bonn streets *en masse* in December to protest the terms of the EC–US compromise. The BML remained silent on the issue, although its officials issued frequent reminders that any GATT resolution had to be consistent with – and not go beyond – the painful CAP reforms agreed to in May. The provisional Blair House Accord of December 1992, and its subsequent yet exceedingly difficult acceptance by the negotiating parties over a year later, brought the matter to a conclusion.[86]

On the domestic front, the slow, painstaking move toward a structural policy for agriculture based on an efficiency rationale, which dates from the early 1980s, received a substantial push from unification. As a DBV official put it, "We ... are in the middle of a full-blown debate about structural policy," adding that the association was forced to change its standard approach and recognize the claims of the larger farms.[87] In the words of a BML official, "The new Länder have given added impetus to the principle of competitiveness, as opposed to the preservation of the farming way of life, in agricultural policy."[88] With the addition of large farming structures in the east, there now existed an *internal* reference point (as opposed to one in France or Britain) for political debate, which had a galvanizing effect.[89]

In part, the accelerating shift in government policy was reflected in intangibles like the tenor of the national "discourse" on agricultural policy. According to a BML official in Bonn, Kiechle's successor as agriculture minister, Jochen Borchert, referred more frequently to efficient farming structures, and made far fewer allusions to the mythical

---

[85] Interview with BML official, Bonn, June 11, 1992.
[86] See Keeler, "Agricultural Power in the European Community."
[87] Interview with DBV official, Bonn, July 8, 1992.
[88] Interview with BML official, Bonn, May 11, 1992.
[89] Interview with BML official, Bonn, May 16, 1994. In 1994, family farms accounted for only 20 percent of the acreage farmed in the new Länder. Bundesministerium für Ernährung, Landwirtschaft, und Forsten, *Agrarwirtschaft in den neuen Bundesländern: Aktuelle Situation und Maßnahmen* (Bonn, 1995), 4.

bäuerliche Familienbetrieb, than did his predecessor.[90] That said, Borchert was politically astute, and frequently cautioned against abdicating control over agricultural policy to free marketeers.

At a more concrete level, the BML in 1992 began to advocate changes in the GAK designed to bring it in line with the needs of larger, more efficient farms as well as with the growing EC/EU emphasis on environmental goals. Basically, these involved streamlining and concentrating assistance measures; giving higher priority to efficiency and environmental goals; lifting assistance restrictions on larger farms; and moving toward a uniform set of national policy instruments. Officials hoped that a uniform assistance framework would dampen the east–west tensions that had plagued GAK policymaking since 1990,[91] and help to forge a community of interest between larger, more efficient farms in the east and those aspiring to the same status in the west.[92] In March 1995, GAK assistance levels and ceilings for dairy concerns were lifted, and financial support for farm mergers was expanded. The BML opted to leave unchanged assistance measures for the east, but planned to address such long-range reform questions after 1996.

Reform of the GAK necessitated reform of the CAP, since aid ceilings and the like were regulated by European, not national, guidelines. Indeed, BML officials decided to hold off on GAK reform until sufficient room for maneuver could be created in Brussels; as one official described it in 1992,

It makes no sense to enact reforms, which are in any event going to be quite controversial, before an adequate opening has been created in Brussels. Otherwise, Germany runs the risk of having a hard-won reform package unraveled by the Commission.[93]

In 1993, Bonn won Commission approval of its request to extend the eastern German derogations to the CAP assistance guidelines up through the end of 1996; this was seen as essential to the eventual success of agricultural restructuring in the new Länder, and as a means

---

[90] Interview with BML official, Bonn, May 11, 1992.

[91] For example, in the GAK's Agricultural Credit Program, six additional categories of assistance existed for eastern German farms over and above those available to western enterprises. These and other special conditions were the cause of growing irritation among western German farmers, particularly as the economic performance of their eastern competitors improved and even overtook them in some categories by 1994. See Bundesministerium für Ernährung, Landwirtschaft, und Forsten, *Agrarbericht der Bundesregierung 1995* (Bonn, 1995).

[92] According to a BML official interviewed in 1994, farming interests in the west no longer looked upon eastern German agriculture as an evil to be smashed by the government; instead, their demands were for treatment on a par with eastern German farms, so as not to be locked into small, inefficient structures by government policy. Interview with BML official, Bonn, May 16, 1994.

[93] Interview with BML official, Bonn, December 4, 1992.

of buying valuable time to develop proposals for a comprehensive reform of EU regulations in line with Bonn's new structural aims. The reform of the CAP regulations was completed in November 1994, opening the way to a reorientation of national-level structural policies for agriculture in western Germany toward larger units and greater efficiency and competitiveness. A BML official noted that Germany was willing to go much further than the eventual Council decision, but had to settle for what was politically acceptable to other members. He added that Bonn was "in something of a strange position, since it was calling for things like the complete abolition of size thresholds that it had originally inserted into the CAP regulations back in the 1980s!"[94]

Beyond agricultural structural policy, however, the Germans showed little enthusiasm for further revisions of the CAP, preferring instead to defend the letter and spirit of the May 1992 decision. To the extent that the Federal Republic picked up the mantle of reform, it sought to bring about a simplification of CAP administrative procedures, which Bonn argued were placing intolerable burdens on individual farmers. With support from Britain, France, and Italy, Germany submitted a ten-point reform program in June 1994, which bore some fruit later that year when several suggestions were adopted by the Commission.[95]

Bonn also remained extremely vigilant on behalf of the new Länder. In 1993 grain production in the new Länder exceeded the aggregate acreage limits established under the MacSharry reforms, and the Commission moved to impose sanctions, which consisted of automatic reductions in set-aside premiums and compulsory but uncompensated set-asides. Brussels reminded Germany pointedly that Bonn, not the Commission, had furnished the original data on which the acreage figures were based. Germany, supported by the DBV and eastern farming interests, argued that the penalties would have disastrous consequences for a region already reeling from rural unemployment rates approaching 50 percent in some areas, and demanded that the Commission simply raise the acreage limits for the region by the excess amount, since the old figures, in the opinion of German officials, were clearly in error. After Bonn threatened to instruct its Länder to refuse to carry out the punitive aspects of the set-aside program if Brussels failed to produce an acceptable way forward, the two sides agreed to a compromise in December 1993 that removed the threat of EU sanctions. In July

[94] Interview with BML official, Bonn, May 28, 1995.
[95] By pushing this administrative reform agenda for the CAP, Bonn hoped to defuse criticism from the Länder; around this time, Bavaria was in the process of developing proposals for a radical "regionalization" of the CAP, i.e. the transfer of many agricultural policymaking responsibilities from Brussels to the regions in the name of subsidiarity.

1996, the Council approved an extension of the special derogations for the new Länder decided on in May 1992.

Bonn took a dim view of most proposals for market reform. BML minister Borchert insisted on "a phase of tranquillity and consolidation," and rejected calls for "a reform of the reform."[96] The ministry was cautious about extending the MacSharry cereals formula to other product areas, such as sugar, wine, and dairy products, and repeatedly resisted Commission attempts to push through price reductions on cereals and other products. In mid-1996, Bonn derailed a Commission proposal to reduce direct compensation payments to grain farmers as a means of coping with rising CAP expenditures as a result of the British "mad cow disease" crisis. When the combination of drought and the effects of the 1992 reforms led to grain shortages in the EU markets and higher world prices, Germany opposed a series of French-backed initiatives commenced in 1994 to reduce mandatory set-asides, arguing that it represented a possible step backward toward the days of chronic overproduction. Between 1994 and 1996, the Agriculture Council reduced the mandatory set-aside rate from 15 percent to 5 percent over German objections.[97]

Bonn's innate conservatism on market and price issues remained intact in other areas too. Beginning in 1992, the BML fought long and hard to retain the CAP's agri-monetary system – the "switchover" mechanism introduced in the mid-1980s[98] – when renewed instability in the EMS reopened the possibility of reductions in German agricultural price levels to offset the effects of appreciations in the Deutsche Mark. The Commission and other member governments rejected Bonn's demand on the grounds that it condemned the CAP to ever higher prices, and therefore operating costs. According to one official, "The Germans have to recognize that every time the switchover is triggered, they're paying a third of the bill, while their farmers are only getting about a quarter of the take."[99] Nevertheless, the compromise reached in

---

[96] "Borchert kritisiert die Agrarpreisvorschläge," *Frankfurter Allgemeine Zeitung*, February 11, 1993, 13.

[97] A BMWi official described this as "a naked assertion of French national interests." Interview with BMWi official, Bonn, May 26, 1995.

[98] The switchover mechanism tied the green exchange rates to the Deutsche Mark, effectively ruling out agricultural price reductions for countries with appreciating currencies (e.g. Germany); CAP adjustment to broader currency fluctuations took place solely through price increases in member states with depreciating currencies (e.g. France).

[99] The Commission estimated that over the preceding decade, the switchover had contributed to a 21 percent increase in Community agricultural prices and had come with a price tag of DM12 billion (ECU6 billion). David Gardner, "EU Plans to Scrap Farm Price Cushion," *Financial Times*, November 16, 1994, 2.

1996, which eliminated the switchover, still left the Germans in a solid position to protect farm incomes through EU direct income payments and national compensation programs.

German efforts to the contrary notwithstanding, the looming prospect of eastern enlargement, coupled with unremitting GATT pressures, kept the issue of CAP reform very much alive. As part of the Agenda 2000 initiative (see chapter 2), EU Agriculture Commissioner Franz Fischler began to circulate a comprehensive CAP reform proposal in mid-1997, one designed to facilitate the enlargement of the Union while at the same time avoiding a return of the food mountains and lakes that had plagued the CAP in the past. Building on the MacSharry reforms but aiming well beyond them, Fischler's initiative envisioned reductions in EU price support of up to 30 percent in cereals, beef, and dairy products, in exchange for which farmers would receive partial compensation through direct income payments. The Commission proposals resurrected the principle of modulation by proposing a fixed ceiling on the amount of direct aid payments any farm could receive. The Commission plans also recommended that national governments be given more freedom to allocate a sizable portion of production subsidies tied to beef and dairy support programs.[100] If implemented, the reforms would cause annual CAP expenditures to increase in the short term.

Britain, the Netherlands, and Sweden, which had already emerged as major proponents of radical reform (dismantling price supports, reorienting CAP price supports toward the world market, scrapping production quotas, and ending set-aside payments), immediately embraced the Commission's proposals. Germany, along with France and most other member governments, condemned the initiative. Jochen Borchert, with an eye on federal elections as well as a Bavarian Land contest in the fall of 1998, described the combination of price cuts and partial compensation as an unacceptable burden on German farmers, and warned that the payment ceilings advocated by the Commission would disadvantage eastern Germany's larger, more efficient, yet still vulnerable agricultural enterprises.[101] Borchert added that he would oppose in principle any

---

[100] Proponents of radical regionalization of the CAP, such as the Bavarian state government, criticized this nod in the direction of subsidiarity as inadequate. See Bayerische Ministerrat, "Memorandum der Bayerischen Staatsregierung zu den Vorschlägen der Europäischen Kommission in der 'Agenda 2000'," September 16, 1997.

[101] Borchert's warning shot across the bow of CAP modulation was by no means a lone incident; other member governments with agricultural sectors populated by large farms, such as the United Kingdom, France, and Denmark, expressed similar doubts about the Commission's proposals.

CAP reform package that added to Germany's already intolerable financial burdens in the EU budget.

After numerous bilateral consultations with the member governments and several full-scale discussions in the Agriculture Council, the Commission released its formal CAP proposals in March 1998. Although the basic outlines of the reform survived intact, on the question of modulation evidence of tacking to the prevailing political winds blowing out of Bonn was unmistakable. In place of a single ceiling, there now stood a series of graded thresholds: farmers were to be paid in full for the first ECU100,000 of direct income claims; thereafter, they would receive 80 percent of the next ECU100,000 in claims, and 75 percent of all claims above ECU200,000.

Bonn officials were quick to claim an important victory on behalf of eastern German agriculture, and set their sights on winning yet another extension of the special derogations for the region beyond 1999. At the same time, the government pledged to the rest of the national farming sector a sustained fight on the question of price reductions.[102] In May 1998 agriculture ministers from the sixteen Länder issued a joint position paper calling on Brussels to return substantial competencies over farm policy to the regions. The initiative, spearheaded by Bavaria, quickly won the endorsement of senior figures in the government, including the Chancellor.

Conclusions

In both cases examined here, the German government attempted to stick to its established pre-unification position after 1990, but eventually was forced into a formal shift in objectives by the concerted efforts of the eastern Land governments. This chain of events is clearest in the case of the structural funds; for the CAP, external pressures for change flowing from the Uruguay Round must also be credited with a significant causal effect. The ability of the Länder to mount successful lobbying campaigns in both Bonn and Brussels can be traced back to the institutionalized "position" they enjoy in the domestic policy process and, by extension, the Community-level programs in each of these areas.

[102] "Bonn Strongly Opposed to Reform of European Agriculture," *Agence France-Presse*, March 19, 1998.

7   A new Germany in Europe

United Germany's place in Europe is intact. Bonn (soon to be Berlin) remains an ardent proponent of the overarching goals of integration, and along with France continues to occupy the activist political fulcrum in Brussels. Since the collapse of the wall in November 1989, the German government has contributed vital support to the ambitious goals of political and economic integration enshrined in the Maastricht Treaty and its more staid progeny, and it has made eastern enlargement a central objective of the European Union. The Federal Republic's integration policy reveals new accents since 1990, to be sure: a greater frugality and a more sober appraisal of the limits of the European project, to name just two. Nevertheless, the appearance is one of seamless continuity with the past.

Yet beyond the glamor and glare of grand bargaining in Brussels, conspicuous shifts in Germany's approach to European regulative policies have emerged since, and in many instances because of, unification. In sum, the preceding chapters reveal a complex pattern of change and continuity, stretching across both the constitutive and regulative dimensions of Community politics. In this final chapter, I delve more deeply into the empirical findings, and construct explanations based on the analytical framework outlined in chapter 1. I then consider the long-term implications of constitutive continuity underpinned by regulative change for the larger relationship between an integrating Europe and a unified Germany as the twentieth century draws to a close.

The politics of continuity: constitutive outcomes

The automatic, even unreflective nature of Germany's "decision" to maintain and even intensify its ties to the West and to the EC after November 9, 1989 can be attributed in large part to the fact that elites and ordinary citizens viewed Europe not as an instrumentality, but as a starting premise – an internalized, intrinsic component of German identity *and* political economy. To recall a core assumption of this study, member governments will strive to replicate or, at a minimum, secure at the European level the constellation of ideas, interests, and institutions that they find (or would find) most advantageous at the domestic level. And given the success that West Germany enjoyed in building a successful model of political economy embedded within a stable, supportive relationship to Europe, it is hard to imagine another EC member with better reason to pursue policy continuity after 1990. And try Germany did. The Bonn government sought to preserve the postwar equilibrium in interests, institutions, and ideas between Germany and Europe via a policy of comprehensive institutional transfer at the national and supranational levels.

German officials enjoyed unprecedented autonomy during the period immediately surrounding formal unification, conferred on them by the sheer uncertainty accompanying these momentous developments and the virtual absence of mobilized interests in the new Länder. The decision to pursue policy continuity via a comprehensive transfer of the German model in Europe flowed not from precise or even approximate calculations of the vector of group interests, but rather from their reflexive belief in the restorative powers of the West German model in Europe.[1] Political and economic elites looked at the *Wirtschaftswunder* – a macroeconomic boom ushered in by a swift, decisive currency reform in 1948 followed by rapid implementation of the social market economy within an integrating Europe – and concluded that history could repeat itself four decades later.

The post-unification period revealed with brutal clarity the fatal flaws in the ideational foundations of the government's approach.[2] In retrospect, the original script drafted in Germany's provisional capital looks positively Panglossian. When the predicted economic take-off in the new Länder sputtered and then stalled in mid-1991, national policymakers suddenly found themselves in uncharted territory, holding ideational road maps that in many instances bore little relation to the new

---

[1] This belief was in fact widely held in Germany at the time. For *Ossis*, hope gave rise to conviction, whereas to most *Wessis* it rested on faith.

[2] Lehmbruch, for example, laments the fact that a myth – the 1948 currency reform – and a symbol – the social market economy – guided government policymakers as they crafted the terms of GEMSU, with disastrous consequences. He takes particular issue with the 1948 analogy, pointing out that there were crucial differences between the starting points obtaining in the western occupation zones immediately after the war and in East Germany *circa* 1990. For example, in the former, firms emerged from the war largely intact and with state-of-the-art production capabilities; what held back the economy were deficiencies in transportation and communication as well as anemic consumer purchasing power. Moreover, West German firms found shelter under the nonconvertibility of the Deutsche Mark for a good part of the 1950s. Thus, 1948 in no way provided an accurate map of the likely effects of economic and currency union in 1990. Lehmbruch, "Institutionentransfer," 58–59.

terrain. And as social-market-economic orthodoxy faltered and economic distress mounted throughout Germany, political challenges to government policies, both at home and in Brussels, multiplied. Yet these challenges were aimed not at the broader integration goals pursued by the Federal Republic – testament to the resilience of these core political values and the national framework of institutions that uphold them – but at the regulative aspects of German policies toward Europe.

The politics of continuity and change: regulative outcomes

Within a broader tapestry of continuity in European constitutive politics, the German government's regulative policy responses unfolded in a manner consistent with the "sectorized" nature of the national policy process, i.e. piecemeal and often uncoordinated.

Table 7.1 reveals a complex pattern of change and continuity since unification. First, in *trade* and *internal market* affairs, there is an unbroken line of continuity across the 1989–90 divide. Second, German *environmental* and *energy* policies reveal subtle shifts in the post-unification period. At the domestic level, the government adopted a more measured approach to national environmental regulation (although not for the new Länder) and a greater emphasis on market liberalization in the energy sector. At the supranational level, the German government remained committed to its ambitious European agenda for the environment, but resorted less frequently to solo policymaking when progress in Brussels proved elusive. In energy policy, the changing terms of the national debate after 1990 allowed the Germans to push openly for an internal energy market program they had always supported in principle, but had been unable to advance because of domestic roadblocks and disagreements with the Commission over means to the desired end.

Finally, Germany's approaches in the remaining policy areas exhibit marked changes after 1990. The German government formally changed its positions on the *structural funds* and the *CAP* in order to address novel problems in the new territories. *Vis-à-vis* EC/EU policy on *state aid*, Bonn's position remained unchanged only in a formal sense, i.e. the government insisted that it still supported and adhered to a strict application of stringent competition rules. However, after a succession of decisions on individual aid cases, the German government cumulatively altered its praxis in this policy area.

How to explain this pattern of outcomes? The seven case studies together reveal several plausible causal chains. For example, it is clear that national officials, who controlled a reasonably intact institutional

Table 7.1. *Policy comparisons*

EC/EU policy	Opposition in new Länder? (1)	Counter-opposition in western Germany? (2)	Organization of policy: Germany (3)	Organization of policy: EC/EU (4)	Policy model congruence? (5)	Δ in national policy? (6)	Δ in EC/EU policy? (7)
Trade	Yes[a]	No	Federal	All supranational	Yes	N/A	No
Internal market	No	No	Federal	Mostly supranational	Yes	N/A	No
CAP	Yes[b]	Yes[a]	Shared	Mostly supranational	Yes	Yes	Yes
State aid	Yes[b]	Yes[a]	Federal	Shared	Yes	Yes	Yes
Structural funds	Yes[b]	No	Shared	Shared	No	Yes	Yes
Environment	No	No	Federal	Shared	No	Yes	No
Energy	No	No	Federal	Some supranational	No	Yes	No

Notes: [a] Producer group-led.
[b] Land government-led.

Table 7.2. *The locus of post-unification conflict*

None	Outside Eastern Germany	Eastern Germany
internal market	energy environment	trade structural funds CAP state aid

apparatus in the federal bureaucracy and employed a coherent model of political economy, did not confront uniform domestic pressures for EC policy change; the cases reveal considerable variation in the intensity, composition, and organization of domestic opposition, as well as differential access to the federal and EC policy process. Moreover, national officials were subject to variable pressures from above. In some cases, the interests and ideas embraced by national and EC-level officials were congruent, creating strong currents in favor of policy continuity. Conversely, in at least one case – the structural funds – EC/EU officials pursued a markedly different agenda from their counterparts in Bonn, and used the opportunities presented by unification to press for changes in long-standing German positions.

Taking a broad overview of the seven regulative policy areas covered in this volume, three distinct clusters of cases take shape: those within which the locus of conflict after unification originated in eastern Germany; those in which the locus of conflict resided outside eastern Germany; and those in which conflict simply failed to materialize. The three case clusters, which are depicted in table 7.2, serve as an organizing framework for the ensuing causal analysis.

Explaining policy outcomes: the absence of politicization

The internal market case provides support for the front end of the first working hypothesis outlined in chapter 1.

H1: If eastern German actors do not press for change in government policy toward Europe, government policy will not change. Conversely, if eastern German actors press for change in government policy toward Europe, national officials will adjust policy to meet their expressed needs.

The constancy of the government's approach can be traced to the failure of the SEA to resonate politically in the new Länder. The federal government came under no pressure whatsoever from political constituencies in the new territories to alter its approach to Project 1992, and western German interests remained as enthusiastic as ever about the initiative. The result was (and is) policy continuity. Of course, unification led to a revival of the *Standort* debate, which carried implications for German domestic politics and, indirectly, environmental and energy policies, but not for the internal market.

Explaining policy outcomes: western Germany as a locus of conflict

A similar correlation between the absence of political mobilization in the east and policy continuity in Brussels surfaces in both energy and the environment, but the parallel is superficial. In contrast to internal market affairs, unification clearly made a difference in these policy areas, leading eventually to perceptible changes in national energy and environmental policies. Yet the eastern German *problématique* featured hardly at all in these policy deliberations; instead, debates and decisions addressed systemic requirements – the health of the German *Standort* – rather than singular problems in the new territories.

Adjustments in energy and environmental policy arose out of concerns about the international competitiveness of the German economy. Unification catalyzed this national debate, and thus its effects on outcomes in these regulative policy areas can be characterized as largely indirect. By altering the terms of the national discussion, unification altered the cost-benefit matrix that national policymakers used to formulate environmental and energy policies at both the national and European levels. This was a debate carried out for the most part by western German political and economic elites, although, as chapter 4 makes clear, eastern German actors contributed to the discussion; business-as-usual in Bonn on matters relating to coal and especially the environment spelled disaster for fledgling business concerns in the new Länder, and they responded accordingly.

Ultimately, preserving and improving the competitiveness of German export industry counseled greater caution on the environment and greater activism on the energy front. These conclusions were applied for the most part at home, however. Indeed, what is intriguing about the changes observed at the European level in these two cases is that they in no way reversed or altered the long-standing substantive objectives of the Bonn government. German officials continued to count themselves among the most ardent supporters of strict environmental regulations at the supranational level, and they continued to adhere to a deregulatory energy agenda.

In contrast to the four cases examined in the next subsection, the eastern interests that mobilized around both environmental and energy policies did not place unique pressures on Bonn decision-makers, since they paralleled domestic political line-ups that already existed in the west. The basic consensus in the new Länder on the need to bring the region up to the existing environmental standards of the west matched sentiments expressed on the other side of the former border almost perfectly. Eastern German entreaties to Bonn to refrain from putting too much daylight between itself and its European partners on environmental regulation, or to cut subsidies to hard coal to free up resource transfers to the new Länder, dovetailed with the positions of many western interest groups and, particularly in the case of coal, with the objectives of the federal government.

Although eastern German actors reinforced the structure of the pre-unification debates in both energy and environmental policy, it would be inaccurate to attribute changes in national policy approaches to their emergence on the political scene after 1990. Actors in the new Länder did not "tip the scales" in favor of an environmental moratorium or energy market deregulation. Rather, unification transformed the national economic context, which in turn transformed the national political context. The stakes attending the rejuvenated *Standort* debate were now much higher, a situation that proponents of national policy change in energy and the environment (often the same groups) used to their advantage.

As debates over environmental policy and energy deregulation unfolded in Bonn, national officials referred frequently to developments and precedents in Europe to strengthen their hands domestically. This was most evident in the case of energy; the Bonn government insisted that the EU's internal energy program, shorn of its *dirigiste* elements, virtually dictated parallel reforms at the national level. Convergence to the emerging European energy model was essential if German economic interests were to be safeguarded. On the environment, Bonn officials exhibited an intense desire to continue living up to their image as the EU's *Musterknabe*. The subtle changes introduced at the national level, which entailed more a change in pace rather than a change in direction, presented few obstacles.

Explaining policy outcomes: eastern Germany as a locus of conflict

Turning to the cases in which unification prompted a mobilization of eastern German actors opposed to government policies, one quickly encounters anomalies that spell trouble for an unalloyed interest-based explanation consistent with the second half of the volume's first working hypothesis. Simply put, the emergence of eastern German opposition in no way guaranteed a shift in government policy. Although concerted eastern lobbying campaigns galvanized Bonn officials into adjustments on the Common Agricultural Policy and the structural funds, the same cannot be said for trade, a highly contentious issue area after 1990. There, an eastern German coalition, led by THA firms and organized labor, pressed vigorously but in the end unsuccessfully for radical changes in Bonn's Eastern trade policy.

Perhaps the solution to the puzzle lies in western Germany.

H2: Regardless of the interests of eastern German actors, national officials will administer policy in a way that meets the expressed needs of western German actors. When western groups demand policy continuity, continuity will ensue. When they demand policy change, change will ensue.

It turns out that western German pressure group activity is an equally erratic predictor of change and continuity in Bonn's European policies. The failure of the eastern trade lobby cannot be laid at the doorstep of powerful, entrenched business interests in western Germany, which, keen on reaping the benefits of Eastern trade themselves, successfully blocked government efforts to improve the export prospects of potential competitors in the new Länder. Although plausible, this argument is not supported by the empirical evidence. Western firms mobilized neither against the special trade conditions nor for a bigger share of the Eastern trade pie. The issue of special trade arrangements with Russia was not a zero-sum game pitting east against west, since Russia played such a small part in overall western German trade relations.[3] Perhaps more significantly, in two key cases – the CAP and state aid – eastern German reform agendas prevailed over bitter western opposition.

Clearly, an unadorned domestic-interest-based explanation – changes in societal vectors of group interests produce changes in policy – appears plausible in some but not all of the cases covered in this analysis. It covers elements of the internal market, structural funds, CAP, and state aid cases, but completely misses trade and fails to capture relevant aspects of the politics of energy and the environment. A careful examination of some of these cases underscores the importance of incorporating two additional clusters of explanatory variables – institutions and ideas – as well as a second level of analysis – the supranational.

---

[3] An alternative hypothesis would hold that western firms contributed to the eventual policy outcome by vigorously opposing any change in German policy that might threaten the international trade order and its liberal norms. Although no such evidence materialized, this account is consistent not with an interest-based explanation, but with one that assigns causal weight to institutionalized ideas (see below).

Trade Policy

This case reveals that policy continuity arises not just from non-events (e.g. the absence of pressures for change in internal market affairs), but also from a politicized process culminating in a conscious decision to maintain the existing contours of government policy in the face of societal opposition. Intense demands from eastern German firms, trade unions, and state governments for trade subsidies came at a time when Bonn was politically vulnerable to the charge that its unification policies had failed. The federal government responded by declaring the problem of Eastern trade to be of paramount concern, initiating a wide-ranging debate, conducting a thorough policy review, and ultimately standing pat. Had the federal government acquiesced, the ramifications for Germany's liberal trade orientation could well have been momentous. In this instance, continuity resulted from the interaction of ideas and institutions.

The empirical evidence suggests that the German government ulti- mately chose the policy option most consistent with the prevailing set of ideas about the proper role of the state in trade policy. The government expressly declined to shift its approach toward open trade subsidies when it became clear that existing policy instruments had lost efficacy in light of changed circumstances, and that proposed policy alternatives would require a marked departure from long-established orthodoxy. In short, the doctrine of the social market economy served as a road map, providing federal policymakers with a means of interpreting reality and selecting avenues of action.

Essential to policy continuity in trade, however, was not the mere presence of a coherent economic belief system, but the fact that it was institutionalized within the federal bureaucracy; the full weight and authority of two key ministries – the BMWi and the BMF – lay behind the justification for Bonn's course of action. These parts of the German federal bureaucracy entrusted with responsibility for trade policy had emerged unscathed from the formal unification process, and were in an advantageous position to resist pressures emanating from the eastern Länder for open-ended subsidy schemes.[4]

Moreover, the institutionalized belief system that informed the gov- ernment's decision drew on critical support beyond the domestic level. The framework of international trading norms and rules in which the

---

[4] As a case in point, the BMWi left the department responsible for economic trade relations and policy toward the Eastern bloc countries (*Abteilung VC*) largely untouched in the aftermath of unification. The department head remained in place throughout the period of study, and the few personnel changes involved lateral and upward moves by officials already working within the department.

Federal Republic had embedded itself for nearly fifty years provided conceptual orientation and political backbone for federal bureaucrats, who consulted frequently with responsible officials in Brussels and Paris. OECD and EC trade regimes by no means determined German policy responses, but they formed an integral part of the Bonn bureaucracy's resistance to policy options that entailed open trade subsidies for eastern German exporters.

State aid, agriculture, and structural funds

In each of these cases, mobilized coalitions of eastern actors launched major and ultimately successful initiatives to change government policies both at home and in Brussels. In two of the three cases, these eastern coalitions overcame substantial opposition from western groups. In light of the negative example of trade policy, where eastern pressure failed to move policymakers in Bonn, these three instances of regulative policy change deserve close scrutiny.

Across the board, eastern Land governments provided the main impetus for change, a fact that stands in contrast to trade, where the eastern German lobby was led by THA firms and producer groups. These eastern political coalitions led by the Länder either prevailed in the absence of any meaningful countervailing pressure from the west (structural funds) or triumphed over western opponents consisting of producer groups (state aid) or of a coalition of producer groups and certain western Länder (agriculture). The crucial role played by the eastern Länder provides an important clue in our search for causal factors: what enabled them to achieve such prominence in the policy process, and why were they so effective? The explanation can be traced to variations in the organization of the policy process generated by domestic institutional transfer, which influenced the composition of pressure coalitions mobilized in the east and their political efficacy. In short, we find at least partial confirmation of the fourth working hypothesis presented in chapter 1:

H4: Where eastern German actors opposed to government policy toward Europe are included in the national policymaking process, national officials will adjust policy to meet their expressed needs.

The two German policy positions to undergo substantial and official changes during the post-unification period were those in which domestic policymaking was shared between Bonn and the Länder; both regional policy and agricultural policy are "joint tasks" in Germany, resting on elaborate policymaking arrangements that elevate the Länder to the status of virtually co-equal participants in the federal policy process.

During unification, institutional transfer in these areas entailed the immediate incorporation of the eastern Länder into the federal policy framework. Consequently, they were positioned to influence national policies directly as participant-insiders, not as lobbyist-outsiders. Insider status also gave the Länder access to information that enabled them to mobilize eastern German interests more effectively at both the national and European levels. Furthermore, joint policymaking arrangements helped eastern interests find win–win solutions in tandem with representatives from the western Länder, and thereby minimize the possibility that east–west conflicts would undermine their bargaining position in Bonn. Where federal government and the states shared policymaking authority, the forbearance of the western Länder was won, either immediately as in the case of the structural funds or eventually as in agriculture.

Länder prominence in the state aid case also stems from institutional sources, but of a different origin than those at work in agriculture and the structural funds. The key to their eventual success was the Treuhandanstalt, a product of "reverse" institutional transfer during unification. On the surface, this suggests support for the third working hypothesis:

H3: Where unification results in a modification of national policy institutions, eastern German actors opposed to government policy toward Europe will enjoy greater success in effecting change.

Did the THA, a GDR import, serve as a Trojan horse for the eastern Länder? Not exactly. In fact, the THA entered the gates of the Federal Republic as a highly insulated agency. The turning point came in 1991–92, when the eastern Länder succeeded in bringing about the penetration of the agency on the grounds that their constitutionally defined responsibilities for structural and economic policies were at stake. Following the integration of the THA into German federalism, the new Länder used their new-found access to push federal policy on state aid (but not official doctrine) in a direction more consistent with their needs. The transitional nature of the THA agency helps to explain the "unofficial" nature of the changes in this policy area – Bonn was unwilling to recognize or otherwise acknowledge in Brussels either the permanence of the situation in the new Länder or the enduring nature of their demands for a more forgiving regime on state aid.

The results of domestic institutional transfer in these three cases contrast markedly with trade, internal market affairs, the environment, and energy, where the federal government retained an exclusive grip on policymaking, free of Länder co-participation. As a result, eastern actors enjoyed few opportunities, even where they were so inclined (e.g. trade policy), to shape the federal policy process from within.

Turning to the institutional characteristics of the supranational policy process – specifically, the distribution of policy responsibilities between national and European-level authorities – the evidence of systematic causal effects, as suggested in the sixth working hypothesis, is inconclusive.

H6: Where eastern German actors opposed to government policy toward Europe are excluded from the national policymaking process but enjoy access at the European level, they will have greater success in effecting a change in their government's policy.

In large part, this is due to the fact that where eastern actors were denied access to the federal policy process, national-supranational congruence worked to deny them access at the European level as well. Trade policy is perhaps the most obvious example; the eastern lobby, stymied in Bonn, found no point of access to the EC policy process either, which effectively ended their campaign to change the government's approach to trade with the former communist bloc. Even the much touted regular consultations between Delors and the prime ministers of the new Länder, which took place outside formal policy-making channels at both the national and supranational levels, failed to generate any movement on this issue.

A stark contrast to trade is provided by the structural funds where the eastern Länder were able to combine their formal roles in both the national and supranational policy processes so as to influence the content and implementation of EC/EU policy, with significant ramifications for the national scene. The absence of a formal role for the Länder in European agricultural policy, however, did not appear to harm their ability to achieve desired shifts on structural questions both at home and in Brussels. In sum, to the extent the organization of the supranational policy process had any systematic effects, it worked to reinforce, not undercut, patterns of access and influence obtaining at the national level.

In trade, ideas worked to reproduce policy continuity after unification. What role, if any, did ideas play in the three cases of policy change?

H5: Where unification results in a modification of the national belief system attached to a particular policy area, eastern German actors opposed to government policy toward Europe will enjoy greater success in effecting change.

H7: Where eastern German actors confront a situation in which the prevailing national policy model they oppose does not correspond to the prevailing European policy model, they will have greater success in effecting change.

Did policy models governing the structural funds, agricultural policy, and state aid simply disintegrate, or were they systematically ignored or overruled? It appears that neither of these is the case. In each instance, the prevailing policy models employed at the European and German levels persisted into the post-unification period, but were sufficiently elastic to accommodate the changes contemplated and ultimately adopted in agriculture, regional policy, and state aid. The CAP reform's explicit formula of social compensation in exchange for efficiency-oriented market adjustment was entirely consistent with social market orthodoxy in postwar Germany, and even though it represented a rebalancing of priorities within the farm policy sector, it resonated with long-standing, albeit embryonic, concerns about agricultural efficiency in the FRG. Germany's heightened interest in an efficiency-oriented structural policy for agriculture dovetailed with the policy model advanced by the Commission as well as the interests of a pre-existing coalition in the Council of Ministers supporting large farming structures. Indeed, the schizophrenia exhibited by Germany's CAP policies after 1992 – reformist on structural questions, conservative on market and pricing policies – fits comfortably inside the evolving CAP regime of the 1990s.

Policy shifts in the structural funds were even easier for the federal government to justify, particularly once the economic gap between east and west had been established with precision. The principle of assisting the worse-off regions had always occupied a prominent place in the overall Bonn economic policy model, and furthermore it found institutional expression in federal regional policy. The ideational framework supporting the EC/EU's structural funds was similarly accommodating to Bonn's emerging demands on behalf of the new Länder.

Real tensions with existing policy norms developed only in the realm of competition policy; eastern German demands for a more relaxed approach to state aid clashed with strictures of the social market economy, which had always tied firm-specific and sectoral aid to efficiency gains and competitive viability. Objectively, these were harder to argue in the case of eastern German industry, although federal officials increasingly made the attempt as the deindustrialization debate intensified. Strife between the Commission and Bonn over subsidy practices in the new Länder, although it marked a clear departure for Germany, represented nothing atypical in a more general sense; state aid practice in the EC/EU has always been the subject of open controversy between the Commission as defender of the market on the one hand, and the member governments advancing particularistic demands on the other. Not only are conflicts over state aid an ever present reality in

Brussels, they are a legitimate reality – Commission and member governments expect to clash over such matters.

What *is* noteworthy about state aid is Bonn's attempt to have its cake and eat it too, i.e. to retain its reputation as strict disciplinarian on subsidy practices while receiving a blanket exemption to subsidize eastern German industry on the basis of Article 92(2c) of the Rome Treaty. The Commission's rejection of this legal reasoning landed Germany, however unwillingly, in an established camp of subsidizers in the Council of Ministers, who were only too happy to welcome a new wayward companion.

Overall, a high level of flexibility characterizes the policy models for these three areas of EU activity, a fact that stands in marked contrast to trade policy. Although the policy frameworks governing the CAP, state aid, and the structural funds are comprehensive and for the most part transparent, each sanctions a fairly broad range of activities on the part of member governments and subnational actors, which encourages political wheeling and dealing in the Council that often results in compromise solutions. That said, it should be emphasized that in each of these three cases, the flexibility of the ideational frameworks came into play only because eastern German actors (the Länder) gained institutionalized access to the policy process, and actively pressed their federal government for changes in national and European policy.

The same cannot be said for trade, which combined a much less flexible set of governing principles with a much more insulated policy process. As a consequence, the lower level of negotiability in trade strengthened the federal government's hand against domestic interests pressing for radical policy initiatives on behalf of the eastern region.

All of this suggests that the degree of policy model congruence between the national and supranational levels, highlighted in hypothesis H7, is not a critical factor in producing policy change or continuity after unification. Policy change in fact occurs where congruence is both present and absent (e.g. state aid, structural funds), as does policy continuity (e.g. trade, energy). That said, the case comparisons suggest that policy *in*congruence comes into play, in that it can create a situation in which the federal government is forced to accept changes in policy – admittedly on the margins – that it does not support. Supporting evidence comes from the structural funds, which operate according to principles at odds with Germany's federal regional policy regime. Although Bonn did not confront any difficulties with the basic *principle* of EC/EU cohesion assistance for the new Länder, once obtained it created significant problems for the government because of the lack of policy congruence. Specifically, the needs of the new Länder, quite similar in content to those of the southern periphery, coincided with the Commission's larger substantive and political agenda in this policy area. For Bonn, the price of structural assistance for the new Länder was the importation of a "foreign" model of regional development into the new Länder.

Interests, institutions, and ideas: a reprise

The analytical framework based on interests, institutions, and ideas captures not only basic contours of the pattern of change and continuity in German policies toward Europe, but its many nuances. Beyond explaining a significant historical outcome, does the study of unification and union lend any insights into comparable cases or larger theoretical issues? In this section, I will sidestep the former question; German unification strikes me as a singular event, with little to recommend itself as a model for other realized or potential unifications.[5] Instead, I will focus on its relevance to theory.

A perennial challenge for political economists who explore the inter-action of interests, institutions, and ideas is that their explanatory variables of choice change so infrequently, and when they do, the pace is often glacial. Viewed in this light, German unification presented a propitious natural experiment; in a historical instant, the constellation of interests, institutions, and ideas within Germany changed within a larger supranational context – the European Community – marked by continuity. Scholars were thus able to observe the effects (or non-effects) of much larger variations in these three categories of variables over a much shorter time frame than is typically allowed by real world events. What generalizations emerge from this unique social scientific opportunity?

The case of unification and union confirms a consistent theme in the literature – namely, that institutions and ideas, particularly where they have developed in tandem, are enormously resistant to change, however strong the shock to the system might be. The supreme confidence and faith placed by German elites in the German model in Europe, and the vigor with which they carried out institutional transfer, attests to this property. Institutional and ideational continuity played a large part in producing the continuity that characterized much of the new Germany's approach to Europe after unification.

Their "stickiness," however, does not always impede change. Recalling the examples of the two policy areas examined in chapter 6, where

[5] Examples include the People's Republic of China (PRC) and Hong Kong, the PRC and Taiwan, and the two Koreas.

the policy of institutional transfer granted particular types of access to eastern German actors, the government changed tack within a relatively short time frame. New interests used old institutions and the flexibility inherent in dominant policy models to elicit a shift in government approaches to both federal and European policies. More generally, this suggests that institutional frameworks and the policy models they uphold are independent of the interests that gave rise to them in the first place – leaving open the possibility that change initiated by new interests is quite possible.

This case-oriented study also sheds light on the outer limits of an assertion that appears frequently in institutionalist and idea-centric studies in political economy – specifically, that institutions and/or ideas shape, inform, or otherwise influence the formulation of interests. What this volume shows is just how "hard" material interests are, or at least can be. Contrary to expectations in Bonn, eastern German interests, grounded in a material world vastly different from the one that had developed on the other side of the Elbe, did not converge to the range of preferences held by western German actors. In fact, these interests remained largely impervious to the conditioning effects of the (West) German model in Europe, thereby perpetuating, indeed cementing, a lack of fit between material interests circumscribed by the eastern territories and the constellation of interests, institutions, and ideas buttressing national and European public policies that impinged on those interests. This was a recipe for political conflict and, in some instances, policy change.

This last observation could be read as suggesting that the debate over which variable warrants placement at the top of the causal hierarchy – interests, institutions, or ideas – has moved a long step closer to resolution: interests matter most of all. That, however, would constitute a highly selective interpretation of the volume's empirical evidence and conclusions. Naturally, the activation of new interests through unification made a huge difference to the potential for political conflict and to the possibility of policy change at both the national and European levels. Only through interaction with certain kinds of institutional frameworks and ideational systems did new interests lead to new policy directions, however. If anything, these conclusions provide strong reasons for moving beyond the research agenda of causal one-upmanship.

Finally, this study demonstrates that the multilevel interactions of interests, institutions, and ideas are not only ubiquitous, but reveal systematic properties, in terms of both process and outcomes. What confers regularity on these interactions is the bounded nature of the system; in this case, a national political economy embedded within a supranational framework. Given the complex and often subtle nature of these interactions, and the high degree of contextual and historical specificity they exhibit, there is no reason to believe that these patterns of interaction and their outcomes will travel, i.e. that they will replicate themselves perfectly in other times and places. Put another way, this study lends support to the notion that interests, institutions, and ideas will combine systematically elsewhere too, but the logic may well differ from locus to locus.[6]

United Germany in Europe

What is Germany's place in Europe, now that the Berlin Wall has been consigned to the trash-heap (and mantelpieces) of history and the continent is no longer divided? Put another way, which Germany will take a seat at Europe's council table: a descendant of the assertive, aggressive state that roamed the continent for almost three-quarters of a century after 1871, or the "model and magnet"[7] that sat quietly and comfortably at Europe's center after 1945? The short answer is neither, although the Germany emerging from the settling dust of unification bears a strong familial resemblance to its immediate predecessor.

Unification failed to launch a sweeping reevaluation of Germany's place in Europe, either at home or abroad. In spite of the domestic and international upheavals unleashed by the events of 1989–90, the causal substructure of Germany's distinctive blend of constitutive and regulative politics remains for the most part intact; these include domestic conceptions of interest and identity, institutionalized policy models at both national and supranational levels, as well as international expectations concerning acceptable German behavior. Thus, in the late 1990s Germany's general approach to integration remains consistent with its pre-unification past. The Federal Republic remains solidly anchored in Europe, its exaggerated multilateralism and "culture of restraint"[8] undiminished. Still, to describe the united Germany's relationship with Europe in terms of seamless continuity would be grossly inaccurate. Something has changed since 1990, rendering Germany less of a model and magnet for other European countries, but no less central to the continent's future peace and prosperity.

The changes have been largely domestic in origin, and intimately bound up with unification. Initially, the German government, buttressed

---

[6] This is consistent with arguments advanced by, among others, Charles Ragin, Raymond Boudon, and Alan Zuckerman. See notes 2 and 3 in chapter 1.
[7] Garton Ash, *In Europe's Name*, 408.
[8] See Peter Katzenstein, "Introduction," in Katzenstein, ed., *Tamed Power*.

by broad public support in both the western and eastern parts of the country, held to the pre-unification formula: EC regulative politics (where possible) as a means to and (where necessary) subordinate to constitutive ends and domestic system requirements. In the Maastricht Treaty, the Federal Republic projected elements of its domestic model onto Europe,[9] whereas on regulative issues it acted for the most part as a policy-taker during the first two years after unification, submitting to established EC procedures and outcomes. Meanwhile, however, domestic pressures were growing that would eventually call into question long-standing German assumptions and approaches in several EC policy areas.

Many (but by no means all) of these pressures originated in the new Länder, i.e. from newly arrived actors whose material interests were ill served by Bonn's EC priorities. Their demands began to resonate in an increasingly charged political atmosphere in Bonn. The softening of domestic consensus over Europe can be traced in part to unification and the ensuing crisis of the national political economy. It can also be attributed to widespread public disillusionment and frustration with contemporary developments on the European continent, from EMU to Bosnia to mad cow disease. Along the way, core elements of the German model were subjected to domestic scrutiny and challenge, with significant ramifications for German objectives in Europe.

Germany's European policies after 1989 continue to be driven by concerns about process and principles, but Bonn officials are paying closer attention to distributive outcomes and net pay-offs in the short term. In the words of a Foreign Ministry official,

We are used to placing the goal of integration above all else, which requires a certain propensity toward generosity. Integration had to be advanced, even if it ended up costing Germany something in the bargain. This is no longer possible. We have to totally reorient ourselves.[10]

Such behavior, quite common for other member governments, is unusual for Germany, which in the past acted in a more rule- and norm-regarding manner than other Community members, particularly the large ones.[11] Precisely because elements of its domestic model of political economy found prominent expression or support in many EC regulative policy areas, West Germany consistently threw its weight behind outcomes that spoke more to the integrity of the rule frameworks

---

[9] This is characterized as "direct institutional export" in Bulmer, Jeffery, and Paterson, "Germany's European Diplomacy," 42–45.

[10] Interview with Foreign Ministry official, Bonn, November 20, 1992.

[11] On the subject of "normalcy" and German foreign policy, see James McAdams, "Germany after Unification: Normal at Last?" *World Politics* 49 (January 1997), 282–308.

themselves than to "who got what." This is tangibly less true in the 1990s. Increasingly, Germans are scrutinizing the bottom line in Brussels.

What of it? In purely practical terms, it obviously translates into a more arduous integration process. Up to and including the Maastricht Treaty, integration advanced on the basis of an implicit formula: in exchange for the invisible economic benefits provided by the internal market and the opportunity to reaffirm its innate multilateral credentials, Germany agreed to underwrite regional integration and to wield its influence unobtrusively. Unification rocked the foundations of this cozy arrangement. Germany's diminished inclination to foot the bill for expensive ventures like eastern enlargement and EU institutional reform, coupled with a less starry-eyed approach to Europe and a growing interest in securing a fair share for itself from various regulative policies, has already complicated EU constitutive bargaining post-Maastricht, and will continue to slow the pace of integration and raise the level of discord among the member states.[12]

Given the deep and abiding concerns expressed across Europe about the flawed democratic credentials of the EU, perhaps this is not a bad thing at all.[13] And if a somewhat more ponderous integration process is all that results from the new Germany in Europe, then basic postwar continuities will surely have endured. It is possible, however, that these subtle changes we are witnessing in Germany's basic approach to integration, the consequence of a far-reaching domestic transformation begun in 1989, are just the tip of the iceberg. To adopt the analytical terminology employed in this volume, as German national officials reconcile themselves to the fact that their country has been permanently and in some respects profoundly changed by unification, they will seek to adjust their regulative and constitutive agendas in Brussels to reflect the new facts on the ground. In other words, as the content of the German model undergoes a transformation, so too will the assessment of the supportive superstructure desired in Brussels.

Whether this transformational scenario will in fact materialize, and

---

[12] Bulmer notes that sectorization and its attendant lack of coordination often played to Bonn's advantage in the past, rendering its gains less visible and therefore less open to criticism from its EC partners. This may no longer be the case – although sectorization persists, Germany is raising its visibility across many policy areas as it pursues a more equitable share of the proceeds. See Bulmer, "Shaping the Rules?"

[13] See Michael Newman, *Democracy, Sovereignty, and the European Union* (New York: St. Martin's Press, 1996); Antje Wiener and Vincent Della Sala, "Constitution-making and Citizenship Practice – Bridging the Democracy Gap in the EU," *Journal of Common Market Studies* 35 (December 1997), 593–614; and Jeffrey Anderson, ed., *Regional Integration and Democracy: Expanding on the European Experience* (Boulder: Rowman & Littlefield, 1998).

where it will lead, is anybody's guess – there are far too many variables and too little available data to venture concrete predictions at the present time. What can be said right now is that Germany may well see fit to undertake major adjustments in the kinds of demands and the types of goals it pursues in Europe, both at the regulative and the constitutive levels. The question is whether the political environment in Brussels will facilitate or impede such changes.

As we have seen, unification reshuffled the cards inside Germany, transforming the domestic context in which European policy is made. New material interests now sit along established ones, overlaid by still intact but increasingly contested institutional and normative frameworks. This renders it much more difficult, even impossible, for the German government to satisfy domestic constituencies with traditional policy priorities and a self-effacing deportment in Brussels. The only real question now is how much and how far German policies toward Europe will change.

Now more than at any time since 1945, however, Germans are expected to walk, talk, and act softly – in short, to be good (West) Germans. Unification rekindled deep anxieties among its neighbors about German power and intentions. Although manifest concerns have subsided, they persist in latent form, and are easily resurrected. Many EU member governments, usually *sotto voce*, ascribe dark intentions to German demands for institutional reform or eastern enlargement, seeing in them thinly veiled attempts to cement its growing power and influence in the EU.

So what? One can start by recalling that the post-unification continuities discussed in earlier chapters originated *inside* Germany; that is, they resulted from the conscious and sometimes reflexive choices of the German government. To date, continuity is "Made in Germany." But the rumblings expressed by EU members about departures from the West German template smack of externally imposed continuity, which is certain to elicit a far different reaction within Germany, both among elites and the general public. The risk is not the return of the Third Reich, but the emergence of yet another UK in Europe – a second awkward partner, skeptical and often unconstructive on the European stage. Europe can ill afford that outcome. EU member governments and their citizens would do well to reflect on the fact that, while Germany's European interests may be changing, they still fit comfortably with its uniquely positive European identity.

As this book went to press, Germans filed to the polls on September 27, 1998 to elect a new Bundestag. In many respects, the campaign had been a referendum on Helmut Kohl and unification; the plight of eastern Germany featured prominently in the contest, with both major parties giving iron-clad commitments of continued financial support for the troubled region. In the end, eastern Germans turned their backs on the unification chancellor. When all the votes were tallied, the CDU/ CSU had registered its worst election defeat since 1949, and an SPD-Green coalition, led by Gerhard Schröder, looked set to take power for the first time in the republic's history.[14]

Does this change in the partisan composition of government augur still more upheaval in the country's policies toward Europe? At this point in time, all we have to go on are public utterances of the leaders of the new coalition partners, but little else. If their policy pronouncements are genuine, the answer to the above question is "no." In fact, we are likely to observe the same mix of policy continuity and change over the next four years, coupled with an accentuation of the tensions that have been generated by and since unification.

On issues relating to constitutive politics, the policies set down by Germany since 1990 will persist. Trade and internal market policy will carry on as before. With the Greens in power (and in control of the environment ministry), the new government will be willing to drive the EU environmental agenda with domestic legislative initiatives, thereby restoring Bonn-Berlin's pre-unification approach in this policy area. The SPD's new-found political base in eastern Germany, coupled with its commitment to centralize the administration of economic policy for the new Länder while maintaining support for troubled regions and localities in the old, will heighten the tensions with Brussels over subsidy policy and the structural funds already established under Kohl. In agriculture, the SPD-Green government almost certainly will support continued protection for the sector, but will lay greater emphasis on the market, efficiency criteria (which bodes well for eastern German farmers), and environmental objectives in the reform of the CAP and domestic policy.

Only in energy is a departure from the course charted by the Kohl

---

[14] Final election results were:

	percentage of popular vote
CDU/CSU	35.2
SPD	40.9
FDP	6.2
Greens	6.7
PDS	5.1
Others	5.9

Source: "SPD-Greens To Have 10 Seat Majority," *Agence France-Presse*, September 28, 1998.

government possible; the Social Democrats harbor major reservations about their opponent's approach to domestic energy market liberalization, arguing that it does not take sufficient account of the interests of domestic energy producers and local authorities. Even here, modifications to German energy policy are likely to occur on the margins only; the new government will be unwilling to launch a frontal assault on the Commission's IEM project, much of which is already in place thanks in part to German votes in the Council of Ministers.

All of which brings us back to the basic conclusions reached in this volume. Against all confident predictions and pious hopes of western German politicians and public, the Federal Republic did not emerge unscathed from the cauldron of unification. Domestically, the political and economic constitutions are still recognizable, but they function differently, often subtly so, but differently nonetheless. The changes have not been sufficiently sweeping to prompt dramatic changes in Germany's self-defined place in Europe, at least not yet. Nevertheless, they have bubbled up in complex and fascinating ways, generating shifts in some policy areas and continuity in others, the sum total of which constitutes a new Germany in Europe. The twenty-first century will reveal the direction of this ongoing, evolving relationship between unification and union.

Bibliography

Abelshauser, Werner, *Der Ruhrkohlenbergbau seit 1945*, Munich: Verlag C. H. Beck, 1984.

Allen, Christopher, "The Underdevelopment of Keynesianism in the Federal Republic of Germany." In Peter Hall (ed.), *The Political Power of Economic Ideas*, Princeton: Princeton University Press, 1989.

"From Social Market to Mesocorporatism to European Integration: The Politics of German Economic Policy." In Michael Huelshoff, Andrei Markovits, and Simon Reich (eds.), *From Bundesrepublik to Deutschland: German Politics After Unification*, Ann Arbor: University of Michigan Press, 1993.

Anderson, Jeffrey, "Skeptical Reflections on a 'Europe of Regions': Britain, Germany, and the European Regional Development Fund," *Journal of Public Policy* 10 (October–December 1990), 417–47.

The Territorial Imperative: Pluralism, Corporatism, and Economic Crisis, New York: Cambridge University Press, 1992.

"Hard Interests, Soft Power, and Germany's Changing Role in Europe." In Peter Katzenstein (ed.), *Tamed Power*, Ithaca: Cornell University Press, 1997.

Anderson, Jeffrey (ed.), *Regional Integration and Democracy: Expanding on the European Experience*, Boulder: Rowman & Littlefield, 1998.

Anderson, Jeffrey and Celeste Wallander, "Interests and the Wall of Ideas: Germany's Eastern Trade Policy after Unification," *Comparative Political Studies* 30 (December 1997), 675–98.

Armstrong, Harvey, "The Role and Evaluation of European Community Regional Policy." In Barry Jones and Michael Keating (eds.), *The European Union and the Regions*, Oxford: Clarendon Press, 1995.

Arp, Henning, "Technical Regulation and Politics: The Interplay between Economic Interests and Environmental Policy Goals in EC Car Emission Standards." In J. Duncan Liefferink, Philip Lowe, and Arthur P. J. Mol (eds.), *European Integration and Environmental Policy*, New York: Belhaven Press, 1993.

Banchoff, Thomas, "Germany's European Policy: A Constructivist Perspective," Working Paper Series no. 8.1, Program for the Study of Germany and Europe, Minda de Gunzberg Center for European Studies, Harvard University, 1998.

Baun, Michael, *An Imperfect Union*, Boulder: Westview Press, 1996.

Berger, Thomas, "Norms, Identity, and National Security in Germany and

Japan." In Peter J. Katzenstein (ed.), *The Culture of National Security: Norms and Identity in World Politics*, New York: Columbia University Press, 1996.

Bertsch, Franz, "Wie gut ist der Wirtschaftsstandort Deutschland?" Inter Nationes, Basis-Info Working Paper Series, 3–1997.

"Beschluß zur Gründung der Anstalt zur treuhänderischen Verwaltung des Volkseigentums (Treuhandanstalt) vom 1. März 1990," *Gesetzblatt der Deutschen Demokratischen Republik*, part I, no. 14, (March 8, 1990).

Biersteker, Thomas, "Locating the Emerging European Polity: Beyond States or State?" In Jeffrey Anderson (ed.), *Regional Integration and Democracy: Expanding on the European Experience*, Boulder: Rowman & Littlefield, 1998.

Blyth, Mark, "'Any More Bright Ideas?' The Ideational Turn of Comparative Political Economy," *Comparative Politics* 29 (January 1997), 229–50.

Boll, Bernhard, "Interest Organization and Intermediation in the New Länder," *German Politics* 3 (April 1994), 114–28.

Bongaerts, Jan, "Harmonization of the EC Environmental Policy after Maastricht." In Otmar Höll (ed.), *Environmental Cooperation in Europe*, Boulder: Westview Press, 1994.

Boudon, Raymond, *The Crisis in Sociology*, New York: Columbia University Press, 1980.

Bryson, Phillip J. and Manfred Melzer, *The End of the East German Economy: From Honecker to Reunification*, New York: St. Martin's Press, 1991.

Bulmer, Simon, "The Governance of the European Union: A New Institutionalist Approach," *Journal of Public Policy* 13:4 (1993), 351–80.

"European Integration and Germany: The Constitutive Politics of the EU and the Institutional Mediation of German Power," paper presented at the Conference on "The Influence of Germany and the European Union on the Smaller European States," Budapest, Hungary, May 31–June 3, 1995.

"Shaping the Rules? The Constitutive Politics of the European Union and German Power." In Peter Katzenstein (ed.), *Tamed Power*, Ithaca: Cornell University Press, 1997.

Bulmer, Simon, Charlie Jeffery, and William Paterson, "Germany's European Diplomacy: Shaping the Regional Milieu," paper prepared for the Forschungsgruppe Europa of the Centrum für Angewandte Politikforschung, Munich, December 1996.

Bulmer, Simon and William Paterson, *The Federal Republic of Germany and the European Community*, London: Allen & Unwin, 1987.

"Germany in the European Union: Gentle Giant or Emergent Leader?" *International Affairs* 72 (1996), 9–32.

Bunce, Valerie, "The Empire Strikes Back: The Evolution of the Eastern Bloc from a Soviet Asset to a Soviet Liability," *International Organization* 39 (Winter 1985), 1–46.

Bundesminister für Umwelt, Naturschutz, und Reaktorsicherheit, *Stellungnahme der Bundesregierung zum Programm der Europäischen Gemeinschaft für Umweltpolitik und Maßnahmen im Hinblick auf eine dauerhafte und umweltgerechte Entwicklung*, Bonn: 1992.

Bundesministerium für Ernährung, Landwirtschaft, und Forsten, *Agrarpolitik der Bundesregierung in den neuen Bundesländern*, Bonn, 1992.

Agrarbericht der Bundesregierung 1995, Bonn, 1995.

Agrarwirtschaft in den neuen Bundesländern: Aktuelle Situation und Maßnahmen, Bonn, 1995.

Bundesministerium für Umwelt, Naturschutz, und Reaktorsicherheit, *Basic Guidelines for Ecological Recovery and Development in the New Länder*, Bonn: 1991.

Bundesregierung, *Ausfuhrgarantien und Ausfuhrbürgschaften der Bundesrepublik Deutschland: Bericht über das Jahr 1991*, Bonn, 1992.

Ausfuhrgarantien und Ausfuhrbürgschaften der Bundesrepublik Deutschland: Bericht über das Jahr 1992, Bonn, 1993.

Ausfuhrgarantien und Ausfuhrbürgschaften der Bundesrepublik Deutschland: Bericht über das Jahr 1993, Bonn, 1994.

Cameron, David, "The 1992 Initiative: Causes and Consequences." In Alberta Sbragia (ed.), *Euro-Politics: Institutions and Policymaking in the "New" European Community*, Washington, DC: The Brookings Institution, 1992.

"British Exit, German Voice, French Loyalty: Defection, Domination, and Cooperation in the 1992–93 ERM Crisis," paper prepared for delivery at the Annual Meeting of the American Political Science Association, Washington, DC, September 1993.

Campbell, John, "Institutional Analysis and the Role of Ideas in Political Economy," paper presented to the Seminar on the State and Capitalism since 1800, Center for European Studies, Harvard University, October 13, 1995.

Checkel, Jeffrey, "The Constructivist Turn in International Relations Theory," *World Politics* 50 (January 1998), 324–48.

Commission of the European Communities, "The Internal Energy Market," *COM*(88)238, Luxembourg: Office for Official Publications of the European Communities, 1988.

XXIIIrd General Report on the Activities of the European Communities 1989, Luxembourg: Office for Official Publications of the European Communities, 1990.

"The European Community and German Unification," *Bulletin of the European Communities* (Supplement 4/1990), Luxembourg: Office for Official Publications of the European Communities.

"European Industrial Policy for the 1990s," *Bulletin of the European Communities* (Supplement 3/1991), Luxembourg: Office for Official Publications of the European Communities.

Der EFRE 1989, Luxembourg: Office for Official Publications of the European Communities, 1991.

The Regions in the 1990s, Luxembourg, Office for Official Publications of the European Communities, 1991.

Der Zustand der Umwelt in der Europäischen Gemeinschaft: Überblick, Luxembourg: Office for Official Publications of the European Communities, 1992.

Community Structural Funds, 1994–1999: Revised Regulations and Comments, Luxembourg: Office for Official Publications of the European Communities, 1993.

Competitiveness and Cohesion: Trends in the Regions, Luxembourg: Office for Official Publications of the European Communities, 1994.

"Green Paper: For a European Union Energy Policy," *COM* (94)659, Luxembourg: Office for Official Publications of the European Communities, 1994.

Agenda 2000, 3 vols., Brussels: Office for Official Publications of the European Communities, 1997.

Czada, Roland, "Die Treuhandanstalt im politischen System der Bundesrepublik," *Aus Politik und Zeitgeschichte* 43–44 (October 28, 1994), 31–42.

Dennis, Mike, *German Democratic Republic: Politics, Economics, and Society*, London: Pinter Publishers, 1988.

Deutscher Bauernverband, *Für Marktausgleich gegen Preissenkung: Der Deutscher Bauernverband zur Reform der EG-Agrarpolitik*, Bonn, 1991.

Deutsche Bundesbank, *Monatsbericht November 1993*, Frankfurt, 1993.

Monatsbericht Juli 1995, Frankfurt, 1995.

Deutscher Bundestag, *Unterrichtung durch die Bundesregierung: Das energiepolitische Gesamtkonzept der Bundesregierung: Energiepolitik für das vereinte Deutschland*, 12. Wahlperiode, Drucksache 12/1799, December 11, 1991.

Dornbusch, Rudiger and Holger Wolf, "East German Economic Reconstruction." In Olivier Blanchard, Kenneth Froot, and Jeffrey Sachs (eds.), *The Transition in Eastern Europe*, Chicago: Chicago University Press, 1994.

Downs, Anthony, *An Economic Theory of Democracy*, New York: Harper and Row, 1957.

Dyson, Kenneth, "West Germany: The Search for a Rationalist Consensus." In Jeremy Richardson (ed.), *Policy Styles in Western Europe*, London: George Allen and Unwin, 1982.

Dyson, Kenneth and Stephen Wilks, "Conclusions." In Kenneth Dyson and Stephen Wilks (eds.), *Industrial Crisis: A Comparative Study of the State and Industry*, New York: St. Martin's Press, 1983.

Esser, Josef and Wolfgang Fach, "Crisis Management 'Made in Germany': The Steel Industry," in Peter Katzenstein (ed.), *Industry and Politics in Germany*, Ithaca: Cornell University Press, 1989, 221–48.

Esser, Josef and Wolfgang Fach (with Kenneth Dyson), "'Social Market' and Modernization Policy: West Germany." In Kenneth Dyson and Stephen Wilks (eds.), *Industrial Crisis: A Comparative Study of the State and Industry*, New York: St. Martin's Press, 1983.

Ewringmann, Dieter *et al.*, *Die Gemeinschaftsaufgabe "Verbesserung der regionalen Wirtschaftsstruktur" unter veränderten Rahmenbedingungen*, Berlin: Ducker and Humbolt, 1986.

Fischer, Wolfram and Harm Schröter, "Die Entstehung der Treuhandanstalt." In Wolfram Fischer, Herbert Hax, and Hans Karl Schneider, *Treuhandanstalt: Das unmögliche wagen*, Berlin: Akademie Verlag, 1993.

Fisher, Marc, *After the Wall: Germany, the Germans, and the Burdens of History*, New York: Simon and Schuster, 1995.

Flockton, C. H., "The Federal German Economy in the Early 1990s," *German Politics* 2 (August 1993), 311–27.

Friman, H. Richard, *Patchwork Protectionism*, Ithaca: Cornell University Press, 1990.

Garrett, Geoffrey and Barry Weingast, "Ideas, Interests, and Institutions: Constructing the European Community's Internal Market." In Judith Goldstein and Robert Keohane (eds.), *Ideas and Foreign Policy*, Ithaca: Cornell University Press, 1993.

Garton Ash, Timothy, *In Europe's Name*, New York: Random House, 1993.

Giersch, Herbert, Karl-Heinz Paqué, and Holger Schmieding, *The Fading Miracle: Four Decades of Social Market Economy in Germany*, New York: Cambridge University Press, 1992.

Goetz, Klaus and Peter Cullen, "The Basic Law after Unification: Continued Centrality or Declining Force," *German Politics* 3 (December 1994), 5–46.

Goldstein, Judith, *Ideas, Interests, and American Trade Policy*, Ithaca: Cornell University Press, 1993.

Goldstein, Judith and Robert Keohane, "Ideas and Foreign Policy: An Analytical Framework." In Judith Goldstein and Robert Keohane (eds.), *Ideas and Foreign Policy*, Ithaca: Cornell University Press, 1993.

Goodman, John, "Do All Roads Lead to Brussels?" In Norman Ornstein and Mark Perlman (eds.), *Political Power and Social Change*, Washington, DC: American Enterprise Institute, 1991.

  Monetary Sovereignty: The Politics of Central Banking in Western Europe, Ithaca: Cornell University Press, 1992.

Görtemaker, Manfred, *Unifying Germany, 1989–90*, New York: St. Martin's Press, 1994.

Gourevitch, Peter, *Politics in Hard Times*, Ithaca: Cornell University Press, 1986.

Gowa, Joann, "Bipolarity and the Postwar International Economic Order." In Peter Katzenstein (ed.), *Industry and Politics in Germany*, Ithaca: Cornell University Press, 1989.

Grabitz, Eberhard and Armin von Bogdandy, "Die Europäischen Gemeinschaften und die Einheit Deutschlands – die rechtliche Dimension," *Integration* 14 (April 1991), 47–64.

Gröner, Helmut, "Energy Policy in Eastern Germany." In A. Ghanie Ghaussy and Wolf Schäfer (eds.), *The Economics of German Unification*, New York: Routledge, 1993.

Groeben, Hans von der, *The European Community, The Formative Years: The Struggle to Establish the Common Market and the Political Union (1958–66)*, Luxembourg: Office for Official Publications of the European Communities, 1987.

Hall, Peter, *Governing the Economy*, Oxford: Oxford University Press, 1986.

  "The Political Economy of Adjustment in Germany." In Frieder Naschold *et al.* (eds.), *Ökonomische Leistungsfähigkeit und institutionelle Innovation. WZB-Jahrbuch 1997*, Berlin: Wissenschaftszentrum-Berlin, 1997.

Hall, Peter (ed.), *The Political Power of Economic Ideas*, Princeton: Princeton University Press, 1989.

Hanrieder, Wolfram, *Germany, America, Europe*, New Haven: Yale University Press, 1989.

Härtel, Hans-Hagen, Reinald Krüger, *et al.*, *Die Entwicklung des Wettbewerbs in den neuen Bundesländern*, Baden-Baden: Nomos Verlagsgesellschaft, 1995.

Hasse, Rolf, "German–German Monetary Union: Main Options, Costs, and Repercussions." In A. Ghanie Ghaussy and Wolf Schäfer (eds.), *The Economics of German Unification*, New York: Routledge, 1993.

Heilemann, Ullrich and Reimut Jochimsen, *Christmas in July? The Political*

Economy of German Unification Reconsidered, Washington, DC: Brookings Institution, 1993.

Heinze, Rolf and Helmut Voelzkow, "Der Deutsche Bauernverband und das 'Gemeinwohl'." In Renate Mainz (ed.), *Verbände zwischen Mitgliederinteressen und Gemeinwohl*, Gütersloh: Verlag Bertelsmann Stiftung, 1992.

Heisenberg, Dorothy, "The Mark of the Bundesbank: Germany's Role in European Monetary Cooperation," unpublished Ph.D. dissertation, Yale University, 1996.

Hendriks, Gisela, *Germany and European Integration: The Common Agricultural Policy: An Area of Conflict*, New York: St. Martin's Press, 1991.

Herrmann, A., W. Ochel, and M. Wegner, *Bundesrepublik und Binnenmarkt '92: Perspektiven für Wirtschaft und Wirtschaftspolitik*, Berlin, 1990.

Hichert, Ingo, *Staatliche Exportabsicherung*, Cologne: Deutscher Instituts-Verlag, 1986.

Hirschman, Albert, *Exit, Voice, and Loyalty*, Cambridge, MA: Harvard University Press, 1970.

"Exit, Voice, and the Fate of the German Democratic Republic: An Essay in Conceptual History," *World Politics* 45 (January 1993), 173–202.

Hoffmann, Reiner *et al.*, *German Industrial Relations under the Impact of Structural Change, Unification, and European Integration*, Düsseldorf: Hans-Böckler Stiftung, 1995.

Hull, Robert, "The Environmental Policy of the European Community." In Otmar Höll (ed.), *Environmental Cooperation in Europe*, Boulder: Westview Press, 1994.

Jachtenfuchs, Markus, "The European Community and the Protection of the Ozone Layer," *Journal of Common Market Studies* 28 (March 1990), 261–77.

Jachtenfuchs, Markus, and Michael Huber, "Institutional Learning in the European Commuity: The Response to the Greenhouse Effect." In J. Duncan Liefferink, Philip Lowe, and Arthur P. J. Mol (eds.), *European Integration and Environmental Policy*, New York: Belhaven Press, 1993.

Jacobson, John Kurt, "Much Ado about Ideas: The Cognitive Factor in Economic Policy," *World Politics* 47 (January 1995), 283–310.

Jarausch, Konrad, *The Rush to German Unity*, New York: Oxford University Press, 1994.

Jarothe, Sabine, "Konfliktfeld deutsch–deutsche Landwirtschaft," *Politische Studien* 43 (January–February 1992), 97–106.

Jeffery, Charlie, "The Länder Strike Back: Structures and Procedures of European Integration Policy-making in the German Federal System," Discussion Papers in Federal Studies FS94/4, University of Leicester, September 1994.

Jeffries, Ian, "The GDR in Historical and International Perspective." In Ian Jeffries and Manfred Melzer (eds.), *The East German Economy*, London: Croom Helm, 1987.

Jepperson, Ron, Alexander Wendt, and Peter Katzenstein, "Norms, Identity, Culture, and National Security." In Peter Katzenstein (ed.), *The Culture of National Security: Norms and Identity in World Politics*, New York, Columbia University Press, 1996.

Katzenstein, Peter, *Policy and Politics in West Germany: The Growth of a Semi-Sovereign State*, Philadelphia: Temple University Press, 1987.

"Introduction: Alternative Perspectives on National Security." In Peter J. Katzenstein (ed.), *The Culture of National Security: Norms and Identity in World Politics*, New York: Columbia University Press, 1996.

"Introduction." In Peter Katzenstein (ed.), *Tamed Power*, Ithaca: Cornell University Press, 1997.

"United Germany in an Integrating Europe." In Peter Katzenstein (ed.), *Tamed Power*, Ithaca: Cornell University Press, 1997.

Keeler, John, "Agricultural Power in the European Community: Explaining the Fate of CAP and GATT Negotiations," *Comparative Politics* 28 (January 1996), 127–50.

Kelleher, Catherine, "The New Germany: An Overview." In Paul Stares (ed.), *The New Germany and the New Europe*, Washington, DC: Brookings Institution, 1992.

Klemmer, Paul, "Harmonisierung der Umweltpolitik in der EG," *Wirtschaftsdienst* (May 1991), 262–68.

Klodt, Henning, "Europäische Industriepolitik nach Maastricht," *Die Weltwirtschaft* (September 1992), 263–73.

Kohler-Koch, Beate, "Die Politik der Integration der DDR in die EG." In Beate Kohler-Koch (ed.), *Die Ostwerweiterung der EG: Die Einbeziehung der ehemaligen DDR in die Gemeinschaft*, Baden-Baden: Nomos Verlagsgesellschaft, 1991.

Krakowski, Michael, Dirk Lau, and Andreas Lux, "Auswirkungen der Wiedervereinigung auf die Standortqualität Westdeutschlands," *Wirtschaftsdienst* (September 1992), 464–71.

Kramer, Heinz, "The European Community's Response to the 'New Eastern Europe'," *Journal of Common Market Studies* 31 (June 1993), 213–44.

Kreile, Michael, "The Political Economy of the New Germany." In Paul Stares (ed.), *The New Germany and the New Europe*, Washington, DC: The Brookings Institution, 1992.

Kühl, Carsten, "Finanzierung der Altlastensanierung in den neuen Bundesländern," *Wirtschaftsdienst* (April 1991), 180–87.

Kuschel, Hans-Dieter, "Die Einbeziehung der ehemaligen DDR in die EG," *Wirtschaftsdienst* 71 (February 1991), 80–87.

Lange, Peter, "The Politics of the Social Dimension." In Alberta Sbragia (ed.), *Euro-Politics*, Washington, DC: Brookings Institution, 1991.

Läufer, Thomas, *Europäische Gemeinschaft Europäische Union: Die Vertragstexte von Maastricht*, Bonn: Presse- und Informationsamt der Bundesregierung, 1992.

Layne, Christopher, "The Unipolar Illusion: Why New Great Powers Will Rise," *International Security* 17 (Spring 1993), 5–48.

Lehmbruch, Gerhard, "Die deutsche Vereinigung: Strukturen und Strategien," *Politische Vierteljahresschrift* 32 (December 1991), 585–604.

"Institutionentransfer: Zur politischen Logik der Verwaltungsintegration in Deutschland." In Wolfgang Seibel, Arthur Benz, and Heinrich Mäding (eds.), *Verwaltungsreform und Verwaltungspolitik im Prozeß der deutschen Einigung*, Baden-Baden: Nomos Verlagsgesellschaft, 1993.

Leptin, Gert and Manfred Melzer, *Economic Reform in East German Industry*, Oxford: Oxford University Press, 1978.

Liefferink, J. Duncan, Philip Lowe, and Arthur P. J. Mol. "The Environment and the European Community: The Analysis of Political Integration." In J. Duncan Liefferink, Philip Lowe, and Arthur P. J. Mol (eds.), *European Integration and Environmental Policy*, New York: Belhaven Press, 1993.

Lippert, Barbara, "Die EG als Mitgestalter der Erfolgsgeschichte: Der deutsche Einigungsprozess 1989/90." In Barbara Lippert *et al.*, *Die EG und die neuen Bundesländer*, Bonn: Europa Union Verlag, 1993.

Lucas, Nigel, *Western European Energy Policies*, New York: Oxford University Press, 1985.

Mäding, Heinrich, "Die föderativen Finanzbeziehungen im Prozeß der deutschen Einigung." In Wolfgang Seibel, Arthur Benz, and Heinrich Mäding (eds.), *Verwaltungsreform und Verwaltungspolitik im Prozeß der deutschen Einigung*, Baden-Baden: Nomos Verlagsgesellschaft, 1993.

Marer, Paul, "The Political Economy of Soviet Relations with Eastern Europe." In Sarah M. Terry (ed.), *Soviet Policy in Eastern Europe*, New Haven: Yale University Press, 1984.

Markovits, Andrei, *The Politics of the West German Trade Unions*, New York: Cambridge University Press, 1986.

Markovits, Andrei and Philip Gorski, *The German Left: Red, Green, and Beyond*, Oxford: Oxford University Press, 1993.

Markovits, Andrei and Simon Reich, *The German Predicament: Memory and Power in the New Europe*, Ithaca: Cornell University Press, 1997.

Marks, Gary, "Structural Policy in the European Community." In Alberta Sbragia (ed.), *Euro-Politics*, Washington, DC: Brookings Institution, 1991.

Marks, Gary, Liesbet Hooghe, and Kermit Blank, "European Integration from the 1980s: State-Centric v. Multi-Level Governance," *Journal of Common Market Studies* 34 (September 1996), 341–78.

Marsh, David, *Germany and Europe: The Crisis of Unity*, London: Heinemann, 1994.

Matthies, Klaus, "Hindernisse auf dem Weg zum Energie-Binnenmarkt," *Wirtschaftsdienst* (March 1993), 143–46.

McAdams, James, "Germany after Unification: Normal at Last?" *World Politics* 49 (January 1997), 282–308.

McGovern, Karsten, "Kommunale Umweltpolitik in den neuen Bundesländern: Innovationsbedarf und Umsetzungsprobleme." In Susanne Benzler, Udo Bullmann, and Dieter Eißel (eds.), *Deutschland-Ost vor Ort: Anfänge der lokalen Politik in den neuen Bundesländern*, Opladen: Leske + Budrich, 1995.

McGowan, Francis, "The European Electricity Industry and EC Regulatory Reform." In Jack Hayward (ed.), *Industrial Enterprise and European Integration: From National to International Champions in Western Europe*, Oxford: Oxford University Press, 1995.

Mearsheimer, John, "Back to the Future: Instability in Europe after the Cold War," *International Security* 15 (September 1990), 5–56.

Mény, Yves and Vincent Wright (eds.), *The Politics of Steel*, New York: Walter de Gruyter, 1987.

Messal, R., and A. Klein, "Finanzlasten und Eigenmittelstruktur der Europäischen Gemeinschaft," *Wirtschaftsdienst* (July 1993), 375–83.

Michalski, Anna and Helen Wallace, *The European Community: The Challenge of Enlargement*, London: Royal Institute for International Affairs, 1992.

Milner, Helen and Robert Keohane, "Internationalization and Domestic Politics." In Robert Keohane and Helen Milner (eds.), *Internationalization and Domestic Politics*, New York: Cambridge University Press, 1996.

Milward, Alan, *The European Rescue of the Nation-State*, Berkeley: University of California Press, 1992.

Moravcsik, Andrew, "Negotiating the Single European Act: National Interests and Conventional Statecraft in the European Community," *International Organization* 45 (Winter 1991), 651–88.

"Preferences and Power in the European Community: A Liberal Intergovernmentalist Approach," *Journal of Common Market Studies* 31 (December 1993), 473–524.

"Why the European Community Strengthens the State: Domestic Politics and International Cooperation," paper presented at the Conference of Europeanists, Chicago, March 31–April 2, 1994.

Moyer, H. Wayne and Timothy Josling, *Agricultural Policy Reform: Politics and Process in the EC and the USA*, Ames, IA: Iowa State University Press, 1990.

Müller, Harald, "German Foreign Policy after Unification." In Paul Stares (ed.), *The New Germany and the New Europe*, Washington, DC: Brookings Institution, 1992.

Müller-Armack, Alfred, *Wirtschaftslenkung und Marktwirtschaft*, Hamburg: Verlag für Wirtschaft und Sozialpolitik, 1948.

Nägele, Frank, "Strukturpolitik wider Willen? Die regionalpolitischen Dimensionen der Treuhandpolitik," *Aus Politik und Zeitgeschichte* 43–44 (October 28, 1994), 43–52.

Newman, Michael, *Democracy, Sovereignty, and the European Union*, New York: St. Martin's Press, 1996.

Nugent, Neill, "The Deepening and Widening of the European Community: Recent Evolution, Maastricht, and Beyond," *Journal of Common Market Studies* 30 (September 1992), 311–28.

Paarlberg, Robert, *Leadership Abroad Begins at Home*, Washington, DC: Brookings Institution, 1995.

Padgett, Stephen, "The Single European Energy Market: The Politics of Realization," *Journal of Common Market Studies* 30 (March 1992), 53–75.

Parker, Mike, *The Politics of Coal's Decline*, London: The Royal Institute of International Affairs, 1994.

Parnell, Martin, *The German Tradition of Organized Capitalism: Self-Government in the Coal Industry*, Oxford: Clarendon Press, 1994.

Petite, Michel, "The Treaty of Amsterdam," Harvard Jean Monnet Chair Working Paper Series No. 2/98, 1998.

Pierson, Paul, "The Path to European Integration: A Historical Institutionalist Analysis," *Comparative Political Studies* 29 (April 1996), 123–64.

Pollack, Mark, "Obedient Servant or Runaway Eurocracy? Delegation, Agency, and Agenda Setting in the European Community," Working Paper No. 95–10, Center for International Affairs, Harvard University, 1995.

Pond, Elizabeth, *Beyond the Wall: Germany's Road to Unification*, Washington, DC: Brookings Institution, 1993.

Porter, Michael, *The Competitive Advantage of Nations*, New York: The Free Press, 1990.

Press and Information Office of the Federal Government, *Basic Law of the Federal Republic of Germany, promulgated by the Parliamentary Council on 23 May 1949 as amended up to and including 21 December 1983*, Wolfenbüttel: Roco-Druck GmbH, 1989.

Presse- und Informationsamt der Bundesregierung, "Das Program zur Vollendung des EG-Binnenmarktes: Ein Ziel gewinnt Kontur," *Aktuelle Beiträge zur Wirtschafts- und Finanzpolitik*, November 17, 1992.

Unsere Landwirtschaft, Bonn, 1992.

Priewe, Jan, "Die Folgen der schnellen Privatisierung der Treuhandanstalt," *Aus Politik und Zeitgeschichte* 43–44 (October 28, 1994), 21–30.

Putnam, Robert, "Diplomacy and Domestic Politics: The Logic of Two-Level Games," *International Organization* 42 (Summer 1988), 427–60.

Ragin, Charles, *The Comparative Method: Moving Beyond Qualitative and Quantitative Strategies*, Berkeley: University of California Press, 1987.

Ress, George, "The Constitution and the Maastricht Treaty: Between Cooperation and Conflict," *German Politics* 3 (December 1994), 48–74.

Rogowski, Ronald, *Commerce and Coalitions*, Princeton: Princeton University Press, 1989.

Ross, George, *Jacques Delors and European Integration*, New York: Oxford University Press, 1995.

Ruggie, John Gerard, "Multilateralism: The Anatomy of an Institution." In John Gerard Ruggie (ed.), *Multilateralism Matters*, New York: Columbia University Press, 1993.

Sally, Razeen and Douglas Webber, "The German Solidarity Pact: A Case Study in the Politics of the Unified Germany," *German Politics* 3 (April 1994), 18–46.

Sandholtz, Wayne, "Choosing Union: Monetary Politics and Maastricht," *International Organization* 47 (Winter 1993), 1–39.

"Membership Matters: Limits of the Functional Approach to European Institutions," *Journal of Common Market Studies* 34 (September 1996), 403–30.

Sandholtz, Wayne and John Zysman, "1992: Recasting the European Bargain," *World Politics* 42 (October 1989), 95–128.

Sbragia, Alberta, "Thinking about the European Future: The Uses of Comparison." In Alberta Sbragia (ed.), *Euro-Politics*, Washington, DC: Brookings Institution, 1991.

"EC Environmental Policy: Atypical Ambitions and Typical Problems?" In Alan Cafruny and Glenda Rosenthal (eds.), *The State of the European Community*, vol. II, Boulder: Lynne Rienner Publishers, 1993.

Schaaf, Peter, *Ruhrbergbau und Sozialdemokratie*, Marburg: Verlag Arbeiterbewegung und Gesellschaftswissenschaft GmbH, 1978.

Scharpf, Fritz, "The Joint-Decision Trap: Lessons from German Federalism and European Integration," *Public Administration* 66 (Autumn 1988), 239–78.

Crisis and Choice in European Social Democracy, Ithaca: Cornell University Press, 1991.

Scharpf, Fritz *et al.*, *Politikverflechtung*, Kronberg/Ts.: Scriptor Verlag GmbH, 1976.

Schattschneider, E. E., *The Semi-Sovereign People*, New York: Holt, Rinehart, and Winston, 1960.

Schiffer, Hans-Wilhelm, "Einführung einer CO2–Energiesteuer?" *Wirtschaftsdienst* (July 1992), 362–67.

Schmitt, Dieter, "Energiepolitik nach dem Scheitern der Konsensgespräche," *Wirtschaftsdienst* (January 1994), 12–18.

Schmitter, Philippe, "Interests, Powers, and Functions: Emergent Properties and Unintended Consequences in the European Polity," Stanford University, April 1992.

Schütterle, Peter, "EG-Beihilfenkontrolle über die Treuhandanstalt: Die Entscheidung der Kommission vom 18.9.1991," *Europäische Zeitschrift für Wirtschaftsrecht* 2 (November 10, 1991), 662–65.

Seibel, Wolfgang, "Die organisatorische Entwicklung der Treuhandanstalt." In Wolfram Fischer, Herbert Hax, and Hans Karl Schneider, *Treuhandanstalt: Das unmögliche Wagen*, Berlin: Akademie Verlag, 1993, 114–47.

"Strategische Fehler oder erfolgreiches Scheitern? Zur Entwicklung der Treuhandanstalt 1990–1993," *Politische Vierteljahresschrift* 35 (1994), 3–39.

"Das zentralistische Erbe," *Aus Politik und Zeitgeschichte* 43–44 (October 28, 1994).

"Innovation, Imitation, Persistenz: Muster staatlicher Institutionenbildung in Ostdeutschland seit 1990," unpublished paper, Universität Konstanz, 1995.

Shackleton, Michael, "Keynote Article: The Delors II Budget Package," *Journal of Common Market Studies* 31 (August 1993), 11–25.

Shonfield, Andrew, *Modern Capitalism: The Changing Balance of Public and Private Power*, Oxford: Oxford University Press, 1969.

Sikkink, Kathryn, *Ideas and Institutions*, Ithaca: Cornell University Press, 1991.

Singer, Otto, "The Politics and Economics of German Unification: From Currency Union to Economic Dichotomy," *German Politics* 1 (April 1992), 78–94.

Sinn, Hans-Werner and Gerlinde Sinn, *Kaltstart: Volkswirtschaftliche Aspekte der deutschen Vereinigung*, Tübingen: J. C. Mohr, 1991.

Smyser, W. A., *The German Economy: Colossus at the Crossroads*, New York: St. Martin's Press, 1993.

Soskice, David, "The Institutional Infrastructure for International Competitiveness: A Comparative Analysis of the UK and Germany." In A. B. Atkinson and R. Brunetta (eds.), *Economics for the New Europe*, Basingstoke: Macmillan, 1991.

Spence, David, "Enlargement without Accession: The EC's Response to German Unification," The Royal Institute of International Affairs, *RIIA Discussion Paper* 36, 1991, 37–38.

"The European Community and German Unification." In Charlie Jeffery and Roland Sturm (eds.), *Federalism, Unification, and European Integration*, London: Frank Cass, 1993.

Streeck, Wolfgang, "German Capitalism: Does It Exist? Can It Survive?" In Colin Crouch and Wolfgang Streeck (eds.), *Political Economy of Modern Capitalism: Mapping Convergence and Diversity*, London: Sage Publications, 1997.

Streibel, Günter, "Environmental Protection: Problems and Prospects in East and West Germany." In Paul J. J. Welfens (ed.), *Economic Aspects of German Unification: National and International Perspectives*, New York: Springer-Verlag, 1992.

Sturm, Roland, *Die Industriepolitik der Bundesländer und die europäische Integration*, Baden-Baden: Nomos Verlagsgesellschaft, 1991.

Swann, Dennis, "The Social Charter and Other Issues." In Dennis Swann (ed.), *The Single European Market and Beyond*, London: Routledge, 1992, 214–29.

Swinbank, Alan, "CAP Reform, 1992," *Journal of Common Market Studies* 31 (September 1993), 359–72.

Tetsch, Friedemann, "Bund-Länder-Gemeinschaftsaufgabe: Verbesserung der regionalen Wirtschaftsstruktur," *Die Neue Verwaltung* (May–June 1993), 24–28.

"Gemeinschaftsaufgabe 'Verbesserung der regionalen Wirtschaftsstruktur' am Scheideweg," *Stadt und Gemeinde* (8/1994), 3–8.

Thelen, Kathleen, *Union of Parts: Labor Politics in Postwar Germany*, Ithaca: Cornell University Press, 1991.

Treuhandanstalt, *Dokumentation 1990–94*, 15 vols., Berlin: Treuhandanstalt, 1994.

Turner, Lowell, *Fighting for Partnership: Labor and Politics in United Germany*, Ithaca: Cornell University Press, 1998.

Viertel, Grit, "Gemeinsame Agrarpolitik und neue Bundesländer." In Barbara Lippert *et al.*, *Die EG und die neuen Bundesländer*, Bonn: Europa Union Verlag, 1993.

Vogel, David, "Environmental Policy in the European Community." In Sheldon Kamieniecki (ed.), *Environmental Politics in the International Arena*, Albany: State University of New York Press, 1993.

von Weizsäcker, Ernst U., "Environmental Policy." In Carl-Christoph Schweitzer and Detlev Karsten (eds.), *The Federal Republic of Germany and EC Membership Evaluated*, London: Pinter Publishers, 1990.

Wallace, Helen and William Wallace (eds.), *Politics and Policy in the EU: The Challenge of Governance*, Oxford: Oxford University Press, 1996.

Wallace, William, "Europe as a Confederation," *Journal of Common Market Studies* 20 (September–December 1982), 57–68.

Waltz, Kenneth, "The Emerging Structure of International Politics," *International Security* 18 (Fall 1993), 44–79.

Waniek, R., "EG-Regionalpolitik für die Jahre 1994 bis 1999," *Wirtschaftsdienst* (January 1994), 43–49.

Weale, Albert, "Ecological Modernization and the Integration of European Environmental Policy." In J. Duncan Liefferink, Philip Lowe, and Arthur P. J. Mol (eds.), *European Integration and Environmental Policy*, New York: Belhaven Press, 1993.

Werner, Klaus, "Der Außenhandel der neuen deutschen Bundesländer mit Osteuropa," *Wirtschaftsdienst* (April 1992), 206–14.

Wiener, Antje and Vincent Della Sala, "Constitution-making and Citizenship Practice – Bridging the Democracy Gap in the EU," *Journal of Common Market Studies* 35 (December 1997), 593–614.

Wilks, Stephen and Lee McGowan, "Disarming the Commission: The Debate over a European Cartel Office," *Journal of Common Market Studies* 32 (June 1995), 259–73.

Wolfers, Arnold, "The Goals of Foreign Policy." In Arnold Wolfers (ed.), *Discord and Collaboration*, Baltimore: Johns Hopkins University Press, 1962.

Zelikow, Philip and Condoleezza Rice, *Germany Unified and Europe Transformed: A Study in Statecraft*, Cambridge, MA: Harvard University Press, 1995.

Zimmermann, Klaus, "Ecological Transformation in Eastern Germany." In A. Ghanie Ghaussy and Wolf Schäfer (eds.), *The Economics of German Unification*, London: Routledge, 1993.

Zuckerman, Alan, "Reformulating Explanatory Standards and Advancing Theory in Comparative Politics." In Mark Lichbach and Alan Zuckerman (eds.), *Comparative Politics: Rationality, Culture, and Structure*, New York: Cambridge University Press, 1997.

Index

Agenda 2000, 53–54, 70–71, 188
agricultural policy (joint task), 173, 175,
178–79, 185, 199–200

Bauernverband der DDR, 176
Beteiligungs-Management-Gesellschaft
Berlin (BMGB), 126
Blair House Accord, 184
Borchert, Jochen, 184–85, 187, 188, 188
n.101
Breuel, Birgit, 71, 118 n.15, 136
Brittan, Sir Leon, 131, 136
budget, EC/EU, 50–52, 54, 171–72, 189
Bund für Umwelt und Naturschutz
Deutschland (BUND), 90
Bundesamt zur Regelung offener
Vermögensfragen (BARoV), 126
n.40
Bundesrat, 9, 31, 42, 45, 45 n.62
Bundestag, 31, 71, 122, 139, 143, 209
Bundesverband der Deutschen Industrie
(BDI), 66, 67, 74, 76, 78 n.68, 79, 80,
119, 148, 180
Bundesverband des Deutschen Groß- und
Außenhandels (BGA), 66, 67
Bundesverband für vereinigungsbedingte
Sonderaufgaben (BvS), 126, 139

cohesion fund, 160, 164, 171–72
Comecon, see Council for Mutual
Economic Assistance
constitutive politics, 6, 13, 15, 34, 45,
190–92, 206, 207, 208, 210
convergence criteria, 42, 47, 48, 49, 108
n.66; see also economic and monetary
union
Copenhagen summit, 61
Council for Mutual Economic Assistance
(CMEA), 57, 58, 61, 62, 63, 64, 72
n.48

deindustrialization, 40, 121, 131 n.56, 137,
142, 143, 202

Delors II, 50, 54, 117 n.10, 160, 162, 163,
164; see also budget, EC/EU
Delors, Jacques, 33, 34, 161, 162, 166
n.33, 181, 201
Deutscher Bauernverband (DBV), 172,
176–77, 180, 181 n.76, 183, 184,
186
Deutscher Gewerkschaftsbund (DGB),
121
Deutscher Industrie- und Handelstag
(DIHT), 80 n.73
Dublin summit, 35–36, 156
Duisenberg, Wim, 50

economic and monetary union (EMU), 14,
34, 45, 46–50, 207
Edinburgh summit, 50–51, 164
Einigungsvertrag, see Unification Treaty
Eko Stahl, 62, 62 n.13, 72, 125, 142–47
enlargement, 52–54, 188, 190, 208, 209
Essen summit, 53
Europe Agreements, 53, 61, 62, 72
European Economic Community (EEC),
172
European Free Trade Association (EFTA),
52
European Regional Development Fund
(ERDF), 152, 153, 154, 166–67, 169
Exchange Rate Mechanism (ERM), 47

federalism, 9, 13–14
Fischler, Franz, 188
Fonds Deutscher Einheit, see German Unity
Fund

*Gemeinschaftsaufgabe "Verbesserung der
Agrarstruktur und des Küstenschutzes"*
(GAK), *see* agricultural policy (joint
task)
*Gemeinschaftsaufgabe "Verbesserung der
regionalen Wirtschaftsstruktur"* (GA),
see regional policy (joint task)
Gemeinschaftswerk Aufschwung-Ost, 38

225